WIDOWER

WIDOWER

Scott Campbell
with
Phyllis R. Silverman, Ph.D.

Prentice Hall Press • New York

While the case studies described in this book are based on interviews with real persons, the names, professions, locations and other biographical details about the participants have been changed to preserve the privacy and anonymity of the men taking part in the study. The psychological analysis following each case study is based on Dr. Silverman's review of the case studies themselves and upon her professional experience and expertise. None of the men described in the book are known to Dr. Silverman.

The poem on page 142 is used with permission of
The Helen Steiner Rice Foundation,
Suite 2100, Atrium Two, 221 East Fourth Street,
Cincinnati, Ohio 45202.

Published by Prentice Hall Press
A Division of Simon & Schuster, Inc.
Gulf + Western Building
One Gulf + Western Plaza
New York, NY 10023

PRENTICE HALL PRESS is a trademark of Simon & Schuster, Inc.

Library of Congress Cataloging-in-Publication Data
Campbell, Scott.
    Widower.
    1. Widowers—United States—Psychology—Case
studies. 2. Bereavement—Psychological aspects—
Case studies. I. Silverman, Phyllis R. II. Title.
HQ1058.5.U5C36 1987   306.8'8   86-43105
ISBN 0-13-959503-1

Manufactured in the United States of America

Designed by Irving Perkins Associates

10 9 8 7 6 5 4 3 2 1

First Edition

*To
the Survivor
in All of Us*

Acknowledgments

I owe a lot of people my thanks for helping to bring this book about:

For supplemental research support, I am enormously grateful to the National Funeral Directors Association, without whose help this effort might not have had the scope it has.

For moral support and early guidance, my thanks to Mary Ann Petti, Ed Myers, Evelyn Gladu, Tom Welch, and Gail Gruner.

For information and referrals, thanks go to Ruth Loewinsohn and Edie Smith at the American Association of Retired Persons, Frank Reissman at the National Self-Help Clearing House in New York, Roberta Halporn at the Center for Thanatology Research & Education, Amy Rokicki at the National Center for Death Education, Ralph Vaccari, Herbert Patchell, Eleanor Robinson, Adina Wrobleski, Carole Katz, Louis, Mary, and Laura.

For faith and friendship, Arthur Kurzweil, Anne Starr, and Richard MacMillan.

And for her insightful stimulation, good company, and superb croissants, my co-author Phyllis R. Silverman.

But most of all, for their courage and faith and generosity, both Dr. Silverman and I owe our thanks and deep respect to the men who shared their experiences for this book. We wish them the peace and good life they deserve.

Contents

WIDOWER

What Happens to Men When Their Mates Die

THERE are more than 12 million widowed people in the United States. Each year, for every three women who are experiencing the loss of a mate, two men experience the same loss—creating nearly a quarter of a million new widowers every year.*

Until recently, not very much has been known of what happens to these men, but if you have lately joined their number, this much we can tell you:

- Your chances of being killed in a car accident have increased 300 percent
- Your chances of committing suicide have increased 400 percent
- Your chances of dying from heart disease have increased 600 percent
- Your chances of dying from a stroke have increased 1000 percent

As a result of the increased stress on your immunological system, your susceptibility to illness has also increased dramatically, especially if you are predisposed to hyperthyroidism, diabetes, cancer, or cardiovascular disease. And if you're over 75, you have just joined a group of men whose rate of alcoholism is the highest in the country.

*In the population at large, the ratio of widowed women to widowed men is more like 5 to 1 because so many men remarry so fast, and once they are remarried they are no longer considered widowed. But according to calculations made by the American Association of Retired Persons, based on the annual death rate, in any given year the ratio of women who lose their husbands to men who lose their wives is 3 to 2.

Those are just the immediate dangers. Failure to accommodate your loss appropriately can also predispose you later on to psychiatric and medical problems. Not to alarm you or anything, but if you've been feeling shaky, at least now you know there are good reasons for it.

Chief among those reasons is stress. Losing a spouse is at the top of the list of life's most stressful events. It is the event by which all other stressful events are measured. It is more than the fact that you have lost a friend and companion and mate, more than the fact that you are now single in a coupled society, more than the fact that you have lost a caretaker and social connector.

It is also the fact that you have been brought to the very brink of the Mystery, and then you have been left behind. It is true that men often look on women as somehow more attuned to the mystery of life, because they bear life. And to the extent that is true for you, you may feel cut adrift not just from your friend and companion and lover, and from your social circuit, but from the whole human community, from the entire metaphysical cosmos. The loss of a mate can create an inexplicably potent sense of aloneness. It can even create in you a sense that somehow *you* have died.

But stress and bottomless loneliness are not the only reason men do so poorly when faced with the loss of a mate. The simple fact is that many men just don't know how to take care of themselves. Recent studies show that even in this post-feminist era, working women still do between 67 and 90 percent of all household chores. Because of that kind of disproportion, some men don't know how to boil a potato. They can't run a washing machine or dishwasher. They can't go on a trip because they don't know how to pack a suitcase. They can't even write a check.

And if men are unprepared in physical terms to be alone, their psychological readiness is even less developed. In three out of four marriages, it is the husband who dies first. Men don't *expect* to be left alone.

This book will not release you from the problems you are facing, nor will it prescribe a cure. What it will do is show you how some other men have dealt with this situation, and how they have survived it. It contains the stories of twenty men, ranging in age from 30 to a grand old gentleman of 94. They have lost their wives to cancer, diabetes, murder, and suicide. They have lost them to strokes, infections, kidney disease, heart attacks, and alcohol. One of them helped his wife kill herself. Another pulled the plug.

One of these men was widowed only six weeks when he was interviewed. Another has been alone thirteen years. Some of them have married again, some have chosen not to. Many thought of killing themselves—one even had the gun in his mouth—but every one of them has survived. Some have even been transformed. All of them deserve to be heard.

Within the past fifteen years, an increasing amount of literature has appeared on the subject of death and dying. In just one decade, in fact, more books and articles were written on this subject than had been written in the course of the previous 150 years. This enormous growth in the literature reflects a significant change in our culture, as we have begun to face death more squarely and to reconsider the ways by which we deal with it.

But most of the research that has not focused on the dying themselves has focused on the problems of widows. Statistically, surviving widows do outnumber widowers, and certainly women face special problems when they are left alone—problems that deserve the close attention they have gotten. But little attention so far has been paid to the problems of widowed men.

In spite of all the evidence we have to the contrary, our prevailing wisdom is that women grieve and men replace. It is assumed that widowers have it easier than widows, that men don't grieve as long or as much, that men just want a housekeeper, or that men just want sex, and that men prefer to talk to women about their most intimate feelings. But in fact, men have as hard a time with bereavement as women do, and often for as long or longer. At the same time, they are often willing to learn how to run a household themselves, they often not only don't want sex, they are incapable of it, and they often find it difficult to talk to another woman in intimate terms after losing their wives.

You see the problem you're facing, then. You are in a life-threatening situation, you have lost the one single person who more than anyone helped you sustain your life, you may be, to a large extent, without the skills you need to survive, and the people who have appointed themselves to minister to your needs have an entirely false image of you.

If, on the other hand, you are not a widower yourself, but you find yourself in the position of trying to help a widower—as a family member, friend or lover, or as a professional—you are also in a tight spot. Not only do you have a dearth of information to work with, you are also very likely to have an unwilling recipient.

Considering their health statistics, you might expect widowers to go to the doctor more often during bereavement, but studies show no such thing, in fact. Most widowers do not ask for help, and when they are successfully drawn into a helping situation, they are reported to be among the most recalcitrant and difficult of people to assist.

If you are a family member, you should know that families are often very limited in what they can do. If you are a friend, you should be aware that friends are also often not able to be a lot of help. And in any case, in a culture where 25 percent of the population moves to a different geographic location within any five-year period, family and friends are often simply not around.

Finally, if you are a woman about to get involved with a widower, you may be interested to know that your chances of marrying him are quite good—52 percent of these men remarry within the first 18 months. But you should also be aware that it is estimated over half of these early remarriages end in divorce or abandonment, leaving the widower and his new wife much worse off than they were before.

When I decided to write a book about the problems of widowers, I thought it might be a good idea to get some help from an established expert in the field. But when I started asking around, I soon discovered to my amazement that there is no such thing as an expert on widowers in this country—a pretty astonishing fact in a culture which has such a craving for experts. I also found, however, to my increasing interest, that one name cropped up on nearly everyone's list of bereavement experts: Dr. Phyllis R. Silverman.

In 1964, Dr. Silverman was asked by the director of the Laboratory of Community Psychiatry at the Harvard Medical School to determine what types of intervention might be most helpful to newly widowed people. In talking to the staffs of social service and mental health agencies, in talking to funeral directors and clergy, and in talking to the widowed themselves, she soon came to recognize that the needs of the widowed change over time.

She came to recognize further that any attempt to help them would have to focus on their ability to accommodate that change, to accept the fact that they could not return to the way things were before their spouses died. She also concluded that such a service would have to be custom designed for the widowed, rather than a subset of some other helping service.

One of the questions she asked herself was, who should offer the help? She had found that the widowed do not make use of human service agencies because they feel such agencies are for people with psychological problems. She had found that the widowed do not turn to clergy and physicians for long because they find those professionals seem to lack the skills to respond to the special needs of the newly widowed.

And although funeral directors were reported to be most helpful at first, because they knew what to do at the time of death, Dr. Silverman found that later on it was other widowed people who were reported to be the most helpful because they understood better than anyone else what the widow or widower was experiencing. When she came across some mutual-help groups that some enterprising widowed people had set up for themselves, she found the members did indeed have a compelling ability to be of help to each other.

As a result, Dr. Silverman developed the concept of the Widow-to-Widow Program, a program that would be run by widows to be of help to other widows. (Widowers were not included because no widowers could be found with enough free time to volunteer.) Helpers would reach out to every new widow in a community at the very time that her need would be greatest, when she would be too stressed to seek and find the most appropriate help. The outreach would come from another widow, from a woman who had successfully accommodated her own loss and wanted to help others.

In the years that have elapsed since Dr. Silverman's pioneering study, the Widow-to-Widow Program has been replicated many times throughout the United States, Canada, and Western Europe. In the largest-scale effort to date, the American Association of Retired Persons has begun the Widowed Persons Service, with more than 135 local programs for widows and widowers. Today it is accepted practice for hospice programs, funeral services, and other bereavement-related groups to sponsor programs for the widowed.

Studies of these programs show that widows receiving their services adapt better and more quickly than those who do not participate. Other studies show that such mutual help leads to greater positive change than professional help, and that the more intense a person's involvement, the better the outcome is likely to be in terms of increased self-esteem and reduced depression. A recent study by the National Academy of Science pointed out that everyone needs some kind of help in bereavement, and that while many people will get that help from their existing social networks, many others, lacking such networks—or finding they cannot get the kind of help they need from existing networks—may need to search out specialized help in the community.

It is a disarming result, in a way, to find widowed people can be of more help to each other than professionals can. We have devoted a lot of our resources in our society to the development of "helping professions," professions based on the concept that with the proper set of skills, a dispassionate observer can help anyone through anything. But according to Dr. Silverman's work, in the case of widowhood what you need is a *passionate* observer, a peer with a palpable sense of your pain.

Part of the reason for that may be the nature of the event. Death is such a profound and disruptive experience that if someone tries to approach it with dispassion, you feel they are doing it a violence. It is not a subject about which one can be objective and indifferent.

Another reason may be that we are all always looking for role models. As we move into new eras of our lives, we look for people who have been there—freshmen look to sophomores, newcomers look to old-timers, children look to older siblings. Their first-hand experience is the most valuable kind of information we can get in these circumstances because it directly addresses our problem. It is the oldest form of learning—learning by oral tradition, by oral history.

As a widower, you have certainly embarked on a new era of your life. It's important to learn how others have handled this situation before you, not because they can, in any way, hand you a solution. But because by seeing what they have done, you can begin to mark off the boundaries of the playing field. You can say, I wouldn't want to do that, or, that seems like a good idea. The more role models you have, the more clearly you can mark those boundaries and structure yourself a new game, so to speak.

It is also easier to learn from a peer than from an authority figure, because a peer can talk your own language. There are studies that show first-graders learn arithmetic more quickly from sixth-graders than they do from teachers. A recent study at Iowa State University has shown that men who have a male friend for a confidant are better able to adjust to widowhood than those who have a child, a sibling, or a woman for a confidant.

Unfortunately, however, it is a thoroughly documented fact that men don't have these kinds of friends. We have colleagues in business, companions in sport, but those involve competition. We are not attuned to each other in terms of our vulnerabilities. So we find ourselves more adrift in widowhood than women do, more alienated from the people who could help us most.

Add to that the fact that as men we are reluctant to seek out help, or to accept it when it is offered, and the problem gets more complicated. Where are widowers to find peers?

That's why we've written this book.

Over the course of about a year, I talked with these twenty widowers at some length about their experiences. I found them in Maine and California, in the Midwest and the South. I then spent about a month with Dr. Silverman going over their stories, drawing out the commonalities and comparing their experiences with the experiences of widows in light of what we know of bereavement and adult development. From those discussions, we have fashioned a commentary on each story to help put it in perspective.

We have not been able to include every thought these stories provoked. But we have tried to develop those that seemed to us most important, those that seemed to have the most pervasive implications and to resonate most with the other stories. We hope that these stories will provoke in you many more responses and while all of this was written primarily with the widower in mind, it is also very decidedly for those who want to help widowers—whether you are a family member, a friend, a health professional, a clergyman, a funeral director, a hospice worker, or a lover. And to the extent that it deals with universal problems in grieving, it will also be of interest to you if you are a recently widowed woman.

In any case, it is not a book you will probably want to read in one sitting. If you are newly widowed, you are very likely having trouble reading anyway. You might want to keep this book on your bedstand, to read when you go to bed at night, or when you awake at 3:00 A.M. and can't get back to sleep.

It is an easy book to read in installments. Every one of these stories contains a life, and the loss of a life. Every one of them deserves its own time and deserves to be considered. You may find some of these men speak especially eloquently to you, and that you want to read them more than once—to make friends with them, in a way. You may also want to dip in and out of this book, to read the stories at random, but if you do read the stories in sequence, you will get a sense of progression from initial loss to accommodation.

This brings up the stages of grief. Most books on bereavement parcel grief out in stages—they tell you first you'll experience this, then you'll experience this, then this. We adamantly do not do that. Grief is not an orderly process. It is true that there is a period of numbness at the beginning that helps to get you through the first few weeks, and that that is followed by a recoiling, a confrontation with the reality of what has happened. But after that, it is more like a maelstrom than a progression of stages. Everything goes on at once—anger, guilt, sadness, remorse, hurt and loneliness, depression—and any of these feelings can come careening at you at any moment. While it's true that different elements of the experience may have more emphasis at one point than they do at another—your anger, for instance, may tend to be more dominant at the beginning—to present it to you as a neat and orderly process would be to do you a disservice.

By the time you have finished this book, however, you should have a pretty good idea of what you can expect to go through, as well as a lot of examples of different ways of dealing with it—both in terms of practical matters and in terms of adjusting yourself to accommodate your new situation.

We hope you'll have gained something else, as well. Because in seeing other men in the midst of this life crisis, we have an opportunity to understand each other in ways we have not understood each other before.

As men, we are taught not only to guard our feelings, but to guard them most especially from each other. Because of that lesson, intimacy is generally thought to be more difficult for men than it is for women. And indeed, men usually form fewer intimate relationships than do women, and almost none with other men. For many men, the only true intimate in their lives is their mate.

Having that mate torn away exposes the nature of that intimacy. It is not the most perfect of metaphors, but it is something like a geode: cut away half of it and you can see all the detail inside. Take away half of a couple, and you can see the private emotional workings of the remaining half. By sharing that with each other, we may get to see each other as we have not seen each other before, to understand each other as we have not understood each other before, and to befriend each other as we have not befriended each other before.

One word of warning before we begin. There is a measure of pain in these pages—particularly in the first chapter—and because that pain will stir your own, you may want to set this book aside and never touch it again. We urge you strongly not to do that. The pain is included because it's the truth, and that's why it stirs your own. If you turn your back on the pain in this book, you will miss the joy and enlightenment that eventually grows out of it, just as, if you ignore your own pain, you may miss what it has to teach you. If this book gets too hot, set it down for a while. But please come back to it.

We believe you will gain from this book a sense of your situation as a hopeful one. If you are very recently widowed, it may be difficult to believe this, and you may not really much care at this point, but trust that it is true and that at some point it will matter to you. Widowhood is, for all its horror, an opportunity. In Chinese, the written character for the word "crisis" is a combination of the written characters for "danger" and "opportunity": a crisis is seen as being composed of both those qualities. As we have said, the danger you feel as a widower is in some ways real.

The opportunity is also real—to grow, to change, to become a more fully developed person than you were, more capable of living and loving, more giving, more taking, more human. There is no consolation in that; given the choice, of course you'd choose to have your partner back. But you do have the opportunity to gain strengths you never had before. It will not happen without some work, you will have to apply your will when the time is right to nudge and nurture yourself in the right direction. But by the time you have finished this book, you should have gained at least a glimmer of how that might happen for you.

This is a book about loss. It is also a book about love. As much as it is about death, it is also very much about life and the living, about love and how it heals its own loss, about caring and dignity and growth. In the end, it its focus on death, it is a profound affirmation of life for those who are most in need of it. And we are always, all, in need of it.

George

GEORGE is 62. He is an internist. He met Carol when he was 20 years old through a friend who was dating her at the time. Because he was in the army, they courted primarily through the mails and were married just a few months after he returned from the war. In the course of thirty-nine years of marriage, in addition to two miscarriages, they had two children together: Katherine and Peter, both now grown and living on their own.

Shortly after her fifty-ninth birthday on January 12, Carol was diagnosed with cancer. She had surgery in March, and the doctor said there was a good possibility they had gotten it all. She started getting stronger, started working and working out again, but in June the doctor found lumps in her neck—a clear indication the cancer had spread—and she started chemotherapy. By September, the lumps had shown no change, so she started radiation treatment. In early November, the doctors discovered that the cancer had spread to her liver. Carol had seen her mother suffer and die from cancer of the liver, and when she heard the diagnosis, she raised her hand and turned down her thumb. Exactly one week later, she died. George is sure it was by her own choice.

This interview was conducted only two months after her death.

She died at 6:15 in the morning.

I had awakened at about five o'clock. Couldn't sleep. And I came out a number of times and listened quietly by the door to see if Carol was awake yet, or whether Ellen, the nurse, was awake. But I didn't hear anything. So I went back into the guest room. Then Ellen came out and said to me, "I can't. . . . I think your wife has died. I can't seem to get a pulse." And I walked in, and there was. . .

I knew.

My mother died two years ago. My brother died the year before that. So I've had a lot of loss, and I knew. I knew exactly what to do. I had done it for my brother, my mother. I did it for my father. So I mean, you know, the procedure was not anything unknown to me. And I did it. I was able. I did it.

I called the police. They were wonderful. Organized. Sensitive. Good. I called my daughter, I called my son, I called one of Carol's closest friends. And then the network started. Very quickly, several of her closest friends were here.

Then an amazing thing happened. You know, when I first had looked at her, her mouth was open, her eyes were staring. She didn't look comfortable or well. But within a half an hour—I don't think it was any longer than that—it was incredible! I'm sure there's an explanation for this, because I saw it with my mother. My mother died a terrible death, and she had a look of agony and scorn and everything else, my mother. And then about forty minutes later, she looked at peace. And the same thing happened with Carol. Her face had actually changed. It's not that that's how I wanted to see her, or that, you know, some process in me made me see her that way. She had actually changed.

About 11:30 or 12:00, we went over to a place where every member of my family has had their funeral service. Not far from here, across the park, half a mile away. I met with the guy I had worked with on my mother's funeral, my brother's too, but he seemed slower somehow. He didn't move fast enough, didn't grasp . . . And the room was cold. I kept my coat on. I told him to heat the goddam room. I was very impatient, angry. Christ, I was a bitch on wheels. I mean, it wouldn't have taken much for me to have become physical, and I'm not a physical person.

I knew very clearly what my wife wanted. The only major question was where she was to be buried. My family has a very large, imposing mausoleum. It would be like staying at the Park Lane, as compared to a neighborhood guesthouse. But obviously, she wants to be with . . . *wanted* to be with her family. And I respected that. She would talk to me about the pressure she knew she was putting on me, wanting *me* to commit that I would be buried, you know, in *her* family plot. I mean, we had conversations about it. Like, one night, after we were in bed . . .

I don't know whether we had made love or had had a fight or what. Whichever, something intense had gone on. And she said to me, "You know," she says, "I think when *we* go . . ." She always talked as if the two of us would go together. One time when I queried her on that, she said, "Well, I'm not leaving you." This was long before she was ill. So she said, "You know, when we go, I picture us stretched out just this way, and there's one tombstone for the two of us, and our epitaph is, It Was A Fair Fight." Later I was to remind her she said this, and to tell her how flattered I was that she had put me in the same class.

So anyway, we worked out the details. And I simmered down. Came home. Sat with my children. With friends. Cried. Talked. Took a walk by myself. I couldn't get comfortable anywhere. I'm not aware of having eaten. I lost ten pounds within a week. I was turned off to everything. I came back here. Ellen was here. And my sister-in-law was here. And my son and his wife, my daughter, her husband. It took a very long time to work out where everybody was going to sleep. I think by the time we figured it out, it was 12:15 or so. At one point my son-in-law, Randy, was calling hotels to try to get a room, because, you know, he didn't want . . . I don't know what he didn't want. So anyway, Ellen slept on the couch. And Pete and his wife slept over on one side of this huge king-size bed I have, and I slept on the other. I ended up sharing my marriage bed that night with my son and his wife.

Subsequently, my daughter was to sleep in that bed with her husband, and I slept in the guest room. I remember the next morning she said, "You know, your electric blanket's broken. You're gonna need a new blanket." I said, "All right." She said, "You know, you can buy them in any store." I said, "I know I can." She said, "Maybe Marshall Field's." I said, "Oh, all right, Marshall Field's." I'm having some tea and I'm trying to read the paper. It's been hard for me to read, by the way, since my wife died. And she said, "You'll get one with *single* controls." I looked up from the paper. "*Single controls?*" I said. "You won't need double controls," she said. So I said, "Well, how do you know I won't want to stretch *across* the bed, and want the entire bed warm?" I was *infuriated*. It was the *height* of obtrusiveness. I said, "Who knows? Someday there may be somebody else in that bed who will want it warm." "Oh," she said. "Well, then, perhaps you ought to get *double* controls." "Well," I said, "I don't know. Maybe they make them with *triple* controls?" Then everybody laughed, and that was the end of that.

That time.

But there were a lot of incidents in which my anger got riled. I got a couple of very inappropriate condolence notes, for instance. Really inappropriate. Here. I'll read you one. This is from a colleague of mine:

> Dear George,
>
> Linda told me Tuesday that your wife had died. I'm sorry for your loss and pain. If I had some magic words, I would give them to you. But I don't. In the end, a loss is a loss. Time will help. I thought of what my life would be like without Esther, and that prospect scares the hell out of me. On the lighter side, there must be sixty women who are thinking of how to match the most eligible doctor in town—a.k.a. you—to their best single girlfriend. I hope that you will handle the pressure. I saw Jack Hemp in your position about three years ago. It was a bit wild.
>
> Best regards,
> Barry

Isn't that amazing? That prick.

Here's another one, from a woman:

> Dear George,
>
> I heard yesterday that you had just lost your wife. Since Margaret told me I have felt that emptiness associated with death, and have thought about my own losses and have been feeling sad and lonely for you. I recognize that there is little consolation from a note. Nonetheless, I wanted you to know that Charles and I [that's her husband] are thinking about you, and that we held each other a little tighter last night as we became aware once more of the fragility and brevity of precious relationships . . .

Well now, you know, I experienced "we held each other a little tighter" as being among the more insensitive things that could have been said to me. It made me feel my own deprivation. I mean, there are wonderful letters that talked about what Carol meant, which I experienced as being warming, consoling, helping the healing process, but I didn't experience these in that way. Some people were so *insensitive*.

13

The funeral took place on Wednesday. The night before, we were sitting around, and I heard my children describing Carol, and it was all so obvious. Oh sure, all those words apply to her. She had charm, she had wit, beauty, intellect. She had all those things, there was no question. But all of a sudden it dawned on me that probably her most unique feature—I don't know why it dawned on me; maybe it was all those people coming and calling the day that she died—it dawned on me that my wife had *forty* best friends! Forty women who would swear up and down that they were her best friend! Her quintessential quality was her ability to bond friends. It was a quality that I was somewhat ambivalent about. At times, I was jealous of it. But at other times, it suited my purpose. . .

On Sunday, some forty or fifty of those friends were invited to a memorial service right here in this room. It was like a Quaker meeting, where everybody just sits in silence and whenever someone's moved by the spirit, they get up and speak. I said a few words at the beginning—I think I said "It was a fair fight"—then didn't say anything after that. About two-thirds of the people talked, all saying very personal things about what Carol meant to them. Invariably, everyone came to talk, in one way or another, about Carol's great humor, great wit. I mean, there are people as bright as she was, there are people that were as pretty. But she could have worked for any greeting card company in the world. She had a flashing wit, brilliant wit. Our only argument was as to who was funnier, she or I. So this woman recalled a time at the swimming pool when one of her children was acting so beyond the pale that in desperation she finally give him a kick. And Carol quietly applauded. She remembered Carol for that, for that wonderful applause. It was marvelous. It was wonderful. It helped me to recall her very, very vividly, her presence. And it made me feel such a feeling of oneness with the people that I was with, so close to my family and my friends, so much sharing.

We didn't lionize her. We were realistic about her. Not everyone is, you know. When my mother lost my father, shortly before the Vietnam War, my mother's sense of the magnitude of her loss was that if Papa were alive, we'd never be in Vietnam. While my father was alive, especially in his later years, she experienced him as a very small, a very petty man. But upon his death, he became a giant. My mother went out with a man very briefly, and she complained to me that "He's a nice man, George, but he's really quite short." My father was five-three, five-four. So I said to her, "How tall is he?" She says, "He can't be more than five-four. I'm used to a taller man." So I said, "How tall do you think Papa was?" "Oh," she says, "five-nine, five-ten." I said, "Mother, that's ridiculous. I'm five-eleven and you know he was nowhere near that tall." So she said, "Well, he gave a tall impression." Okay. Fine. What we're talking about is the impression you have.

I went back to work very quickly. I saw my first patient exactly a week after Carol died. Of course, I'm not doing very good work. I don't have a lot to give. I'm impatient. Preoccupied. My patients notice it too. One of them, whom I've known for a long time, actually asked me, if I could come back and start to work so quickly, how deep were my feelings for my wife.

That first week, I accepted anybody and everybody who would invite me anywhere. We all have our ways of anesthesizing ourselves against the feelings. Pete, my son, uses exercise. So he's running more, playing racquetball more. I used social activity. Tuesday night I finished work at maybe 7:30 and went to dinner with friends. Wednesday night, I finished about the same time and went to dinner with friends. Thursday, a little earlier. Then went to dinner with friends. I was nervous about coming home. I couldn't read the newspaper, couldn't listen to television, couldn't keep my eyes open. So I went out all the time. But it was short-lived. I didn't like threesomes. There was always an empty chair at the table. And I'd put my arm on the back of the chair—you know, in the course of conversation—and suddenly I would be aware that Carol wasn't there. She always used to lean toward me automatically when I did that, lean against my arm. And now she wasn't there. I started cancelling appointments.

Then I stayed here, alone.

You know, I know what mourning involves. I know that a successful mourning will mean that I will incorporate Carol—parts of her, the most meaningful parts—deep within my bosom, and that no one will take that away from me. And no one will replace that. But that's a very, *very* hard process. And I am aware that I am distancing myself from some of my feelings. There are parts of it that I am staying far away from. There's a box that she kept—I think the label on it is "Meaningful Letters," or something—and it sits up in the closet. I cannot go near that box at this moment. It is as close to a phobia as I have ever come. Now, I know I *will* go to it, just like I know my wedding ring will come off at some point. But I really can't do it now.

I did dispose of her clothes, however, as quickly as I could. My wife left instructions, a list. I carry it around with me still. I mean, it no longer has any function, but still I carry it with me. Here it is. It's in her handwriting. First of all, it begins, "No fighting! There's enough for everyone." Then there's Kate, that's her daughter, and her daughter-in-law, and Sherry, her sister. Then she talked about "I owe Pete," that's our son, "a dining room table, his wedding pictures. I owe Kate a thousand dollars. And then if there's a balance in my account, divide it between the kids. Aunt Jo, take five hundred dollars—or whatever you need, if that's not enough—and get a red velvet blazer jacket and a winter coat. And Randy—that's her son-in-law—"get something soft and loving, and love it. . ."

Oh Christ! Oh Jesus Christ!

And then she wrote me a special note. . . . I know I've got it somewhere here. I know, I know I couldn't have lost it.

Here. Here. This is it:

More loving and more fighting for us . . .

And there was more loving. There was more fighting.

Oh Christ, what I am going to do?

I have an ache, an ache in my stomach. An emptiness, a feeling sometimes that there's no inside to me. Like this sculpture a friend of mine made before he died of a second heart attack. It's a man with no chest, that's the way he felt. I look at that, that's the way I feel. It's a state beyond aloneness. When you lose somebody, you can have a feeling of missing the person you've lost. But then you can go beyond that, to almost a personal annihilation. And I don't know that I haven't visited that second place sometimes. Where I feel that it's not that I simply lost Carol, but that I've lost . . .

I sometimes have the feeling, where is she? She's coming home, this is a bad dream. It has an unreal quality to it. Maybe the process of grief is to make reality out of what doesn't feel real. It seems like it couldn't have happened. In the mornings, it feels so strange to be. . .

Often, we would have tea together. In the evening, we would have something to eat. We would talk to each other—you know—and I miss her. I miss her desperately. I mean, there's no mystique to the nuts and bolts of living alone for me. But I miss her, I miss her presence, I miss her physically, I miss her, I miss, I mean I want to, I want, when something has happened, I want to talk to her, I want to tell her something, usually something very funny, and sometimes I talk to her, but I usually start to cry when I do, very quickly.

I'm scared of being alone. Of not having anyone. Of wondering what my life will be like. Of knowing I have to restructure it. And I'm angry for having to change my life. We had a comfortable life. And I'm angry for what she didn't give me. And for what she did. I'm angry at her *both* ways—for what she *did* give me that I'll miss, and what she *didn't* that might have still happened. There was always the feeling with Carol that the best was yet to come. And she died just before Thanksgiving; these holidays were a bitch on wheels. That's something else I'm angry about. You know, her timing was really lousy.

And also I feel guilty. What I call survivor guilt. I have this very sad image of my wife in the coffin in the ground. And she's very lonely, it's over for her. The image comes to me when I am at a movie or something I know she would like, and I am enjoying it. And I'm there and she's not. And that makes me feel guilty. You want to talk about anger—I'm angry at her for making me feel guilty. I start to feel good, then I start to feel guilty, then I start to feel angry for feeling guilty. Everything keeps setting everything else off. It makes it impossible to enjoy anything right now.

You know, I denied that Carol was going to die as quickly as she did, but I never denied she was going to die. And there were times when I tried to get into the adventure of it. I mean, like that fucking letter. "There are going to be sixty women out there . . ." Don't forget that I was married when I was 22. Didn't have much experience. Lived a monogamous life. So why not? Black ones, red ones, short ones, tall ones. Why not let it rip? But I can't even get a good fantasy going. I mean, I am turned off at this point.

I had the strangest thing happen to me. I'm waiting at the corner, and a very attractive woman comes over and waits for the light with me. I'm aware she's too close to me. I look at her, and she says, "I am available this evening". It was like she was speaking a strange language. I said, "Available?" She said, "Yes. And I'm very good." I said, "Gee, that's fascinating." She said, "But I'm very expensive." I said, "I can't even make a fist." She says, "With me you don't have to." So I said, "Well, thank you very much. That's the best offer that I've had in I don't know how long." And then I walked on my way. But it was very demoralizing, a very sad experience. Because it put me in touch with the fact that that part of my life seems light years away. My physical responses. I know enough about my body to know that at this moment I would be of no use to anyone, that I would be impotent. I know that this is a likely response, and an appropriate one, and that even this shall pass, but it doesn't make it less agonizing.

If I were going to give advice to a man who has just lost his wife, I would tell him to keep the pictures out. Don't put them away. Don't beat yourself up for running, for using defenses not to feel. But be aware that you're doing that. And be aware that hopefully that will be only temporary, that soon enough you will encourage yourself to remember, to feel, to cry. The way out is, where you want to end up is, with the preservation of the best of what you had in a permanent place where it can't be robbed or taken away from you. And that will involve facing what you got and what you didn't get. What you *really* feel about that person.

I haven't been to her grave. I don't know if it's a custom in other faiths, but in the Jewish faith when you go to the grave, you generally take a little pebble or a rock and you put it up on top of the tombstone. I guess it's to tell others, as well as to tell the deceased, that you were there. If I have a belief at all that I'm going to go and visit Carol, it's to, you know, it's to do that. To do that very specifically. I can assure you that if I go, that there will be no way that I wouldn't leave that little pebble. I'd like a lot of pebbles on her tombstone, because she deserves it. Of course, there won't be a tombstone there until a year from now. That's the custom in the Jewish faith. But who knows, there may be forty pebbles on her grave even as we speak.

In considering George's experience, one of the first things we have to note is how articulate he is. It is unusual for a man of his generation and profession to be so finely attuned to his own psychological and emotional workings, and especially unusual for him to be able to talk so clearly about them. Men who are now in their 60s were raised, for the most part, to rise above their feelings, and people who spend their working day looking into people's orifices are not inclined to spend their evenings looking into how they feel about it.

It's worth a mention in passing, then, by way of explanation, that George has involved himself for several years in psychotherapy, just in the interest of personal growth, and that that practice in talking about his emotions is coming in handy now. For the many men of his generation who have not had that kind of practice, the inability to articulate feelings can be a problem in grieving. If you can't articulate what you've lost, how do you go about grieving it? If you can't communicate your pain, how can anyone understand? And if no one can understand, how do you go about overcoming the isolation you feel?

If you can talk about your experiences the way that George does, it can be to your great advantage. It can help you to understand, by naming your feelings, what's happening to you. But at the same time, it is important to recognize that all of George's articulateness and awareness does not temper his pain in the least. It doesn't matter how well or how long you can talk about it, it still hurts.

But while understanding what's going on doesn't make it any less painful, knowing what to expect does make the process a little less frightening—it lets you know that there is indeed a process involved in grieving, that you can take an active part in it, that there is, if not an end, at least a resolution point, and that intense pain won't go on forever. If you understand, for example, that you're likely to be impotent, it won't be nearly so dismaying to discover you are. It may not make you any more comfortable with it to know that it's expected, but some men have come to believe that they had lost their libido forever, and then had to go through the grieving for *that,* only to find it returned again.

If you don't know what to expect, you can start to feel like you're going crazy—a fear that a lot of men report—and your impulse to short-circuit your grief, to run from it, can be reinforced. And any time you spend running from it is only delaying the grief process, and while the process is being delayed the pressure behind it is building. Later on, we will talk with some men who tried to run from their grief, and you will see what havoc it wreaked in their lives.

George's story gives you a very clear picture of what you can expect in the first few months of grieving—shock, anger, disbelief, despair, a sense of annihilation—and it also gives you a very clear picture of how it all happens at once. There is no orderly progression—everything keeps setting off everything else at every moment—but the element of grief that is perhaps most dominant at this point, at least in George's experience, is an all-pervasive anger. George is angry at everybody, at everything, at every moment. Indeed, anger is among the most dominant early elements of grief, particularly in men.

Anger can also be one of the most problematic elements. Since even under normal stress, people find anger to be among the most difficult of feelings to deal with, it can be especially difficult to deal with in grief. In day-to-day living, it's hard enough to find socially acceptable ways of expressing anger, but in grief—where it's mixed in with so many other unnamed and uncomfortable feelings, and at a time when people are doing their best to be their nicest to you—it can be extremely difficult to experience and express. To the extent that it gets repressed, it can give you health problems. To the extent that it gets expressed, it can create social problems. So if you are practiced at tuning into and expressing your anger, that will come in handy here and, if you tend to have trouble expressing your anger, one thing you might keep in mind is that you have all kinds of license at this particular moment. Most people will make allowances, so you can let it rip if you want— keeping in mind, of course, that there are those who *won't* make allowances. It pays to know who you're talking to.

Another element of grief that can be expected to dominate in the early months of bereavement is a sense of disbelief. It's been two months since Carol died, and George still finds himself speaking of her in the present tense—"I know what she wants . . . I know what she *wanted*." It's very common for widowed people to speak of their spouses this way, in the same way that it's common for an amputee to experience the sensation his missing limb is still there. It isn't even always a slip. One of the men I talked with, on the Christmas after his wife died, sent out Christmas cards from the two of them.

Talking in the present tense, and using "we" instead of "I," reflects a sense of disbelief that can be expected to weave in and out of your perceptions for some time. Right now, you may be solid in the knowledge that your wife is gone. But before you finish this chapter, you may look up to make a comment to her and be surprised to find she's not there. It happens all the time. George is right on target when he says that maybe grieving is making reality of what doesn't feel real. But the reality of this loss is so huge and so pervasive that you can't handle it all at once. So somehow you allow yourself to perceive it at moments, then shut it out, then perceive it again, shut it out again, and so on, until you can face it squarely. It happens both consciously and unconsciously, sort of in the same way that by flinching and looking and flinching and looking, you adjust your eyes to a glaring light.

But however much you may at moments "forget" that your wife is gone, when you crawl into bed alone at night, there is no mistaking her absence. The loss of that nighttime companionship is especially difficult for men because, for many men, their wives were their only source of physical comfort. Women in our culture are allowed to touch in many ways, and so to receive reassurance and comfort. We have even heard of a widow who shared her bed with a woman friend and held her on the night her husband died. But there is no way a man in this culture could receive that kind of comfort from either a man or a woman. In our society, a man never touches a woman except sexually, and he never touches another man except in combat or sport. In many ways, men are the Untouchables of American culture.

None of the men we talked to even mentioned the need for physical comfort during their bereavement. We suspect that is not because they don't need it, but because they have become trained not to expect it. We teach our sons not to expect or ask for physical comforting in any way but sexually. In ordinary circumstances, that can be little more than a peculiarity of the species. But when you have lost your mate in life, when you are under life-threatening stress that can be alleviated by touch, that lesson is painfully constricting.

If you are a widower who finds himself caught up in this bind— needing the warmth of physical touch but not knowing how to get it— the tension that builds up in your muscles as a result of the stress you are under can have a profound effect on your health. Since it isn't likely that you'll become casually demonstrative if you haven't been that way before, you'll need to find some other way to release the tension. Lovemaking is probably not a likelihood for a while, and if you are older, strenuous physical exercise may not be advised (although you may want to start exercising slowly and work your way up). So if you find yourself tightening up, if you are nervous, jumpy, brittle, you might consider alternatives. A good masseur literally can pull the tension right out of your fingertips. The benefits to your health of having a pet around are well documented, not only because they give you the opportunity for physical touching but also because the responsibility can give you some transitional structure. A number of men remarked that having a dog around kept them going. One of them even said that having a dog was what saved his life.

If you are in the position of trying to help a widower, you might consider ways in which you could touch him that would be compatible with his "touching style." A touch on the hand can signal a lot. A hand on the brow can soothe. A shoulder rub can work wonders, and hugs, of course, are top shelf. One man I talked to went on at some length about the way his son hugs him. He told the story with some surprise. It was not a form of affection that he anticipated from his son, or had taught him in any way, and it was certainly not a form of affection that he could openly ask for. But it was clear from the way he talked that it meant an enormous amount to him.

So if you're befriending a widower, see if you can't find a way to slip him a few good strokes. You may not be able to find a way that's comfortable for both of you, but explore it a little anyway. Along with all the other things he's suddenly lost—and he feels as if he's lost about everything—the widower has lost his main source of physical comfort, putting him in need of physical comfort perhaps more than ever before. This need often drives men right back into marriage, which is not always the most appropriate solution to the problem.

People always talk about how difficult it is to know what to say to a widower, and widowers, for the most part, since they don't know what they need to hear, are not very good at giving clues. But George's experience offers a few good examples of what *not* to say. His daughter's comment after spending the night in his bed, for example, makes you wonder what makes people say the things they say.

George is a vital, attractive man, witty and well-off. None of that, we can be sure, has been lost on his daughter, and she very well may have been giving voice to her own fears about having her mother replaced. That may be why she was hinting her father should sleep alone from now on. If, as a widower, you can recognize that intrusive comments like that are often expressions of others' fears, you might be able to handle them better.

But it won't make those thoughtless comments any less intrusive. George's daughter was trying to get him to commit himself to being single at the same time his colleague Barry was trying to get him fired up for going out with sixty different women. Already George has got people trying to push him one way or another, rather than just letting him figure out how he wants to deal with his loss and who he wants to be now. It is to George's credit that he absolutely rejects those attempts. Not everybody at this very vulnerable stage of bereavement is quite so able to draw his boundaries, but all the men I talked with said that most of the advice they got was useless, and all of them, finally, ignored it. So if you're a friend of a widower, you should be prepared for the likelihood that he will reject your advice.

But as useless as your advice might be, your presence is essential. Every widower talks about how much he needs people at this time, not to impose their own agenda of what they want him to do, or what they think he ought to do, or what they would feel most comfortable with, but to do as was done at the memorial meeting George had for Carol.

That meeting provides fine examples of what you *can* say that can be of use.

What a widower needs to hear are the ways in which *you* miss his wife—what you loved about her, and how you share the loss, so that he can know that he is not alone in his loss, that others have lost her too. If you tell him it's going to get better, more than likely the message you're giving him is to hurry up and get over it, which is not what he needs to hear. He needs to be allowed to experience his loss and to share that experience. There is plenty you can say. Just think back about her. What can you remember about her?

How you will remember his wife is one of the most important things you can say to a widower because one of the major tasks he faces now is how *he* will remember her. By telling him your memories, you may be able to help him get a start on working out the ways in which he's going to do it. And it also helps you get a handle on what it is *you've* lost. One of the reasons we always have trouble knowing what to say to someone is that we are having trouble dealing with the loss ourselves. So share a story. Share a memory. It comes up over and over again, how important and helpful that can be.

For all the considerable things that George has going for him—his sense of humor, his circle of friends, his awareness and articulateness— his life is still in disarray. His description of feeling no longer intact, no longer complete, is compelling. He feels as if there is no inside to him, that something's been taken out of him, that he's been annihilated, that his world no longer exists as it did. Widows acknowledge this all the time, but we have never before heard a man describe his loss in terms of such a tremendous disruption of who he is and how he relates to the world.

To his credit, George is absolutely unflinching in his response to this. His world is crumbling all around him, and collapsing within him, and he is not, as many men try to do, pretending otherwise. We suspect that many more people feel this way than are able to say so and that many others are not able to tolerate these feelings at all. When you are faced with such feelings, when you are left with such a raw, open wound, and you find it intolerable, what do you do with it?

Some people, such as Sam and Jim, have systems of belief that allow them to seal the wound right away.

Sam and Jim

SAM is 79, a retired piano and organ retailer. He married his high school sweetheart, Sarah, when he was 22, right after he returned from his two-year mission for the Mormon Church. During their fifty-four-year marriage, they raised five children, three girls and two boys, all of whom now live close by, three of them in the same city.

About ten years ago, Sam and Sarah went on a mission for the church. Two months before they were released, Sarah had a heart attack. She had a bypass operation, they completed their mission and returned home, but over the next nine years, she had two more heart attacks and a stroke. She finally died of a heart attack one February evening at home.

His interview was conducted almost one year after her death.

Jim is 94, a prominent businessman.

He met Laura when he was 16 (she was a classmate of his sister's) and married her when he was 31. Living and working together, they spent nearly twenty-four hours together every day for fifty-eight years (a total, Jim calculates, of 508,080 hours), raising two children and building an internationally famous business. They led prominent, public, extraordinarily productive lives together, until, at 89, Laura suffered a stroke and fell into a coma. She died a few weeks later.

His interview was conducted four and a half years after her death.

Sam: I had given her all the morphine we had, and she was still in pain. So I called my daughter (my daughter is a registered nurse) and she came running down. We tended to her for a while, she and I, and then I went out to the kitchen to talk to her husband for a few minutes. And she called to me, "Dad, come here." And I knew there was something wrong. I went in and she was gone, that quick.

Jim: It came as a complete surprise. I woke up at 5:00 in the morning, and she'd gone to the bathroom. All of a sudden I heard noises in the bathroom. She was on the floor, suffering. I called her physician, and he immediately sent an ambulance. She was in a coma, she'd gotten a stroke, and that was it. She never regained consciousness. She died several weeks later.

Sam: I had never seen anyone dead before. Her head was just flopped over. I picked her head up and talked to her and kissed her a few times. I pleaded with her not to go. But when the ambulance came, they tried to revive her, and it made me angry. They pushed on her so hard, her feet flipped. I said, "You guys are being too rough. Leave her alone. She is my wife." I didn't want her to be brought back. As much as I begged her not to go, I knew it was best for her because of what she'd been going through.

Jim: I was completely unprepared. You have no frame of reference for death. It just hits you like an explosion or a revolution. She was functioning perfectly. She was taking pills for angina, but no one ever would have known it. We would go out and maybe before we went out she would take a couple of pills. But she was joyful and joyous, alive. . .

Sam: She had been in constant pain because of her arteries being plugged up—the heart would try to pump the blood and it couldn't go. Nothing could be worse than having your wife be helpless and lying in bed, unable to talk, in pain. I would rather have had the pain— that's something I always prayed for. But when the spirit leaves the body, there's no more pain and no more suffering. So now she is relieved of pain. Now I have the pain.

Jim: What happens to the pain? It doesn't go away. What it does is, over the months and the years, it gets to be less and less. But it remains with you. Whenever you discuss it or permit yourself to think about it. When you talk about it, you bring it back. But you can't do anything about it. So you just have to accept it as one of life's realities. Trees die. Flowers die. People die.

Sam: When she died, we just phoned the mortuary. We paid for both of our burials, got our caskets picked out and everything, about fifteen years ago. So all we had to do was phone them and they had everything ready. And then, for the funeral service, I took this organ over to the church. I told the guys if they'd get a truck and haul it over, I'd take the organ. 'Cause I know how to make this one sound good. So they put it in the church, and I played her song for her, the song that we had written together. Tears ran down my face, but I did it. I've got a tape of the whole thing. I love it.

Jim: We didn't have any ceremonies, there were no rituals. She had wanted her body to be given to science, so the body was sent to the medical school and that was the end of it. There was no funeral, no memorial service. Ritual is a delusion to me, going through motions that have no meaning in reality. If you deal with life on a real basis, you don't create delusions.

Sam: My wife was a person who loved everybody. And everybody loved her, everybody. When we'd take her to the hospital and take her back that night, the nurses would kiss her on the cheek and hug her. She was that type of person. She was happy and never complaining. I took care of her when she got paralyzed, for two years, and never heard one complaint. She was a beautiful woman. She had a beautiful spirit with her. She was a terrific girl.

Jim: My wife was a brilliant woman, a very helpful woman. She bounced back the ball on any matter that I was interested in. That becomes a pattern of life, so you really feel that two are one. I think the most difficult part is missing that person who was part of you, in terms of empathy, sympathy, understanding, love. To have a cessation of that is a very disheartening element.

Sam: My biggest problem since she died has been lonesomeness. Coming home to a cold, dark house, no one home. That's awful. That's lonesome, I'm telling you. You don't know what to do. The thing that helps me more than anything else is playing the organ. If I can just play for twenty minutes, I feel like a new man. I come home—I don't even bother to turn on the lights. I just sit down and play in the dark. And I feel like a new man, like I just went for a swim or something.

Jim: I plunged myself into work as a distraction from the grief. Even on the day that my wife went into the hospital, when the ambulance came and took her away, even that day I came home and worked. And all through the time she was in a coma and after she died, I never stopped working, except when I went to see her. I found I had enough work to do. And after I worked, I slept. I was tired.

Sam: I also have lots of friends calling on me. I have the people in my ward. Our church is divided into wards, small groups of four to five hundred people. There are lots of wards in the world and I have been in quite a few, on the missions, but I have never found a ward where there are so many good-living people. At Christmastime, I had nineteen families come to the door and give me goodies. And just last Wednesday—even after a year—somebody brought me a plate full of lunch. If I didn't belong to the church, I don't know what I would do. Without it, it would be grim. I'm not fooling with you.

Jim: I've always, since my wife died, had somebody younger living with me. They get free room and board and they can bring their friends here for dinner and live as part of a family. I've had three people, and each one has stayed for about a year and a half. I think that it's a good thing because they're younger and youth has a lot to learn. It's enjoyable, you know, to give advice. If people listen.

Sam: We have people in the church that can give a patriarchal blessing. And about ten years ago, at the end of our mission—when Sarah had just been operated on and had started back on the mission—this man gave her a blessing. I have never heard a more wonderful blessing. So I wrote and asked him for the transcript. I went through it three or four times and underlined it just for me. Then I put some decals on, just to make it look pretty. And when I have a shaky moment, or I'm feeling extra lonely or something, if playing music doesn't work—I read it and it works. Just the same.

Jim: Some of my friends gave me books on death. There are a couple of good ones, but I didn't feel in the mood to read books about death because death was so frightening. People have very little concept of what the death of a loved one really means to the survivor. I can show you a letter from a good friend, a Christian Scientist, who said, "Your wife has not died, she's alive and has just passed on." It was a thought I appreciated, but it didn't assuage my grief. I received 315 letters of condolence from our friends. Five books full of them. They made me recognize the people who loved and respected her, but they didn't modify the facts. Laura is dead. As dead as a tree. As dead as anything else that dies. She just no longer exists.

Sam: I believe my wife is alive. I think she is in the exact same form as we are, only it's not flesh. If I could see her, she would look just the way she always looked here. And I know that I'll be with her again. I know very well that I'm going to have that same sweet spirit, that same sweet person to be with me forever. A lot of people can't believe this. They think I'm nuts to think like I do. But I'll tell you something. Even though I was born into the Mormon Church, it took me forty or fifty years to really be convinced. But now I'm as sure as I'm sitting here that all of it is true. I'm positive it's true.

Jim: Religious people have an entirely different idea of death, because they believe that there's a soul, and that if you're good it goes to heaven and if you're bad it goes to hell. But I don't believe in that. My father made the statement that he would not impose any religion on his children, that we could make our own decisions at 18. So basically, in my adulthood, I've done without organized religion. I believe, with Sigmund Freud, that religion is a creation of men. They develop a world of unrealism to help them meet the sufferings that occur when people who have affection for each other die.

Sam: When I die, I will join her in the spirit world and together we will go to the Celestial Kingdom. I have to go and take her, because to be in the Celestial Kingdom, you have to have a husband and wife married in the temple. One can't enter without the other. And when we're resurrected, if we've lived a celestial life, we will get celestial bodies. The spirit comes down and gets its body, this perfect body that you pick up if you lived a good life.

Jim: If you are religious, my advice would be to let whatever beliefs you have about afterlife satisfy your needs, let them assuage your grief. If, on the other hand, you don't have such beliefs, I would suggest you move closer to your family. I talk to my children every day. I'll call them up or they'll call me.

Sam: If you just lost your wife, the first thing I'd recommend is that you pray. I can't tell you how to pray, cause I haven't got your mind. But if it were me, I would do that. And although you may not know how to pray, you can get on your knees and say, "If there is a God," or something like that. That's the first thing I'd do.

Jim: And then I would urge you to develop whatever distractions you can, by working so hard that it will draw on all your resources, so that you don't go to pieces. That seems the normal thing to do. My feeling is that if Laura were alive, she would agree with me that the way I'm handling it is exactly the way she would want me to. My advice is just to keep on going.

Sam: The other thing that I would do is read The Book of Mormon. 'Cause in the beginning there is a promise that if anybody will read that book with a desire to know the truth, you'll know the truth and be baptized. Just ask the Lord to help you. Everyone in the world is born with the spirit of God in them. No matter if they're Mormon, or whatever they are. Just keep praying, humbly. You'll get the answer, if you're sincere. I know you will. I promise you that.

As different as these two stories may seem, we have cast them together here because they are so much the same. Both Sam and Jim are responding to the devastation of losing their wives by relying on very traditional, firmly entrenched belief systems, systems that give their lives not only meaning but also ongoing structure.

Sam, for instance, may never have to restructure his life the way George will because his world is so highly structured by the Mormon Church, both socially and metaphysically. The Church's system of support is so strong that Sam can turn to emotional Jell-O and that social and metaphysical structure will still hold him up. Whenever he starts to feel shaky, he gets out the blessing and reads it over and reaffirms his beliefs.

He is able to apply that blessing like a balm, to soothe the pain, much as he uses music. It's interesting, in fact, that the cadences of the language in the blessing (which he read aloud to me) are smooth and regular and fluid, like the organ music Sam plays. And what else is there to do, after all, but "play music" to appease the pain? Since he doesn't really have to give his wife up (as do men who don't share his beliefs) he doesn't really have to set about reorganizing his life. Since he considers her still alive and believes he will be with her again, all he really needs to do is bide his time and nurture his beliefs.

It's a pretty good way of handling things, if you can make it work for you. And if you have strong religious beliefs, they can be a great help to you now. But, as Sam points out, it took him fifty years to be truly convinced, and if you haven't been building a system of beliefs like this for years, it's questionable whether you're going to be able to take one on just like that when you need it.

Some people, such as Jim, however, subscribe to secular belief systems that can work almost as well. Jim's absence of a religion is, in a sense, a religion itself—the religion of rationalism. And like Sam's, it is an airtight system. His convictions surrounding life and death are just as firm as Sam's, and he is able, like Sam, to rely on them when they are needed.

Howevermuch Jim disavows rituals, he absolutely has them. His rituals are that you call the doctor, you call the police, you send the body over to the medical school and then you go back to work. Those are the rituals of his "religion," the rituals of the here and now. They are an enacting of his belief that when you die you cease to exist. There is no need to convey the spirit to another realm, no need to pray for intercession, no need to concern yourself with the soul. Laura simply is no more. After ninety years of practicing and reaffirming that belief, maybe Jim *could* just go back to work before the kind of devastation that George described got a hold on him.

If you have that kind of faith in your work, if your work is that meaningful and entwined with your understanding of life, and if, like Jim, you are able to turn to your work even after you've "retired," by all means, plunge ahead. The structure and sense of purpose and distraction you can get from work is a lifeline that can be enormously helpful in pulling you through this time.

But as valuable as work can be, we have reservations about it. Some people use work as a way of hiding from reality, just as other people use religion as a hiding place. In a case like Jim's one wonders what happened to the pain. As much as he may have had a philosophical position prepared for the way he thought about death, and as much as he may have had the ritual of work to turn to, still there had to be pain. He didn't talk much about it, even when pressed, except to say that it had lessened over the years. When he did talk about it, he started tapping his glasses nervously on the desk, as if the mention of the pain might bring it rushing back.

To a large extent, it seems that Jim simply turned his back on his pain. He didn't pretend he didn't *have* it, but rather than dwelling on it, he turned to his strength, his competence. It is the traditional manly way of dealing with emotions, and these days we tend to think that that is not necessarily the "right way." It is certainly a theme of this book that to turn away from your pain, to ignore it, is to run a very high risk, and there is plenty of evidence to indicate that acknowledging and expressing your feelings is healthier, both physically and mentally.

But in Jim's day, men did not learn to "process" feelings the way people do now, and one often finds men of his generation putting painful feelings aside, never letting them come out, never fully allowing themselves to express their grief. In their marriages, these men had their wives "process" feelings for them—there was that kind of division of labor. For men of these generations, to deal with emotions was women's work. It may not be that these men repress intensely painful feelings—it may be that those feelings never reach that pitch of intensity. If you've lived for ninety years with the premise that you are "not emotional," maybe your emotions are never given the room to become as devastating as they are for others.

I described Jim's seeming lack of reaction to a funeral director, to get his opinion on it, and his reaction was, do people that old really need to grieve? It was a curious question, curious not only because he didn't know the answer, but also because the concept seems so wildly unlikely. But maybe it *is* possible that when you are 94, death is so much a part of your existence that you can pretty much take it in stride. There is no law that says you have to experience the kind of emotional devastation that George describes. Feelings like those are extremely difficult to tolerate. And when you're 94, maybe the benefit of exploring those feelings simply isn't worth it. Maybe you need to conserve as much of your energy as you can to survive.

It's also important to remember that Jim was talking four and a half years after Laura died, and that memory is kind. When he taps his glasses against the desk, maybe it's in response to a murky memory of the kind of pain that George described as making him nervous. Maybe Jim chooses not to remember more vividly than necessary, in the same way he chose not to dwell on the pain when it was fresh.

In any case, whatever he went through in the early stages of grief, Jim's way of getting through it worked. He is a healthy, functioning man. In fact, he functions better than many men function at half his age. He keeps up correspondence, he goes to parties, has people over to dinner—for which he cooks and cleans up himself—and goes on speaking engagements. He lives in a big old Victorian house that has one of those little motorized seats to carry one up the stairs, and as we went upstairs to talk, he had *me* ride on the little seat while he walked alongside me.

So who are we to say that turning your back on the pain and returning to work is a "bad" way to handle grief? Any response is a viable one as long as it works. The problem, perhaps, is predicting whether it's going to work or not. Another man who tried to deal with his grief the way that Jim did might have died within the year from neglecting the need to express that grief. And we don't know what's going to happen to Sam in the next few years. But if you're trying to help a widower, you have to keep in mind that whether you share his beliefs or not, you have to let him follow them. If his beliefs don't fit with yours, it doesn't mean they don't work for him. Not everybody functions in the same way.

Unfortunately, many people—most people, perhaps—don't have these kinds of highly developed systems of belief to rely on. But some, like Jan, are lucky enough to have other kinds of structure around them to carry them through the ordeal.

Jan

JAN is 41. He is a high school science teacher. He was fixed up with June by his brother-in-law when he was 35, about two years after he was divorced from his first wife, Sue Ann. He and June lived together three years with Jan's children by that first marriage—Paul, who is now 11, and Lisbeth, who is 8—then decided to get married. "It seemed as though we were going to continue hanging around together, and we thought it would be nice to get old and creaky together—walk around holding hands like old folks—so we might as well get married." June had not been married before and was somewhat scared of having children, but she got along well with Lisbeth and Paul, found she could fill a mother's role, and was starting to consider having a child of her own with Jan. They never got that far.

On a summer day only ten months after she and Jan were married, June was murdered by a "local madman" in the woods near their home. She had left home at 9:00 that morning to walk through the woods to visit a friend, and when she hadn't arrived by 1:00, the friend called Jan at school. He wasn't especially alarmed at first, but when he got home at 3:00 and there was still no sign of her, he called the police, reported her missing, and tried to trace her path through the woods. He searched for the next four hours. Finally, just before dark, he found the dog she'd gone walking with that morning, and it led him to her body.

This interview was conducted nearly two years after her death.

I didn't see her body until I was almost on top of it. She was naked. I touched her and she was cold. I don't know if she'd been raped or not. There is no evidence she was raped, but she was naked and cold and it was obvious she was dead. She'd been hit on the head with a big stone. Her skull was crushed. There was blood. I screamed and yelled and hollered and cursed, ran out of the woods, and called the police.

Right from the beginning, the police had a strong suspicion of who it was. It was known for years that Donald Lacy was capable of this. I had never heard of him, but apparently he had been around. Apparently, he was well known as the sort of person who would go out and stay in the woods for weeks and weeks at a time. The impression I get around town is that he had raped some women out there and had done some other violent crimes out there that had never been reported. It was considered likely, I guess, that he would commit a crime like this. But you can't put people in jail if you know they're going to do something bad. You have to wait until they do it.

I don't think anything more shocking can happen to you than to find your wife murdered. Finding someone dead is not a very nice thing anyway. But finding your own wife naked and dead with her head bashed in is not nice at all. I was absolutely in shock. Fortunately, my children were visiting their mother that day. We got in touch with them, let them know what had happened (I don't know what I said, I don't remember the details at all), and then I stayed at my sister's house for three or four days after that, during all the investigation.

I was sort of a zombie that week. I blocked out all emotion. There was a lot that had to be done, and I submerged myself in it. I had to function. I wanted to. I didn't cry much during that time. The first few hours I was crying—more screaming, really, than crying. More yelling, during those first hours.

An autopsy was done, of course. I had her cremated after that. We had a memorial service at the Baptist church in town. We'd been married by the Baptist minister—in the woods, under a big oak tree—so when June died, we had the memorial service at his church. He evoked feelings that were very, very powerful. I suppose it was very much the same as any other church service, but the mere fact of a ritual is a very powerful thing. I stayed in the church alone for half an hour after the service and cried. Then there was a reception at my uncle's house (I arrived a bit late), and there was music and good conversation.

The next month is all sort of mushed together. Basically I was walking around and doing the things I had to do, but occasionally I'd go off to the woods and scream and just walk around. I don't want to say I talked to trees, but I sort of sat and talked to myself, about nothing in particular, just sort of away from people in a place that had always comforted me.

When times are hard for me, I tend to gravitate to the woods. I go off by myself and just walk around and stare into space and have decisions made for me in my head. Maybe I'm in some state of meditation or something, I don't know, but somehow I know how to think about things after a little while. The solution comes out somehow or other. I don't do anything. My mind just sort of wanders from here to there in a dreamlike state, and something happens. When I get back, I get along better with the things that are of the real world. I don't know how or why. But it seems to work, so I do it.

That's one of the things June and I had in common, that a good part of our sanity was due to wandering in the woods. That's why we got married there. But I'm not comfortable now in the woods, in certain parts of the woods, alone—the place where June was killed, the places where Lacy was known to hang out, places that June and I had walked. If I go with someone else, I'm fine. But if I'm alone, I'm not comfortable. I'm not afraid of something jumping out and grabbing me, but I'm not comfortable either. I don't know if I'll ever be completely comfortable there again. There's always been trouble in there—there's always been strange people walking around of one sort or another—but we were among them, you know. We were some of the strange people.

I have always thought of those woods as *my* woods. June thought of those woods as *hers*. And Lacy thought of them as his. All three of us thought of them as our woods, very personally. The woods that were our comfort, in whatever way they were—differently, certainly, to the three of us—those woods are real important to me. Touching the earth there is a source of a lot of strength. And I still want to build a house up there.

This wasn't the first time I found a member of my family dead. I found my grandmother dead, and one of my uncles, who lived across the street. We knew Grandmother was going to die. She was 91 years old. She'd been an alcoholic for sixty years, smoked two packs a day. And one day, when she decided she didn't want her second afternoon bourbon—she was rationed—we knew the end was near. We called the family doctor. He came right over and said, "You're right, not long." And within a day or two, she died, sitting in her rocking chair. I was the one who found her.

But life goes on, is what happens. My father was one of twelve children, most of whom have died by now, and I've been around and seen all those deaths, right from the time I was very small. To have death be such a part of the normal process of life is unusual now—the world is so sanitized. There are special places for people to die where no one else can see them, except for people whose profession it is to watch people die. But death is something that happens, and it doesn't necessarily happen to people when they're young or when they're old or when it's expected or when it's unexpected. People die. That's what is. The world keeps turning.

I've learned a lot from my family. It is an enormous family. As I say, my father was one of twelve, and almost all of them lived around here. So there are a lot of aunts and uncles and cousins—about fifty of them. It can take a little while to straighten out just exactly who is who. My father's father came here from Finland at the turn of the century. He was a stonecutter in the quarries. When he was about my age, he decided that work was not for him and he used to sit in his yard with the other old Finns and talk about philosophy, religion, and the communists. He had a backyard big enough to keep a cow, raise some chickens. He had eight sons who could go out and work. He sent them all to college. Incredible! Twelve kids and no money, and they all went to college, somehow.

My mother's family summered here. She was a big-city girl, brought up in Rome, Paris, and New York. She went to Bryn Mawr and things like that. She was quite a cultured lady, and an opinionated one, and she married the son of an immigrant. She was a chicken farmer's wife, with no electricity, no running water, and an outhouse out back. It is a relationship that has had its ups and downs for forty-odd years. Their problem is the problem of so many couples like that, they love each other. And that's what I come from. A mishmash of Finnish-American culture.

This mishmash has provided me with a lot of good examples in life. Like my cousin Jamie. He was in an accident in which his neck was broken, and now he's a quadriplegic. But he doesn't feel sorry for himself. He carries on, in his wheelchair. He's a cabinetmaker and carpenter. He has only two or three fingers that work, but he does things that normal people can't do. He does them with half of his hands, from a wheelchair. You work with what you've got and do the best you can. Life isn't always rosy but it does keep going on, and you make the best of it.

When my son was two or three months old, he had spinal meningitis. I went to my parents' house to visit, feeling sorry for myself. Here I've got this kid who's sick and could die, and my dad said, "Yeah, he could, and if he does, he does. You can't feel sorry for yourself. There's nothing you can do about it. It's something that's happening to the kid, it isn't happening to you. There's nothing to do but wait and hope."

Then, one of my uncles, his wife had just died a month or so before June died. I went and talked with him. He's a gentleman in his 80s, a sculptor. I went and sat and had dinner with him. He said, "Go out in the woods and yell at the trees. It will make you feel better." I had done that, but I did it again. I guess it did make me feel better.

I've talked with a lot of other people who have had things happen to them. One of our neighbors had a son murdered several years ago—young, 11 or 12 years old—and I talked with him and his wife about it. And then I talked with my cousin Jamie. I talked with my uncles and with my parents, and they all said the same thing. You can't expect things to happen too fast, but they do get better. You give it a chance, you'll be okay. You'll be a different person, but you'll be a functioning person. You will do all right.

So you see, I'm getting what I need from the people who are close to me. We've all of us talked about it a lot. It's not a taboo subject. But outside the family, it's different. It's like my cousin Jamie. When Jamie goes out with his friends who can walk, he's invisible. People talk over his head. That's the way it is with cripples—you know, the cripple doesn't exist—and I'm a cripple, in that sense. In the teacher's room, conversations come around to violent crime of some sort and people look around and see me and immediately stop talking. It's okay. That's the way we all are. I'm guilty of the same sort of thing. I'm not uncomfortable with conversations about violent crime—I think I've got something to say about it—but nobody wants to hurt your feelings.

I have talked with June's father, too. June's father and I have always sat up drinking homemade wine and talking until all hours of the night. We talked about June, and about her death, and I think that's been helpful also. It's hard for a parent to lose a child. I can get another wife, someone else can fill that role for me, but no one else can be his daughter. And I think that for me, being part of it—even without much consciousness of what was going on—I think that was easier, in a way, than being a hundred miles away and hearing about it on the phone. I didn't have time to stew over it. I was there, I was part of it. June's parents didn't have that advantage.

From June until the end of August, I didn't do much of anything. I just let the whole reality of the situation sink in. I kept to myself and with my family. I didn't see anyone else. A friend took me out a couple of times—told me I had too long a face and he was taking me to dinner—but other than that, I kept to myself, or just within the family. I spent a lot of time with my sister and brother-in-law and with my parents and various uncles and things. I'm not very social anyway. I don't have many close friends that are not family in one way or another. But I've got such an enormous family, it leaves me with no shortage of people I can depend on for comfort.

I guess I let it sink in until August. I wanted to let this whole thing straighten out in my mind somehow. I didn't want to start socializing. I know a man about my age whose wife died in a car crash and he immediately started hanging around with another woman. I didn't really want to do that. I wanted to let things settle a bit.

But I didn't want them to settle too long. When I was divorced from Sue Ann, I went for two years with no companionship. I went to work and had my children and my family, but I didn't have a lady around. And I like to have a lady around. It's something that's very important to me. When I first started hanging around with June, and when it became apparent that I was going to be living with her, I decided if something similar happened I wasn't going to let myself be a hermit again for two years. I wasn't going to spend two years with my jaw hanging down to my belt buckle.

I get lonely when there's no one around. I like to have somebody around. Just someone to share the kitchen with when you're fixing dinner or something. Just someone to be around, just a physical presence to share whatever it is that people share when they're not talking, when they're just around each other. Waking up in the morning with nobody next to you is about as low in the pits as you can get. When you can't roll over and put your arm around somebody warm, it's awful. It is.

So I wanted companionship. But I wanted to be careful. I didn't want to be promiscuous. I'm not promiscuous anyway, but I didn't want the children subjected to ladies coming in and out.

Along about September, I started seeing Delores. She'd played the flute at June and my wedding. When June was murdered, I asked her to play at the memorial service, and she said she certainly would. Then after the service, I went to thank her, and it turned out she was getting divorced. So when I felt that I was ready to go out and be with someone a little, she seemed a safe person to do that with. She wasn't looking for anything, I wasn't looking for anything. But it turned out we got along very well.

After hanging around together for about a month, we realized we were getting serious. That was scary to both of us, that it should happen so quickly. We realized that it was a potentially terrible situation. These on-the-rebound sorts of things are notorious for being just awful. So we decided we wouldn't get married in a hurry, that's for sure. But it's been a year and a half now, and we do seem to get along awfully well. We're assuming that we'll get married probably within a year.

So I'm continuing on with my life. Going about what I go about. I've got a nice lady I hang around with. Got my kids. There's plenty to do.

There's always memories that come back about June when she was around. Things come up that we did together and sort of a "Whoops! There we go again!" feeling. I think that probably every day at one time or another, something will trigger a memory of her. If I'm reading the children a story and it's a story that she had read to them, or that we had all read together, or if we do something in some little way that we would have done with her, all of us sort of go, "Oh. That's the way June did things." There's some sort of drawing together from it. It binds me to what I am.

She's certainly a part of me. If you think of yourself as something that is constantly extending, the part of me that's her is not extending anymore. But it's still there. It's there, and you're aware that it's there, and it will always be there. It becomes a smaller and smaller part of the extending whole over time, but it's always there. It will always be a part of me. Just as Sue Ann will always be a part of me, and Delores.

I haven't buried June yet. I guess I've blocked that out. She's going into the family plot, but I didn't get her in this fall so I have to get her in this spring. The ashes are in my mother's house, and she's been letting me know that it's not appropriate to keep the ashes lying around the house—it gives her the heebie-jeebies. I know if they were here, they'd be giving me the heebie-jeebies. So everyone agrees it's time to get this over with, and get her buried and get the stone. It's one of those things that I think I've drawn a little curtain across. It's like getting your homework done—there's always something better to do.

Only this is a little deeper than that. I think we'll have a little ceremony with the children and me. Just the three of us. We'll just go over there and do it and talk a little bit, sit down and look at the stone and touch it, know that it's there. I think ritual is important.

It took almost a year for the court proceedings to get underway. June was murdered in June, and the trial was in March. The kids were there for three of the days, during selected testimony. There were some parts of the testimony that were really gory, and we didn't want them there for that. But they were there when I testified, and several other days. They had to be involved, they were a part of it. It couldn't be sanitized for them; it shouldn't be sanitized. They knew it happened. They couldn't not go. And they wanted to go.

The trial reopened everything. It was as devastating as the murder. I was buffered from my emotions a lot during the murder and the investigation. I formed a barrier to keep functioning, and a lot of what was happening went by without any memory of it. But the trial was a conscious sort of a thing. When I testified (I testified for a morning, I guess), the whole thing became real again. I wasn't testifying, I was reliving the murder in detail, all the events of the day of the murder, and that was terrifically draining. I was aware of the people around, and Lacy's sitting in front of me, twenty feet away from me, but I was alone in the witness chair. I was reliving the experience of finding my wife's body. It was very, very real. I was sufficiently aware of the courtroom that I described the screaming rather than actually screaming, but I was quite emotional.

I didn't know that I was going to relive it that vividly. I didn't know until I was up there and reliving it. The rehearsals were very matter-of-fact. It wasn't . . . it didn't . . . it wasn't real. But I think the trial was a catharsis. I certainly felt much better after. A huge, huge pressure lifted when the guilty verdict came in. It was just . . . collapse . . . just a tremendous pressure released.

At first, I had hoped Donald Lacy would die. The police had an enormous manhunt with hundreds of people and helicopters and dogs and things like that, and I was hoping they'd have to shoot him. But I think that was the last feeling of that sort that I had about him. I dehumanized him very early. He became an object in the distance. During the trial, it became more and more that he was just another exhibit. Not something to hate, or something to poison my own thinking with. I can't hate him. What's to gain from it? He's an object. He's not a human being. He's a log that fell on her, or a dog that attacked her, or something like that. He's simply an instrument of what happened. My wife died of mental illness—Donald Lacy's mental illness. There's no point in my being bitter at him. I could be bitter at him for the rest of my life. I've got better things to do.

I've always realized that there are all different kinds of people around, and that not every one of them is nice or what they seem to be—and that's okay with me. I'd like to get rid of the crazies but I think the system we've worked out is about the best we can do. I wouldn't want to be living in South Africa or the Soviet Union. I think as a society we have to put up with the crazies, because as soon as we start locking them up, then we start locking up everybody who disagrees with us, and that's a whole lot worse. The best we can do is hope for the best with the crazies that are out there.

All in all, I'd have to say I was handled very well. The state police, the local police, and the FBI are all very professional people. You can complain about them, but their homicide groups are experienced at this, and they handle it very well. The trial was not a circus at all. It was a trial of a criminal in front of a group of his peers, which is exactly what it should have been. It was very gentlemanly.

And the press never got to me. They tried, for probably a week or so, but I stayed with my brother-in-law and my neighbor in the woods. He's a big beer-bellied kind of guy and when he says you can't come in, you simply don't come in, is what happens. There were reporters at the trial, though, and after the trial was over, one of the TV stations got me. All of a sudden there was a camera on me and a microphone in my face and this guy was asking me questions. It was very nicely done. He was smooth, and he didn't ask anything impolite or anything like that. He just sort of said, well, how do you feel now that this has happened? I don't remember what I said. I said whatever I said.

I got a couple of sympathy letters from my students at school. They all knew what had happened, of course. They'd seen me on TV and things, and they'd followed the trial, I guess. I was worried that the students would handle me with kid gloves. I knew I was going to be handled with kid gloves by the other teachers, but I wasn't worried about that. We'd get over that, in time. But there's got to be a give-and-take in my relationships with my students.

For the first few days, things went carefully. In a couple of the classes, we did discuss that, yes, my wife had been murdered. I tried to bring it up, to let them know that it was okay. I think at some point it came up in all of my classes, one way or another. I just made sure they understood that it was something that happened to me and it didn't have to affect the way we got on with each other. If they wanted to call me an idiot for other reasons, that was okay. Of course, they'd have to stay after school . . .

How my kids took it, we're still finding out. They've been through a lot. They've been through their parents being divorced, they've been through having their stepmother murdered, and they've been through all the things that kids ordinarily go through. They've got a lot of things to get straight, and I think that it will be a while before we know how they've gotten it straight.

Lisbeth seems to be okay. She talks about things, she talks endlessly. When she's happy, she lets you know, and why. She lets you know why she's unhappy. When she's mad, she cries and yells. She's just general, all-purpose open about her feelings. Paul doesn't do that. He goes off and hides, things like that. Climbs under his bed and won't come out.

But it seems Lisbeth is keeping the internal bookkeeping done somehow. She seems to be cruising along okay. Well, you can see who she is in this drawing. You want to know who she is? That's her. A princess with a unicorn and a rainbow and flowers. Here's Dad, as a centaur, with a bow and arrow. Here's "Mom." This "Mom" is Delores. This drawing was done at *this* house; she keeps straight which family is which. And there's the caption: "By Lisbeth. This is Fairyland. It is my family. The unicorn is not in the family. P.S. I did this myself." So, see? She seems to be doing okay. But we may find out something's going on when she's about 13. You know, an 8-year-old girl can have Dad around to protect her, the centaur. But when they get to be 13 or 14, when they start being on their own, you start finding out where the pieces are that don't fit exactly right. For now, though, everything seems okay.

But my son is having a very hard time. I was the last person to become aware that he was having problems, but he is having a dreadful time. His mother, Delores, my mother, all were concerned about him before I really saw what they were seeing. I see him in the morning for breakfast, and then we hustle off for the day. Then we come home, and it's a big hustle to do all the stuff that has to be done before they go to bed. His mother and stepfather see him most weekends, his grandparents see him after school. I don't see him ever under really relaxed situations. So for whatever reasons there were, I didn't see what was happening. It had to be pointed out to me.

He's really not coping adequately. He's immoderate in his response to things. He loses his temper, has violent tantrums. He was always a little bit that way, but this is taking what he is and exaggerating it many times. So he's started seeing a therapist. He was the one who said he wanted to see a therapist, to understand why he was losing his temper. He doesn't talk much about his feelings, and the idea of the therapy is somehow to loosen that up. Things haven't opened up enough yet to find out just where his problems are, but June's death is certainly a real significant part of them.

When I was 11, I got angry, but not the way Paul does, you know? It was on a smaller scale, and I learned to deal with it by going off alone into the woods. It's not the appropriate thing, exactly. Therapists always seem to feel you should let your emotions out a lot. I don't. I've learned other coping techniques. I've taken something that's basically an inappropriate response and refined it through years of experience so that it works for me. And because I've had experience with smaller things earlier on, I can handle this situation in this perhaps inappropriate way. It seems to be working for me, so why fix it? But Paul's not old enough to have learned how to handle real bad things. Maybe he's trying to use my way of handling things as a model, and it isn't working for him. I don't know.

I know he has no example of someone who cries and lets emotion out. I've tried, but I don't know how to do it. Delores, she won't take that. She says, "You have to. You will. It's not a question of don't-know-how. You can. You just have to do it." And I guess I do. But this has come on sort of recently, and it takes a while to figure out how do I be emotional without becoming as mad as Paul? How do I moderate that? Because I think I have to. And I think the reason is because I know that just underneath the surface, there's a violent person lurking in me. It's in there. At least when I was a kid, I thought that it was in there. So I developed this way of dealing with that personality. I think. I'm not at all sure that I am what I am because of that. Or that Paul is the way he is because he's modeling himself after me. It's just something that I'm looking at.

Anyway, I've tried to encourage him to be more expressive, but it doesn't work real well. I don't know how to do it. I guess it's important, being conscious of feelings and letting them out, talking about your feelings instead of just letting them take care of themselves. One side of me knows that I guess it's important, but I'm not convinced. I mean, I do talk to people. But I don't know exactly what it is you're supposed to talk about. Apparently I don't talk about it. I don't know quite what it is. It's, you know, it's . . .

Therapists. I ride to work every day with a Dane, and he can sympathize with my apparent lack of emotion. He thinks it's something that's genetic in Scandinavians, and the trouble with the world is, at least for us Scandinavians, that all of the therapists in the world are nice Jewish ladies and Italians and Irishmen. And nice Jewish ladies and Italians and Irishmen really love to cry. There's nothing better than a good cry. But for Finns and Danes, it's not the heritage. One just doesn't cry. You go along and you go through life and you have your joys and sorrows, and they're just your joys and sorrows. They're not everybody else's. That's his theory, anyway. I thought it sounded pretty good. So I'm scouting around for a good Scandinavian therapist who'll say, "Aha! That's the way it is! You bet! That's it, sure enough!

People suggested I go to a therapist. It may have been arrogance on my part, but I thought I was getting along all right. I was sleeping fine, I was eating okay. I was hanging around with Delores and we were getting along very nicely. I seemed to be functioning normally. Sue Ann and I went to a therapist once, a family counselor. A wonderful lady, who wanted us to hug and kiss in her office—you know, everybody always has to be hugging everybody else—and neither of us were comfortable with that. It just didn't seem as if it was getting at what we wanted to get at. So I didn't go to a therapist. Then people told me to go out and go to the single parents' groups, but I had no interest in that at all. I don't think that other single parents have anything to tell me. There's a widows-and-widowers group that meets a couple of times a week, but I don't think they have anything to tell me.

There are a lot of people around me, very caring people. I get what I need from them. Every Saturday at 3:00, there's a sauna bath at my uncle's house. People come from miles around. They have, ever since I was little. We have births, we have deaths, we have weddings and wakes, but nothing interrupts the bath. Every Saturday at 3:00, ever since I was little.

The sauna is very important to me. The people there have all had hard times. They've all had bad things happen to them one way or another, as all of us have, I guess. But they aren't there to say, "Oh, I feel so badly for you, I cried for a week." They are there just to be there. I know that they've had troubles, they know I've had troubles, and we have shared experiences. I don't go to them and say, "Oh I have problems, I feel so bad," and they say, "Well tell me about it." It's simply that they're there.

After school, I go home and sit with my dad and have a glass of beer—he makes beer, he makes very good beer—and we don't talk about much of anything, but he's there and I'm there, and we sort of talk about nothing in particular. It's just the fact that we're near each other. The same thing with my sister, with my brother-in-law, my uncles and cousins. With Delores, it's the same thing. It's the fact that there is somebody there. You don't have to talk about things. Just the presence of somebody does a lot of good.

I don't know why, but it's important. There are these little . . . *things* . . . that run from one person to another. Little things, that run between people and connect them to each other, that take parts of you and mix them together with parts of someone else. They take a part that's not physical, a part that's sort of spiritual, and mix it with somebody else's and that then is sort of a bond, maybe like a chemical bond. At least, that's the way I think of it. You've got to know somebody for a while before those little things will come out, but once they come out, they're there. You don't really have to do much with them. They're there, and when you're with one of those people, those things are busy doing their work, while the people are doing something else. It's another human being that somehow is a part of you. I think we need that. *I* need that.

I don't think I'm in a position to offer anybody advice. Whatever strength you have, you had before you become a widower. You survived this far with it, you can't go looking for something new. You can mourn for a time, be alone for a time, but after a while you have to go back to being whatever you were before. Because that's what you are.

To take the death of a loved one as a call for changing your life around, that sounds like too much to do. You can't become a new person. That would be like going through adolescence again. That would be terrible. You have to take what you already have and use it, as well as you can. The death of someone you love and depend on is a pretty awful thing. It's a time to fall back on what you've got, rather than charging ahead. At least that's the way it's been with me.

I guess people do become transformed by the experience of being widowed, but aren't we all in the process of transforming constantly? That doesn't have anything to do with being a widower. I'm a new person every time I turn around and look. You can't say, "Gosh, I'm a widower, I think I'll become a new person."

Again, my experience with folks around here who have gone through something like this is that they continue on with what they do, first as an automaton, but then gradually they get back to what they were doing with a little creativity—making new relationships, holding onto the old ones. It's important not to withdraw from the old relationships, from the old friends. In my case, it's easy because they're all here and they're all family.

I pity those folks who have moved to California for some dream, and there they are, alone. And I mean *alone*. I don't know what they do. It must be a dreadful thing, a horrible experience. I've lost a big part of what I am, but there's still a big part to rely on. In that way, I'm very fortunate. I have this huge . . . *tribe* . . . that's part of me. June always called my family a tribe. I was born with them, and there they are.

I've always thought very highly of them, this group that I belong to, by birth. I'm mighty pleased about the whole thing. We don't all get along, we don't all especially even talk to each other, but we're there. Walking down the street, that's my cousin. Maybe wave a little bit. Or even not wave, some distant cousin that we don't see very often. But you know that they are there. And you know they're part of you.

After we finished talking, Jan took me to the family bath so I could see exactly how this tribe dynamic worked. It was an enlightening visit. There was a sense of community there that I have not often encountered, perhaps most especially in families. For one thing, of course, everybody is naked, so any attempt at formality or pretense was thoroughly out of place. For another thing, people were tending to themselves in the bath—shaving, cutting hair, and so on—as well as tending to each other, beating each other with those little sticks, as the custom goes in the sauna. It was an atmosphere in which some of people's most basic needs were getting tended to matter-of-factly, without much hullabaloo, in a context of easy sociability. This is unusual in a culture with such Puritan roots as ours, but of course, I was witnessing Finnish culture.

The day I went, a man showed up who had been in a terrible car accident; his body from the waist down essentially had been pulverized. He had been in the hospital for months, getting put back together, and this was his first return, on crutches. It was an education to see how these people dealt with this tragedy in their midst. No one ogled his legs, or avoided looking at the stitches and bruises, and the conversation did not dwell on or shy away from them. His situation was given the same matter-of-fact attention as the weather and real estate. There wasn't anything cold about it; it's just that he wasn't an oddity. He was another fact of life.

A lot of people seem to want to treat life's victims as aberrations, to stare at them and solicit them and get all flustered about them. But life is full of accidents, and all of us are victimized at one time or another. One of the things we don't need at such a time is to be treated as somehow "different," even though our circumstances at the moment are certainly different. To feel part of the community still, even in our new status, can give us a crucial sense of continuity in a disruptive time.

So if you are in the position of trying to help a widower, watch out you don't try to help him too much. He's another person, like you and me. He's having a difficult time of it now, but he hasn't become an alien, and the misfortune that he has suffered is neither an unspeakable horror that needs to be avoided nor a disease that must be examined and cured. If you can treat him with the equanimity with which the folks at the bath treated the man on crutches, you may be doing him a great favor. That is the way a support system works.

It really worked for Jan. People not only treated him as a normal man in abnormal circumstances, they also legitimated his feelings, they gave him a sense he was cared about, and they gave him accurate expectations of what he would be going through. Perhaps most important, they gave him examples of how to get through it.

From seeing people die at home, from seeing his crippled cousin cope, from seeing how his neighbors survived the murder of their child—Jan has lots of models for how to live beyond a crisis. They work not just as role models, but also as something of a standard. He is, as he says, part of these people, and they are part of him, and because of that he has something of a responsibility to their example.

Not that he has to be like them. In fact, there appears to be a lot of respect for individual ways of doing things in this family, which is somewhat unusual. But there does seem to be a collective sense in his family that "we endure." And there also seems to be a feeling that "we can do." Faced with an alcoholic grandmother in their midst, the family members do not pretend the problem is nonexistent, nor do they scorn the grandmother for it. They accept the problem as part of life and address it directly, by rationing her.

Jan is very lucky. He was able to draw on the collective strength and experience of an entire tribe to back him up. If you are a recently widowed man and you have this kind of family around you, or if you have managed to find this sort of community outside your family, you can count your blessings. Unfortunately, this kind of family network is something that few of us have anymore, if we ever did. It used to be like this, or at least we like to think it was like this, when families stayed in one place and communities didn't change for generations. But now, as families scatter and communities become less cohesive, it's rare for a man to find himself with such a well-developed network, so full of meaningful connections and experience. Jan's situation is, in a way, a flashback to the past, and in some ways it may be better than the way we handle things now.

One of the ways we handle things now is that we have come to believe that if you can talk about your feelings, somehow you're doing something right, and that if you don't talk about your feelings, somehow you are not doing your work. But you can talk about your problems ad nauseum and still not have the faintest idea of what in the world to do about them. Talking about your situation by itself is not a solution, and the fact that Jan doesn't talk much about his feelings doesn't mean he isn't dealing with them.

On the contrary, Jan goes off to the woods to be *with* his feelings, and he is clearly doing his work. His attitude toward Donald Lacy is evidence of that. It must have taken a lot of work for Jan to make peace with the fact that Donald Lacy had a claim on the woods, just as he and June did, and to acknowledge that he and June were among the "strange people" that frequented the place, just as Donald Lacy was. Some people can talk and talk about their feelings and never arrive at this kind of philosophical understanding. Others can reach this kind of understanding without *ever* talking about their feelings. So if you are a widower who is being pressed to "talk about it," and you know yourself well enough to know that you handle things better by walking alone in the woods, by all means do what feels most right for you.

But also keep this in mind, while Jan shows wisdom in his faith that the answers will emerge from within him—or, somehow, from the woods—it hasn't stopped him from talking to a lot of other people. He goes and talks to this uncle, his neighbors, his parents-in-law, his parents, even though, ultimately, he understands that the answers will come from him. It is an important concept: There is nobody but yourself who really knows what you need to do, but that doesn't mean you don't need to listen to other people's experiences and gather all the knowledge you can. Other people can make you aware of the range of options that exists. You don't have to talk about every little emotional tic you have, or even necessarily about the big emotional storms, but you do need to be in touch with people, to communicate.

Unfortunately, at a time like this, you aren't always able to communicate as well as you might want to, or need to. This is especially true when it comes to your children. One of the dilemmas of being a newly widowed parent is that at a time when your children are most needy, you have the least to give them. Fortunately for Jan, there were others around who were paying attention to his son, and once they pointed out the problem, Jan was able to respond.

Exactly how to respond to children is another problem. Isn't it interesting how Paul's problem—how to deal with his anger—goes right to the jugular? Kids have a way of doing that, of raising the very issues their parents have always had issues with themselves and forcing them to confront some things they'd really rather avoid, just as Paul forces Jan to have another look at how he deals with his own anger. Under the best of circumstances, kids challenge their parents like that, but in situations like this, the effect can be even more dramatic. And it can create the danger that a single parent in Jan's position will feel at fault for his children's problems, through neglect, or because somehow he feels he should be doing things differently.

But it isn't necessarily so. Paul's problems may have more to do with his biochemistry or his diet than they do with the kind of example Jan sets for dealing with feelings. There is something going on in Paul that we simply don't understand yet. And to insist that Jan be more expressive, more demonstrative, may be entirely off the point. That is not to say that he *shouldn't* reexamine his relationship to Paul and the kind of model he sets for him, it's just to say that in these situations people are often inclined to feel that they are to blame. When you're feeling vulnerable yourself, it's sometimes easy to blame yourself. But while you *are* responsible for your children, and they *are* in a terrible crisis, just because they have some problems doesn't necessarily mean you have to change what works well for you.

It is worth a brief pause to acknowledge that Jan is right in his assumption that Lisbeth will continue to process all of this as she grows, and that problems may surface later. A personality develops in much the same way a helix unfolds, going around and around the same circle, each time at a different level. Each time Lisbeth comes to the point of the circle that is June's death, she may well have a new reaction as a function of her new stage of growth, and the whole event may have to be attended to again.

This is as true for Paul as it is for Lisbeth, and it's also true for Jan. All of us continually develop and go through new stages, and Jan may very well have to deal with the death again in the future. For children who are now only 8 and 11 years old, however, the differences in perceptions from one developmental stage to the next will be much more dramatic. If you have young children, you can anticipate the renegotiating of their mother's loss several times in the future. Recognizing it when it starts can help you help them with it.

It is generally agreed that getting involved with a woman within two months after becoming a widower—as Jan did—is a dangerous thing. On-the-rebound romances can do a lot more harm than good because they are often desperate attempts to avoid the process of coming to grips with the fact that your wife is finally gone, what that really means to you, and accommodating yourself to it. Getting involved again right away is often an attempt to short-circuit that process by replacing your wife with another woman and continuing on as you were (in the way that in soap operas, when an actor leaves the show, another actor is simply hired to play the same role and go on as if nothing were different).

It isn't the speed of the re-alliance that matters as much as the quality of it, and the way that you've dealt with your grief. Jan's involvement with Delores doesn't seem to be a way of short-circuiting his grief. He's conscious of the dangers and is careful not to take it too fast. He's in no hurry to marry her or set up housekeeping with her. There is no quality of frenzy or fear in this re-alliance.

Jan does seem to have done his grieving, and to have found a place for June in his life. Delores is not an attempt to replace her, or to fill the gap she left. She is an independent event. Jan's description of the place that June now has in his life, as that part of an expanding whole that is no longer expanding, is a beautifully visualized concept of an appropriate resolution.

If you are in the position of advising a widower, it might be a mistake to assume automatically that a quick re-alliance is necessarily "bad." Each situation needs to be considered independently. But knowing what we do about the confusion and panic of bereavement, we can suggest that consolidating a new alliance right away by rushing into another marriage is at least a little risky.

For all the risk that might be involved, though, many do remarry quickly. Faced with the devastation that George described in the first chapter, and finding themselves without the kind of support that Sam got from his religion, that Jim got from his work, and that Jan got from his family, most men turn to the support system that has always worked best for them. They turn to another wife.

Hank

HANK is 61. He is a retired salesman. He met Janet when he was in college (she was a registered nurse in the town) and they married when they were both 24. In the course of a thirty-seven-year marriage, they had one son together, Jack, now 32 and married, and living half an hour away.

When Janet was in her early 30s, she had a nervous breakdown (she was diagnosed as manic-depressive) and spent about a year in a psychiatric hospital. It was never clear what brought the condition on, but after she was released from the hospital, with medication, she was able to lead an active life. In fact, according to Hank, "When she was in good shape, she was one of the most enthusiastic people you'd ever want to meet."

Janet remained relatively stable for the next several years, but about four months after Hank retired, she went into a deep depression which got subtly but steadily worse over the next six months. Finally, one April afternoon while Hank was at the hardware store, Janet committed suicide.

This interview was conducted fifty weeks to the day after she died.

Believe it or not, we had been doing the very same chore I was doing today, putting up the screens. We had done that job as a team for years. And after, she lay down on the couch and said, "I'm just so pooped, would you run an errand for me at the market?" I didn't have any indication she was going to do anything. She had never tried this before. And a person with suicide on her mind doesn't say, "I think I'll go downstairs now and commit suicide, will you go to the store?" you know.

So I says, "Sure, Sweetie. You just lay here." And I went off to the store. When I came home, she had hung herself. She'd taken a strand of rope and gone downstairs and gotten up on a chair and jumped off the chair, I guess. It's a whale of a boot in the ass, to come home and find your wife hanging there, it is. It was a tough one. A real tough one. And in her note she said, "I just couldn't face an institution again." It said, "You've done everything you could. I'm sorry to cause all this trouble, but I just couldn't face the prospect of having to go back in an institution. And I never let Dr. Tapscott know how sick I really was."

She'd been seeing this psychiatrist, see—Bob Tapscott—about her smoking. In the last six months, she got very discouraged that she couldn't stop smoking. She was not a heavy smoker, but I had stopped smoking and all her brothers and sisters had stopped and they were on her case because she still was smoking. I says, "Well gee, come on, you know. Six or seven cigarettes a day aren't gonna hurt you. Forget it. Let's go out and do something else." But somehow in the chemistry of these poor folks with depression . . .

Smoking represented a larger issue to her, a much larger issue. She was seeing the psychiatrist on the pretext of helping her stop smoking, but there was much more bothering her that she was hoping he'd help her find. I'm not a psychiatrist, but I think it was the idea that she was not able to cope with this challenge. The psychiatrist said to me that when you have this darn condition, what's a mole hill becomes a mountain.

About a year ago, I noticed that she was starting to lose interest in just about everything. Normally, boy, she couldn't wait to get out and golf on a Thursday morning. I'd come home Thursday night, and she'd replay the golf game for me. This was a very devoted interest, it pepped her up and kept her going. But then all of a sudden she just really didn't have anything for it, you know. She actually stopped playing golf.

Then in the early part of April, we drove down to New Orleans. I really planned this trip for her. I'd been there before, but I wanted her to see this, I wanted her to see that. I'm one of these guys, I get a kick out of organizing things. I'm sort of a trip buff in the fact that I'll say, well gee, we'll try to get this far this day so that will permit us to spend the night with so-and-so, or because there's a good place to eat in that town. . . But things weren't going right for her. All during that trip she was just so tired. And I think this was one of those triggering things—that she felt she had failed, that she had not shown enthusiasm for the things that I'd sort of planned for her benefit.

She had an appointment to see the doctor the day after she took her life. I had sort of resolved in my mind that on that day I would either go with her, or make an appointment of my own with Tapscott, to say, gee, I think Janet needs more help than she gets just once every two weeks meeting with you about smoking. Maybe it's getting tough again. She's been in an institution before. . .

I think I'd mentioned it to her. I think I said, "Well, sweetie, would it help if both of us talked with him?" Not to imply that gee, you're in tough shape, we're going to ship you off to the Funny Farm. Not that sort of a cold thing. But I wish she could have talked to me more. I wish she could have said, "Gee this thing is tough. This thing is harder than hell." I would have said, "I know it's tough. But maybe you could get away and get something that would do you some good . . ." I wish she could have opened up more, maybe we could have gotten more help. But this is the nature of the illness. She wouldn't share it with anyone.

You wonder what could you have done. But I don't know what I could have done. Sure, I snapped at her, she snapped at me, and things like that. But that's the normal conflict of living. You assume these things. You do things that she doesn't like and she does things you don't like. But there were never tremendous pressures. I was happy with our life, she should have been happy too. There certainly wasn't financial worry—we were financially secure—and there were no physical worries. It's not like the guy with terminal cancer whose doctor says, hey you'll be lucky if you're around six months from now.

But you think about these things. I said, "While I'm out at the grocery store I'm gonna go by the hardware store and pick up that paint we were talking about." And she says, "Oh gee, you want to do that?" And I says, "I might as well do it today." And she says, "Well, okay." Whether this was a plea . . . How the hell would I know? "Go ahead and run a quick errand, but you'd better hurry back because you might be able to save me . . ." Maybe that was a plea on her part. Maybe she wanted to be found or something before she died. You figure, well, maybe she would have survived a five-minute trip to the grocery store. But it took me fifteen minutes because the guy at the hardware store was horsing around with mixing the paints . . . Maybe this is something that I conjure up, but it haunts you.

This tremendous onus on the survivor—there's got to be a bigger picture. I think the thing is much broader than that. Mental chemistry is a factor. And dammit, not to be crass about it or anything like that, but should I carry this? Am I wrong in not having this tremendous burden that it's all my fault? Or it's 99 percent my fault? People can really get impacted by this, by going through this horrible thing. If they say "It's all my fault that she did it, I am the one that did it," then they're going to be in as bad a state in six months as their wife was when she died.

This is a very tragic thing. It is a disease. And while you say, What could I have done? What could I have done? you've got to stop it. Good Lord, people don't know much about suicide, you know. There's so much mystery about it. Hundreds of times you say, what could I have done? But objectively, darn it . . . This gal was financially well off. A nice home, as you can see. She had nice interests and things like that. There's just something here that's . . . There's more than just the apparent day-to-day relationships that are responsible for suicide. There's something that's very deep, deep and disturbed and mysterious, and very tragic that's behind it. There's a whale of a lot more to it than just one's individual behavior in a relationship.

I hate to say it but I'm gonna say it. I mean, God, it's gotta be the craziest thing to go kill yourself. I mean, I'd no more jump off a bridge . . . I'm a chicken, you know? That's the way I've always felt. The *determination* you've got to have. The determination—I won't say courage—but the *determination* that things are so bad that you have to take your own life . . . God.

I had to set standards. And one of the first standards I set pretty damned early on in the game was, listen, Logan, don't start feeling sorry for yourself. The problems you have are nothing compared to the problems Janet had, the frustrations of running the house, and so on. That was one premise that I accepted very early on. Pretty damned soon after it happened, I'd say within a week.

Then I talked to this doctor in town. Helluva nice guy, a retired doctor who lost his wife. Dan Conway, swell guy to talk to. I said, hey, let's you and I get out on the golf course and spend a few hours together. I just wanted to talk to him because he was a medical man and he had gone through this himself. So we played golf together once. And he was very helpful. He said, keep busy. Keep your interests going. Don't let yourself climb into despair. This was in the first month or two.

I hit sleeping pills pretty hard those first few months, but then as things got going, I got out of them. And I'd say now I'm pretty well done with grieving. It's a real challenging thing I've been through, but I've bounced back pretty well, because I've had this relationship . . .

This is a major factor in getting me on track and continuing on with my life. For several years, my mother was in a nursing home here in town. And there was another woman like Janet who had a mother-in-law in the place. And this gal, whose name was Dorothy, Janet got very friendly with. She said, Dorothy, don't you come up here and stay at a motel—Dorothy lives several hours away—you come stay at our house. So for five years, this gal has visited us. She was very fond of Janet, and Janet was fond of her.

After Janet went, Dorothy's mother-in-law got very sick, so we started to see quite a bit of each other, just by circumstances. She would come up and stay at the house, you know, to visit her mother-in-law. Dorothy's husband died of cancer ten or twelve years ago, so she was in the same boat that I was, both widowed prematurely, and she had been a good friend of Janet's. And as we got talking, we found that we could talk frankly about losing our spouses, and it developed into a relationship in those first three months. I've seen a lot of Dorothy. It's become a lovely relationship. We're getting along just great. In fact, we're planning to marry this summer.

It may be a little bit sudden, but this is not an impulsive thing. Some guys, you know, get very impulsive. Go into a bar and there's a blond and, boy, doesn't she look sexy! And immediately go head-over-heels. That'll happen sometimes, when a guy goes off the deep end. But this is a person that had been my wife's friend for five or six years before, so I don't feel that it's that impulsive. And Janet liked her very much. I'm sure if it were somebody that Janet hadn't liked, I'm sure the woman would turn me off.

My son's reaction to this is . . . polite. I think to accept a step-mother . . . I don't know. Very frankly, he hasn't got a tremendous enthusiasm. I think he feels that maybe I should have waited a little bit. We had a heart-to-heart and he says, you know, when I was in college I used to tell the younger fellas to get engaged for four or five years. Well, that makes sense when you're 21. But it's different when you're 61. I'd love to see him show some warmth. But I think he can find commonality with his potential stepsisters. He and his wife are career-oriented, and both of Dorothy's girls are career-oriented, and we're hoping this yuppie orientation, the common interests of being young people in their thirties, will create a commonality.

But I lean heavily towards Ed Post, this minister I talked to, a retired minister in town. He said, gee there's nothing to worry about with somebody you've known. Dorothy's a grand gal, and I don't think it's gonna be bad for either one of you. It's not like somebody sets up a dinner party with this beautiful blond that just came in from Texas, and she owns six oil wells or something like that and boy, that sounds good and bingo! within three weeks you're talking marriage or something.

He knows Dorothy, see, from her devotion to her mother-in-law, as being a pretty decent person. Dorothy was the only person this woman had in the world. There were no other sisters or brothers. So Dorothy took on the task of taking care of her mother-in-law, who was not the easiest person. But she did it out of a sense of duty because it was her first husband's mother, and there was no one else in the world to pay much attention to her.

So Ed was pushing this thing early on. I felt a little self-conscious when Dorothy would show up, you know. I wanted to be nice to her, to say, "Come on, use the house, even though we're not married." She'd sleep out in this room and I'd sleep up in my bedroom upstairs. But he said, "Gee, I see you're taking care of Dorothy, that's great. Isn't that nice to open your house. Gee, that's good for you." This kind of encouragement. Because he knew and liked her, you see, and I think he knows and likes me.

Her mother-in-law died in December and we started talking about getting married about the first of the year. I am not making formal announcements until a year after Janet's death, out of respect for her. But Memorial Day weekend, Dorothy will start wearing her ring and stuff like that.

We're going to start off in this house—she's gonna clean out one room and that's gonna be for her stuff—with the understanding that we may both feel more comfortable living somewhere else, because of the memories of Janet. Or we may stay. I'd like to stay, from a selfish standpoint, because this place is an old shoe, and I have lots of friends and lots of things to do, you know. But that's pretty selfish on my part.

She has her roots in Tennessee, and she's cutting herself free from those roots and coming to live among Janet's roots, and I think that takes a lot of courage on this gal's part. People have been very nice to her, but there will always be things like, well, Janet liked to play bridge on Tuesday. Or, you know, comments like this. It's going to be much tougher on her than it is on me because I have my established interests.

But I'll have to make some sacrifices and readjustments, too. This gal had severe financial problems after she was widowed and she had to go back to teaching to make ends meet and educate her girls. Janet, who never worked, concentrated on keeping up the house. This is a conflict that we're going to have to work on. Dorothy has always had to get up in the morning and face a bunch of screaming eighth-graders until 2:00 in the afternoon, and she tends to come home and just flop, and maybe the bed isn't made and maybe the coffee pot isn't cleaned, things like that. I think that that's one thing that we're going to have to concentrate on. But I'm sure we can work it out.

If your wife just committed suicide, I'd say—just from my own experience, not as an expert or anything—hey, you've gotten a kick between the teeth and in the fanny here and, boy it is a toughie. Apparently things were going well and what the heck's the matter? I would say it's gonna bother you, you're always gonna have this constant thing the rest of your life—What could I have done different? What could I have done different? But I think it's important to realize that there's much more to the darn thing than your behavior. There's something in the chemistry, the genes or heredity, God-knows-what, that motivated this person to take her own life. You can't comprehend it. I think this is very important. You cannot comprehend somebody who's going through this kind of thing.

Second, in respect to her and in respect to your family, you've got to somehow continue. Do your best to carry on, do the best with what's left of your life, by keeping your interests up. You've suddenly got a brand new life. Make the best of it. You can.

I would say having this gal who was in the background, so to speak, has made things easier for me. If she hadn't been there, I think it would've been quite a bit tougher. I think it would be awfully easy, without this sort of motivation, to just sort of drag yourself down. I think you can just sort of shrink. Cut out outside interests. I could have just kind of circled my wagons. I don't know. I do not know.

The guy who works at the paint store—in fact, the guy I was seeing the day Janet went—he lost his wife about three or four months before Janet died, and now he goes to his daughter's house every night for dinner. That's his routine, he goes every night. But I wonder if his adjustment of always going to his daughter's house . . . It's a loving thing

on the part of his daughter, but really . . . For him to make more of
an adjustment to what his life should be, he could say, well I'll come
over every Sunday for dinner and maybe you guys live your own life
for the rest of the week. I think if my son said, hey, you've got to come
over, I'd say, you've got your own life. I think I would feel like I was
imposing.

But I have had good training. See, my business life was in sales, and
I think this is a factor. You know 90 percent of your job, when you're
in sales, is rejection. It's a very personal thing. I've been screamed at
in guys' offices—*You and your goddam company, you've completely
messed us up!* I've had guys go ranting and raving and just completely
raking you over the coals, but dammit you have to recover and be cheer-
ful and enthusiastic at the next factory down the road. Twenty years
of that, getting your fanny chewed out six ways to Sunday, then bouncing back—that's good training. You know, sometimes when you've
lost a couple hundred thousand dollars' worth of business, you're feeling pretty low. But if you're going to do your job, you've got to bounce
back and be enthusiastic the next place you go. In that sort of a situation, you just have to say, well gee, that was tough but I've got to keep
going. You have to smile and show enthusiasm to the next guy.

In understanding Hank, it might be helpful to know that to a large
extent this transcript doesn't reflect what he really sounds like. His talk
was so full of false starts and stammers that to make it readable, it had
to be distilled several times before the content was clear. To some extent, that's true for every story in this book—none of these men is quite
as coherent and articulate as he may sound. When you're under emotional stress, your verbal precision can suffer a lot.

But with Hank, the effect was very pronounced, and it demonstrates
the degree to which he is not accustomed to exploring his feelings—or
anyone else's—and articulating them. In that way, he is very traditional. Men of his generation and class, and perhaps of his profession, are
not conditioned to examine or express their feelings. And, as soon as
the feelings get very complex, they may lose track of them altogether.

This makes Hank's task of trying to come to grips with Janet's suicide
especially difficult. If you're not particularly practiced at plumbing the
depths of the human psyche, how do you come to an understanding
of how and why such a thing could happen? If the psychiatrist can't
understand it, how in the world can Hank?

The simple answer is, he can't. Suicide *is* a mystery and very deeply rooted. And it is also true that we don't know a lot about clinical depression. Hank tried to understand Janet's depression in terms of the stress of running the house, but Janet was operating under a different set of rules. When a person is clinically depressed, all our customary assumptions simply do not apply.

Because of all these unknowns, there is tremendous pressure on suicide survivors to take the blame for the death. The pressure comes both from without and within, and it is essentially an attempt to understand what we don't understand. Unresolved mystery makes us nervous, and death is altogether unnerving and mysterious enough without the added question of why someone would bring it on herself. So we seek a cause.

We sometimes seek it with a vengeance. We all have times in our lives when we would just as soon "give up," but we survive on this planet in part because we live by an unspoken covenant that we are all in this boat together. Sometimes it's little more than that that keeps us keeping on. When someone commits suicide, it is a betrayal of that bond with the rest of humanity, a breaking of that convenant. That betrayal makes us angry, and we want to blame somebody. When you are the one who was closer than anyone else to the person who killed herself, it is very easy, in the vulnerability, confusion, and helplessness you feel in that loss, to take the blame on yourself.

Hank is right not to accept that blame. In fact, his resistance to it may well be the strongest card in his hand. Suicide raises a lot of questions. Why would she not talk to me? Why was she so miserable with me? Why did she abandon me? Why did she do this to *me?* The list goes on and on. If you're a suicide survivor, you can get mired in these kinds of questions. Hank is right—within six months, you could be in worse shape than your wife was when she died. If you have lost your wife in this way, be aware of this phenomenon and fight it with all you've got. As deeply as you may need to explain the reasons for your wife's suicide, and as convenient as you yourself may be as a protagonist, it will not do you any good to cast yourself in that role. To a large extent, you may simply have to learn to live with the mystery.

But that doesn't necessarily mean you just take a deep breath and smile at the next one. When Hank first compared the loss of his wife to the loss of a business account, I have to admit I was taken aback. Could this really represent his understanding of what he has lost? Is this his grasp of the situation? But maybe "smiling at the next one" is not the impoverished metaphor it might at first appear to be.

For a man who lived twenty years with a wife who was clinically depressed, the satisfactions of work had to be profoundly influential in
the way he dealt with life. We know that, in any case, work is central
to most men's understanding of life. To that extent, Hank's constant
practice at dealing with rejection at work, perhaps, really did prepare
him for his wife's suicide. It does take a kind of courage, in a way,
to go back on the playing field—to go right back into marriage—after
such a "kick in the teeth." Hank could be demonstrating a courage,
pluck, and resilience that he developed on the job.

Knowing what we do about grief, however, we have to be at least
a little bit skeptical of a man who announces, fifty weeks after he finds
his wife hanging in the basement, that he is "done with grieving."
Grief is not that quickly dispatched. It is a process, it takes time, and
there is work involved in it. You cannot just glide by it, even if it is
your established style to skim the surface of your feelings. There are
depths that will be sounded and you must deal with them.

Many men would much prefer to finesse their bereavement, and the
usual way is to reassemble their lives as they were before, to put another
bridal doll on top of the cake and continue. The fact that Hank committed himself to another woman within three months of his wife's
death raises the question of avoiding or postponing grief. It is very hard
to believe that Hank is actually done with his grieving, especially given
the fact that grieving a suicide is a more complicated process than grieving a "normal" death. What is believable, perhaps, is that Dorothy
is his grieving *agent*. Except for that game of golf with the doctor, which
was cursory at best, it appears the only person with whom Hank talks
about Janet's death is Dorothy. It is with her that he's doing his grief
work, if he's doing it at all. A quick remarriage can work, perhaps,
when the new wife facilitates the grieving and helps the widower find
a way to lay his first wife to rest. While it is estimated that more than
half of all such marriages end in divorce, about half succeed in one
way or another—or if they don't succeed, at least they continue.

In spite of the strikes it may at first appear to have against it (it could
be an attempt to bypass bereavement, and it does not have the emotional support of the surrounding family), Hank's marriage to Dorothy
may succeed. They've known each other for some time, and she apparently shares his values. Since Hank knows Janet would approve, he has,
in a way, her "permission." And finally, they are attuned to the potential for a problem in the fact that Dorothy doesn't exactly fit Hank's
understanding of what a good wife should be: she's not quite the house-

keeper Janet was. To the extent they anticipate such problems, they can address them. If they address them by compromising, maybe they can make it work.

But quick realliances *don't* always work. The pain that can result can be intense for both parties, as we will see with Mark.

Mark

MARK is 30 years old. He is a journalist and a teacher. He met Joanne the summer before their senior year in college, but it didn't turn into a romance until the end of the following summer, and it was a full five years before they decided to get married. The slow pace of the relationship suited them both for different reasons—Joanne, because she loved solitude and insisted on independence, and Mark, because he was reluctant to commit himself to permanence.

From the moment he was introduced to her, Mark knew that Joanne had cancer, but neither of them realized how serious it really was. Periodically, through their courtship and marriage, tumors appeared and were removed and doctors said they had "gotten it all." But the cancers always reappeared, and finally, on their honeymoon, Joanne began to succumb. Six months after they married, she died. Six months later, Mark was involved with another woman—a woman who, incidentally, resembled Joanne physically—and within a year was living with her.

This interview was conducted about a year after Joanne died.

She died on April 21. It was a very rainy day. The day daylight savings went into effect, so she had even one less hour . . . She died at 8:30. Her sisters and her brothers and I stayed in the room for a couple of hours with her body, just kind of watching it change, watching things happen to it . . .

She was in the hospital for the last week. She was medicated with morphine, so she was in and out all the time. She had times of great lucidity and other times she was in a dream world—she'd say funny things and we'd laugh. There were a lot of laughs. It was just so nice not to see her in pain. I knew that she was going to die, but it didn't seem to me like it was going to happen right away. It's too unbearable to think it's going to happen today or tomorrow. Or even the next day. But she slipped into a coma Saturday night, so on Sunday she wasn't really there. All the family was there. But she was, she was already gone. She just started moaning, the moaning . . . on every exhalation, a moan. It went on like that for three hours. And then she just . . .

She was lying in bed and we were all around the bed and I was holding her hand. I had my forehead on her hand, and suddenly there was this gurgling from her throat. And someone said, ''Oh! She's gonna vomit! Turn her on her side!'' Which was absurd, because she hadn't had any food for days: She couldn't have vomited. But we turned her on her side and all this . . . *blood* just came . . . *gushing* . . . *Oh!* Out of her nose and her mouth! And her sister screamed, ''She's *dying!*'' And obviously she was. That gurgle was the death rattle.

And then she was dead. The life had left her hours before. She was gone, there was nothing in her eyes; she looked like a fish, a fish that's been out of water but still twitches sometimes—but this was . . . her body just finally died, stopped trying. We closed her eyes. Her brother and I, we changed the sheets and her gown. And we just stayed in the room and watched her. And it's funny, her body did become less and less like . . . a person. It did become an object. It had this kind of marble look, kind of like a sculpture. I thought she looked Egyptian. She'd lost so much weight, she looked mummified. Her cheeks were so hollow and her cheekbones were so prominent. And her nose was so proud. She'd lost almost all of her hair. I said, ''Look, she looks Egyptian.'' Nobody else saw that.

At first, I was in shock. I was numb. I would find myself saying to myself, ''Why did this happen to me?'' But there was also an element of fascination with the adventure—I mean, to be a widower at the age of 29? The night after she died, her sisters and brothers and I went to dinner at a friend's with a couple of other old, old friends, and I was kind of jovial. I brought this champagne that Joanne and I had gotten for a wedding present and had never drunk, and we drank that and talked about Joanne. I gave them all a minute-by-minute account of how she died. It was fun. At one point somebody said something—I forget what it was—but somebody said something about me and I said, "Well, you can't say that now, because I'm a widower now. Ha-ha." It was a joke. It was funny. There was this unbelievability to it. To be a widower at 29.

It took about a month before the misery of it began to hit me— that's why I say I was numb. I wasn't crying the first two or three weeks after she died. Not the day that she died, not the day after. But starting about a month afterwards, all I was doing was crying. Her sister came to visit one weekend, and when she went home Sunday afternoon—it was a beautiful, sunny day, and I watched her go down the street—I just burst into tears. Couldn't stop. That kind of stuff just started happening. There was just such . . . despair. I hadn't understood that. I didn't know it would be like that. I had never felt anything like it before. I'd felt loneliness and depression before, but never such a sense of loss.

For a while in there, I became devoted to the obituaries. To say it made me feel better doesn't sound quite right, but it made me realize that a lot of young people die of cancer. For a while, I cut out their obits and I'd say, I'm gonna wait three or four weeks and I'm gonna write that person. But I never wrote.

I had tons of rituals like that. It was hard for me to throw away the toothpaste tube that had been in the house when Joanne was last in the house, and I kept it all summer. I got another toothpaste tube and used up another whole tube of toothpaste before I would use that. I had a friend for dinner last summer and he said, "Well, I'm gonna do the dishes!" And he got up and started doing the dishes. And I almost said "Stop!" because he was using the last of the soap, the dish soap . . . And pictures of Joanne. I can't quite . . .

Talk about ritualistic. Joanne was cremated, as she wanted to be, and she wanted her ashes scattered at the beach. So about two weeks after she died, her father and mother and her two sisters and I drove out to the shore, and Joanne's two sisters and I were squished in the back and I was holding this urn. It wasn't an urn, it was a wine bucket that a very good friend of Joanne's had given us to keep the ashes in, an old thirties-style hotel wine bucket, coated with brass. We knew Joanne would have thought that was pretty funny: Here she was in a wine bucket—and I had this thing on my lap. And we were driving to the beach. And Linda, the older sister, the one who looks so much like Joanne—she's a very sexy, sensual person—and we were driving along all squished together and I started getting really horny. It was just academic horniness. But than I started getting an erection, because the urn, the wine bucket, bouncing on my lap . . . And I was just thinking, not for the first time, but in this sick and distracted way, about going to bed with Linda, and meanwhile getting this erection while meanwhile Joanne's ashes in the urn were bouncing on my lap. Those things would happen and I would stand back and think, this is really funny, I really have to remember this.

But then we got to the beach. It was a beautiful day. A real Joanne kind of day. And we were throwing the ashes. And as we'd throw these clumps of ashes, the wind would carry them down the beach, and you'd see the shadow of the ashes following along on the sand, and the ashes would slowly dissipate and the shadow would slowly dissipate, and it was really beautiful. It took about half an hour. And then we all sat down for a while, and there was a little piece of bone right next to where I sat. I picked it up and put it in my pocket. I kept it in my pocket for weeks. It became like a talisman.

In June, I went to Europe. A friend of mine was living in Rome, and I went to stay with him. I wasn't sure what he'd be like. He's a very good, a very close friend, but a very difficult person. He has a hard time with his emotions. As Joanne got sicker and sicker, he had kind of stopped writing. From most people, I would take that kind of bitterly, but from him I realized—the written word is sacred to him. He can't put it on paper unless it's the apex of his feeling. It's got to express it all. And I think what happened was that he just didn't know what to say, so he didn't say anything.

There were some friends like that, who just disappeared. And there were others who called every day. And not always the people you would expect. But I don't take it as a . . . I mean, it hurt in a way, but at the same time I can understand . . . I mean, I'm not sure I wouldn't feel that way too. My landlord died last September of a heart attack— he lived downstairs—and I felt helpless with his widow. I just didn't know what to say. They'd been married sixty years. And I thought, well if anyone should know how to say something . . . But all I could say was, "Wow, I know how you feel." And then at work, a friend of mine, his mother died in the nursing home, and I felt so awkward saying, "Gee, I'm really sorry," just as awkward as I would have felt two years ago. It isn't easy for friends. But I don't know what people do who don't have friends.

So anyway, by the time I came back from Rome, I was crying less, but still crying. I was taking care of things, but feeling very drained of energy. The idea of working, actually working, for eight hours a day was beyond me. It took me a month and a half to do one free-lance article. And that was all I was doing.

But from midsummer on, I guess, I was starting to get back into things. The summer itself helped a lot. I love summertime, eating out under trees and having aperitifs on balconies and all that kind of crap. Meeting for drinks at outdoor restaurants . . . I met this friend from work for dinner at an outdoor café. And we drank about five martinis straight. It was supposed to be a midsummer romantic episode—we were kind of at that time deciding whether we were going to get involved in a relationship—and it was sort of fun. And part of the reason it was fun was because I hadn't been able to do it, because I'd been with Joanne for five years and I hadn't done those things. In that sense, there was a feeling that "Gee, well maybe this isn't *all* for the worst. This is fun to have dates, this is fun to have drinks with people under umbrellas." But it was sort of an act. I was empty. I was really not there. I was going through the motions. In a sense, I think, so was Ann. She was just recently divorced. I met a lot of people like that, a lot. I was drawn to people in pain, and they were drawn to me.

But I just wanted to meet people, I wanted to meet a lot of people. I wanted to meet a lot of women. Not for anything serious. I didn't really *expect* anything. I couldn't. I spent so much of my time thinking about Joanne that I couldn't imagine . . . First of all, I thought any woman who would even consider getting into something serious with me would be crazy, and I wouldn't trust her. Second, I had about one-sixteenth of my emotional self available to someone else. But, I was thinking that I had been involved for seven years with someone and now I was single, and maybe I ought to try to get some enjoyment from that.

I had had a few one-night stands, but I'd forgotten . . . When I was 20 they were fun, but at 30 they're just exhausting. I mean, even when it was fun, even when it was nice, even when I really *liked* the person, it did make me lonely. I remember one night in Rome, I met this woman . . . We spent the night together. It sort of surprised me. I didn't expect it. And I went home the next day and cried and cried. And cried. Because it *had* been nice. It reminded me what it was like to spend . . . I was in such a state of shock that I still, I was like, that kind of feeling, a living person, was something I'd forgotten.

I met Judy in September. I was getting ready to take a ferry. I was in a bakery at closing time and they asked me to latch the screen door—I was standing right by the door—and a moment later she walked up and tried to open it. It was just a screen door, I was standing right there, and in my usual wimpy way I said, "Well, um, the door's locked," when I could have unlocked it and let her in. And she just sort of looked at me like, "Well, you asshole, why don't you open it?" She didn't say that. She just looked it. And she looked real disappointed. So I said, "Well, I'll get you something. What do you want?" And she waited outside and I brought it to her.

She was exotic looking. I thought she was very attractive. I took her for a lawyer. I looked for her on the boat, but I didn't see her anywhere. I figured she *must* be there—that's why everyone was in that part of town at 6:00 on a Sunday night—but there were millions of people. I went all over looking for her—back and forth, back and forth—but I couldn't find her anywhere. So finally I gave up and went to get a drink. And I saw her, sitting alone. Looking out the window. So I asked if I could buy her a drink, and we talked all the way back. And in that space of time I managed to tell her I was a widower—which I'd gotten very good at doing.

I called her up the next week. I'd gotten her number on the ferry. I was totally unbashful. I told her I was just real anxious to meet new people these days and asked "Can I take your number? Or will you take mine?" I'd always been shyer, more aware of the game, whereas now I would say, "Look, I'm a widower. My wife died of cancer six months ago. I'm really in a state of shock and I need to meet people. You seem nice. I'd like to talk to you." People would respond to that. I was trying to remind myself that it's a big, big world and there are lots of people to meet. I can miss Joanne but that doesn't mean I have to not meet new people and not even sleep with them. I was convinced I was going to have another relationship, but I couldn't see how it was going to happen. I figured it wouldn't be right away.

It didn't become a real intense relationship right away—at first I saw her once a week, and then I was seeing her three times a week—but then Thanksgiving came and we were going to be apart for five days and for the first time we realized, "My God, we're going to miss each other." Up to then, we weren't really *involved*.

I suppose I got involved at least in part to shake myself free of Joanne. I was looking for somebody. The women I met during the summer—one was 24, too young. I was bringing too much baggage, and she was bringing too little. The other was 33 years old, and she was married and divorced, and she was definitely interested in children at some point, and was looking to replace her marriage. That was too much for me. Too scary. Judy had been married twice and had two kids and didn't want to have kids anymore. She may or may not have been thinking about getting married again. But in any case she seemed willing to kind of stand back and wait and look . . . I mean, she's nine years older than me. I think that had something to do with it. And also, she didn't seem that affected by my being a widower. I also thought that she was a real nurturing kind of influence. She was very good at understanding, at getting to the core of things, to the core of emotional issues. She's really got a knack for it. And she's very smart and funny. She's really a wonderful person. That's why I feel so bad.

I really can't say what she had to do with it, if she had anything to do with it. I think if she hadn't moved in, I would have gotten depressed anyway. But whatever would have happened, I would have wanted her to move in. Because, for good reasons or not, I would have seen it as a change. Some action taken. A new commitment. Some energy. Some action.

She moved in in February, which is when I got depressed. February 15 was the day . . . I really remember the day it happened. It was like a chemical change. I went running—she went along—and then we went to look at a house. I'd been sort of looking at houses to buy. We were sort of in a hurry after running to make the appointment, and I didn't do cooling down exercises. So we got in the car, very sweaty, and we went to look at the house. And you know that's always sort of tense. We stood outside talking about the house for about fifteen minutes, and I got real cold, then we got in the car and went home. I was feeling really weird. Spacey. Dizzy. Weird. And I laid down on the couch here and I just started to sob. I just started to sob. It had nothing to do with Joanne. But something just came over me. I felt nothing but despair, nothing but depression. I thought, "My life is shit." And I started to sob and I couldn't stop. Judy didn't know. She was reading the paper, and the radio was on and I was lying facing the back of the couch. I didn't want to tell her, to have her think that I was unhappy, after she had just moved in. But all the rest of that evening, I would just start sobbing. I had read something once in the *Reader's Digest* about this guy who had somehow upset his electrolyte balance or something by running, and it had sent him into some sort of a psychotic depression. I really thought I had done something to myself that day, running.

I didn't see this depression coming. It really felt like an ambush.

And it felt to me like I was never going to get out of it, like I was in the grip of something. I really felt suicidal for the first time in my life. It was more than just a passing fancy. It was a real kind of dependence on the idea of suicide as a solution. It would come on the days when I woke up depressed. I had never before woken up depressed. It was like there had been a chemical change. And a lot of it *is* chemical. There are studies that show . . . I would open my eyes and with the first sensation of light in my eyes I would think, "I can't get through this day. There is no reason to get through this day. I don't want to do this. I should kill myself." I'd wake up and I'd say, "I don't think people actually survive this. I think it's a lie that people get through this." Even though I knew . . .

I finally saw what depression is. I finally saw the edge of the cliff. I always knew there was a point where people can't stand it anymore. They go crazy or they kill themselves or they slip into some unreachable place. I'd never had a personal sense of that unreachable place, but for the first time in my life, I was able to see it. There were moments when I could see it. Suddenly there's this huge hollow space that swallows you up. And it's very very hard to get back from. You lose your hold.

I'm not sure I have completely pulled back from the edge of that cliff yet. I think a lot of it had to do with the anticipation of the anniversary of Joanne's death, that I was attaching something to that. That somehow I didn't want to let go. Didn't *want* to get beyond it. Because Joanne's death, her illness and death, had been the most important thing that I had ever done—the most difficult, the most challenging, the most important thing that I had ever done in my life. And there I was. It was over. And mundanity was setting in. While she was sick, it was there every day, that sense of urgency. And I could put aside my stupid job at the newspaper. I could go in and put in my eight hours a day, but my real job was with Joanne. Nothing will be that urgent again. That's all gone now. And I haven't found anything nearly as satisfying, nearly as fulfilling, nearly as important.

The depression finally started to lift a week before the anniversary. It was like an illness—like the flu, when it takes a couple of weeks after you've had it to get back to normal. But this took a couple of months. So I felt much more dragged out. People kept telling me it would pass. And I did believe that. As the anniversary was coming up, I think it was a mixture of—I didn't want it to come. I didn't want it to be there. But then when it actually came, it turned out to be a very nice day, a very restful day. I canceled my class, didn't go to work. I spent the morning here at home, writing in my journal. Then a friend came over for lunch. That night I had dinner with the same group of friends I ate with the night after Joanne died. It was nice. But also it made me feel bad because Judy—she's come to know these friends of Joanne's and mine too, we see quite a bit of them—knew she couldn't be there that night. It was hard. It was hard. Here was this day that I was obviously devoting to . . . An impossible situation.

I think part of the depression was that I was letting myself feel a lot of feelings I hadn't been able to feel the year before because I'd been too busy taking care of Joanne. And I think part of it came from having pushed too hard, having thought that I could just throw myself into this thing with Judy. I don't mean living with her. I don't know how much living with her has exacerbated it. But I think it was just feeling like, "Whew! That's over! Now I can build this new relationship." And there was something in me telling me, "No, you can't. Not yet."

I still have the sense sometimes that I'm waiting for normalcy to return. And when I catch myself doing that, I also find myself feeling that normalcy is living with Joanne. It's not a conscious thing, that I'm waiting for Joanne to return. It's not that. It's that something is terribly wrong and I'm waiting for it to change, to get back to the way it was. And the next thought of course is "with Joanne." I don't expect Judy to be like Joanne. I see her for who she is and I don't expect to feel exactly the same way toward her. They're not the same person, I can't expect the same dynamic. But I think one of the problems is that I expect something of the same relationship. It's not that I'm trying to replace Joanne. It's that I'm trying to replace the relationship. And there is a difference. I just want to be plugged into that.

I think every relationship is a replacement for something else. In the case of grief, it's just more apparent. I mean, I've thought about that. And I think that every relationship I ever have will be trying to replace Joanne in some way or other because that was the first really good relationship I ever had. I think I'm always going to be trying to find that kind of love again.

Sometimes I get really angry at Judy. The anger isn't really at her, it's at the situation. And she's just the target. And then I realize, if we ever broke up, then I'd really be lonely. So then I think, well, what do I want? Who is this magic woman out there that's going to make me happy? And I realize she just doesn't exist. I just don't know anybody . . . I've never even met anybody at a cocktail party, even in my wildest fantasies, I can't think of a slim acquaintance or a movie star or anybody who would be, who might have whatever-it-is that would make me happy. I feel like if I can't create it with Judy, if she and I can't do it, I can't imagine somebody else who would be more appropriate. I don't think it's Judy. I don't think it's something that she's lacking, I don't think it's something she needs or demands, or creates. That's what's scary about it. If I can't do it with her . . .

My biggest regret is that I fear I really fucked Judy over. And I don't know if we can pull out of it. I don't even know if . . . At the time I asked her to move in, I was very convincing to her that this was a real relationship, that I saw her for who she really was, that I was committed to her, herself, not just to replacing something else. Now I'm not so sure of that. I mean, some of it is true. She *is* a wonderful person. I *am* committed to her. But not as much as I thought I was. I think I was lying to her. I think I was lying to myself. It's a big disappointment for both of us—to discover that my commitment was more to replacing Joanne than I realized, and that living together was maybe not such a good idea. I really think it was a kind of leap. I sort of feel like it did bad things to the relationship—too much too soon. But I would have done it anyway. I know myself and I know I've made a lot of mistakes in my life and I've been glad I made them. It's better than not trying.

So I have this new plan to move to the country. What I want to do is buy a little land and a shack and redo the shack. I think that making something, actually forming something, building something, would really absorb me for a while. Three months ago, Judy and I would have been talking about that together, but now I talk about it and don't really invite her to be part of it. I feel like it's gotta be my thing. I think it's a place to be with Joanne. A place where I could go and feel free to think about Joanne, where I could put Joanne's pictures and not feel that I was intruding. That's a little too literal. But I guess I really feel a need to be alone right now and to be alone with Joanne. That's when I'm happiest, in a way. I don't sit and think about Joanne. That would be just too awful. But, in a way, dreaming about this place in the country is a way of dreaming about Joanne. Because I'm alone and I'm free to think. There's no one asking for something from me.

Six months after this interview, I spoke with Mark again. Judy had moved out, he had bought a vacation home in the country that he was making over, and he was leaving for a month-long trip to India with a friend. It was not an altogether surprising epilogue to his story.

Mark has a lot of things going for him. His sense of humor and theater, for instance, are standing him in good stead. There are always funny things going on around you wherever you are—even if you're on your way to scatter your wife's ashes—and just because you're grieving doesn't mean you can't enjoy them. Some people want to put blinders on, to be bereaved around the clock. Well, you are bereaved around the clock, whether you want to be or not, and any respite you can get from that you are entitled to.

It's also to Mark's advantage that he is fascinated with the experience. It is, after all, a part of life and life is fascinating. It's a healthy attitude to take. Of course, when you're only 30 and you were married for less than a year, maybe it's relatively easy to be fascinated with the experience of widowhood. But later on, we'll meet older men who also become fascinated, if not with widowhood itself, then at least with the changes it brings to their lives. To the extent that you can meet this part of your life with a sense of adventure, as crude as that may sound, you may be better equipped to field the curves it is going to throw you.

But just as George's articulateness did not exempt him from the pain, Mark's sense of adventure did not get him off the hook when it came to depression. Eventually, he had to come to terms with the fact that his wife was dead and he was, finally, alone. Not everyone may experience the sadness of that as acutely as Mark did—some people just don't allow it—and certainly not everyone is as articulate as he is about it. But everybody has to deal somehow at some time with this depression, either by stonewalling it or riding it through or escaping it.

Mark's way was to try to escape it, to get involved again before he had to deal with the pain. Like Hank, his immediate reaction—after the first several weeks of numbness, after the shock of recognition and the sense of disbelief—was to turn to what had given him comfort and support in the past—a relationship with a woman. Mark even recognized that he had nothing to give anyone, and that, in any case, he wouldn't trust anyone who would rush into an affair with him at that point.

It was a reflexive reaction, returning to a previous source of comfort, just as Jan returned to the woods, just as Sam turned to his religion and Jim dove back into his work. In all those other cases, the reflexive behavior worked—those previous sources of strength were there, and when turned to, they fulfilled their purpose. But the problem for Mark

was that that previous source of comfort and support—his woman—
was gone. And because every human relationship is a different
phenomenon, a product of the two people involved, he found he
couldn't just substitute another woman in her place.

Many men try to do this, though. They feel driven like Mark to take
action to speed their bereavement along, or to short-circuit it altogether.
And like Mark, many men try to force a change in their circumstances.
Mark set up a whole new life for himself—he got a new lover and started
hunting for a new house, only to find that stepping over the threshhold
of that new life put him over the edge of a deep depression, a depression that lasted for several months.

The depression was there already, but what put him over the edge
of it was trying to make his move too soon. Mark is still very much involved in his relationship with Joanne. For him to live with Judy was
almost, in a way, adultery, because he was still married to his first wife.
He actually said that normalcy for him was living with Joanne, and that
he was "waiting for her to return." He finally came to realize that he
wasn't ready yet to let go, that he didn't really want to get beyond
the anniversary. The struggle, the death, the grieving, all had made
his life somehow meaningful, and getting beyond it was to face the
mundanity of existence.

Before Mark is able to get successfully involved again, he will very
likely have to renegotiate his relationship with Joanne, to find a way
to continue to love her without remaining married to her, so that his
new alliance will not be in conflict with that memory. The men we
talk to later on, who have remarried after some time, confirm that that
is so. They all say, as they got involved again, the new wife did not
displace the first because a place had been found already for the first
wife to be remembered. It was not a competition.

If Mark had understood that he wasn't ready yet to let go of Joanne,
that what he needed at the moment was comfort and sexual release—
and if he had been willing to settle for only what he needed—he might
have spared himself some discomfort and he might have avoided taking Judy on something of a ride. But his reflexes told him that what
he needed was to be married again, to plug into a relationship that
would replace what he'd lost. If you are recently widowed, you very
likely recognize the impulse.

If you are many years older than Mark, this may be a possibility for
you. There are men who remarry within the first year and do, to some
extent, re-create the past with their new wives. If everyone concerned

is happy, that is probably okay. For older men, this re-creation may be more likely than it was for Mark. For these men, marital relationships tend to be more formalized, the roles of each partner more prescribed than they are in "modern" marriages. Men work out in the world, women work at home. Women handle the social engagements, men make all the major decisions. Of course there are as many variations on these themes as there are couples of those generations, but the range of appropriate behavior is more narrowly defined. To the extent that that is true, it may be easier for older men to "replace" their wives, or at least to "replace" their marriages, since the women of their generation have more congruent concepts of what being married is all about.

For men of Mark's generation, such a replacement is more problematic. The dramatic upheaval of women's position in society has not yet settled into a wholly predictable role definition, and the roles of marriage partners are changing to accommodate that flux. We are living in an era of greater individual freedom on many other fronts, as well. Finding a woman whose concept of being a wife is exactly congruent with a wife who has recently died is, for Mark's generation, much less likely.

When love comes into Mark's life again, it will very likely look very different from the way it looked before. Not only will the woman be different, but he will be a different man. He already is a different man. He's now a 30-year-old widower who owns a vacation home in the country and who has been to India—an entirely different animal from a 22-year-old college senior, which is who he was when he met Joanne.

Because he is different, love will come to him in a different way. He may not even recognize it, it may be so different from the love he experienced with Joanne. The work he has to do, if he is to love again, is not to seek love, but to make himself ready for it when the opportunity comes, by healing his wounds, repairing his life, and, perhaps most important, by expanding the boundaries of who he is.

Mark has lost the most important person in his life, the only person who ever really got inside of him and rearranged his emotional furniture. She brought a great deal into his life, things he never knew existed. Now she is gone and the gap she has left is very large indeed. It is no wonder he tried to fill it. But his work, if he chooses to do it—and there is every reason to think he will—may be not only able to fill that gap but also to grow into it. He needs to provide for himself some of those things that Joanne brought to his life—love of solitude, perhaps, the willingness to make a commitment. (Perhaps that is why he bought the house in the country. It is a place to be alone and certainly it is a commitment.)

Obviously, Joanne also brought him things such as companionship which he cannot, by definition, provide for himself. But those qualities that he loved in her, that made her companionship vital, are qualities that he can develop too. He can fill the gap in his life with people and things outside himself, and he can grow, become a bigger person to fill that gap himself.

Mark's story issues two warnings. First, a warning to the widower: Beware of committing yourself to another woman before you have found a way to continue loving the wife you have lost without remaining married to her. The length of time that takes will be different for everyone who goes through it. It is a pretty safe rule of thumb, however, that in the first year or so of your loss, you will have enough to do just dealing with being widowed, without attempting to begin a marriage with another woman.

Another warning is to the woman who might get involved with a widower: A man who has recently lost his wife may not have the slightest idea of what he is or is not capable of. In his desperation to have things as they used to be—or, at least, to have things not as they are—he may be intensely persuasive. And you, because you like him, may desperately want to be persuaded. This is not to say you shouldn't get involved with a widower, but that you should be aware that his agenda may be much more complicated than it at first appears. If you detect a touch too much bravado in his approach to things, that may be the giveaway clue. There is no reason you have to rush into a marriage with him.

When Mark persuaded Judy to set up housekeeping with him, he was at least turning to a source of comfort and support that can work very well when the timing is right. But some men, faced with the loss of a wife, turn for solace to solutions which under the best of circumstances don't work very well. Some men, like Randy, turn to drugs to alleviate their pain and find that then they not only have to deal with their bereavement, but also with drug dependency and the destructive effect of that dependency on the people around them.

Randy

R ANDY is 40. He is a salesman. He met Priscilla when he was 19, while working at a department store. During their marriage, they had three children: Larry, now 17, currently living with Priscilla's sister, and Mickey, 15, and Charlene, 13, both living with their father.

When Priscilla was 36, she was diagnosed with walking pneumonia. One month later, it became clear that she had inoperable lung cancer hidden behind the pneumonia. Seven months later she died. "A strange thing happened during that time. She started pushing me away by making me do things for myself. I didn't know what was going on. It was real painful for me. I knew it wasn't that she didn't love me anymore—there was lots of love going on at that time—but she knew she wasn't going to make it, and she was separating from me."

This interview was conducted five years after Priscilla died, and on the cusp of a new life for Randy—one day before his 41st birthday, one week before he set up housekeeping with his wife-to-be, and two weeks before they were to get married.

I had left St. Mary's the evening before to come home and get some sleep, and the doctor called about 4:00 in the morning. A blood vessel burst. She went very quick. I didn't go back to the hospital. I called her father (he's a funeral director) and he took care of it.

I don't think the kids really understood what was going on. Priscilla and I had decided not to tell them she was dying, just that she was very sick. We didn't lie to them, I don't think. Without coming out and saying she's dying, we were as honest as we could be. Larry must have been 13, and I think he had some understanding of what was going on. But the others were 11 and 9, and I don't know that their concept of death was real well defined at the time. They'd seen a lot of animals die but their grandparents and aunts and uncles all were still around. This was the first time they had ever experienced a person dying.

Of course, they cried when I told them. They wondered what we were going to do now. Same things I was wondering. I think I remember telling them I didn't know exactly. I told them I thought things would be okay. I wasn't convinced, myself.

I sold our house up in the mountains, the one that we had built. I sold everything we had up there—dogs and cows, the horse and the donkey—or gave them all away, and I moved in with my parents. I didn't have a good relationship with my parents at all, but I went and lived with them because I didn't have any place else to go. I felt like I couldn't go back to the mountains 'cause that was where Priscilla had lived. But what it really boiled down to was I needed someone to take care of me. So I could stay mad. And drunk.

And I did. For two and a half years.

What do they say, the first step in the grief process is anger? I stayed in that first step for a long time. I had been angry my whole life—it had made me and a lot of other people miserable—but now my anger was running rampant. All my other emotions shut down, and I was just angry all the time. I was angry at her and at God and at me and I was angry at the kids. I was angry at everything that came into my field of vision.

It was the only defense that worked—the only thing that kept people away. I wanted people's sympathy but didn't want any part of them. It was baffling. So much of what I went through in this time is really just baffling. I had the need to be around people but didn't want to be around them. I wanted them to leave me alone and let me be miserable, I guess. That's no way to live. Drunk or sober, that's no way to live.

I had always been a mellow drunk, but after Priscilla died I started getting my ass on my shoulders. Started getting mean. A bunch of paratroopers jumped me one night at a Howard Johnson's. I don't know how I got out of it, but I got out of it. I musta been shootin' my mouth off.

I think I'd been an alcoholic for a lot of years, but I had always been able to function. I hadn't lost any jobs. I hadn't been in a lot of trouble. But within about a month of Priscilla's death, it started to really escalate. Quick. Within a year, I was in jail on a DUI (driving under the influence). Within two years I had wrecked two cars and never had to pay for them. My dad was covering me at work. I'd go out maybe twice a week and make calls, but I didn't work very hard; he did the work and I got the paychecks. I had a lot of enablers.

Most weeks, I'd probably go out six nights, six out of seven nights, if I wasn't too sick from the night before. My drink of preference was Dewars White Label, but I drank mostly anything. Depending on how quick I wanted to get wasted and forget about things, I would drink tequila. Most of the times, I was with somebody. Or, you know, I'd run into somebody somewhere.

I couldn't stand to stay at home, just couldn't stand it. I can't explain it. I couldn't stand being in that house, with my parents and those kids. I didn't want the responsibility of my kids, you know. I didn't want any part of anything that was happening to me. So I'd stay out until everyone went to bed, and then I'd come fumbling home. I thought I was having a real good time, doing what I wanted to do. I didn't think about Priscilla. I went to the most expensive bars I could find and picked up women. I almost married one of them.

I met her in a bar about a year after Priscilla died. I can't remember her name now . . . Marjorie. That was it. I had to stop and think, ain't that awful? I thought I loved the woman, but . . . I don't know, I guess it was someone to take care of the kids, a babysitter, someone to drink with, that sort of thing. She moved in with me and the kids in this house that I bought about a year and a half after Priscilla died. I knew I couldn't afford this house, but I bought it anyway, just to get out of my parents' house. I've since lost that house to foreclosure. I don't know what would have happened if Marjorie and I had gotten married. It was a sick relationship. Bless her heart, she's a real sick person. I was a sick one, too. One of us probably would have ended up killing the other one.

Fortunately, I finally stopped drinking. It was St. Patrick's Day. It was on a Saturday that year, so I started drinking on Friday. I went

to Flanagan's, then O'Malley's—and that's the last I remember.
Everyone told me I had a good time. But Sunday morning, I got up
about 11:00 and I was sick. Larry had a paper route and I had been
helping him every Sunday. He had over a hundred papers, and the
Sunday paper is a bear, so I'd load them in the car and drive him
around. But I didn't get up that morning. And he asked me, when
I finally got up, how come I didn't help him. I don't know what happened, but something clicked. I couldn't tell the kid that I was too
sick to get up and help him. And something hit me right then, you
know—I had drunk all I wanted to drink. I had one drink that day
to survive, cause I would have died and I knew it, but that was the
last drink I ever had. I had drunk all I wanted to drink.

I called St. Anne's—that's a thirty-day treatment center for drugs,
mainly alcohol—and checked in the next Wednesday for a three-day
evaluation. I took enough clothes for thirty days. I told my mother where
I was going, and she took care of the kids. She came out to see me
one time at St. Anne's. Here I am in the middle of treatment, screwed
up as I can be, and she says, "I just can't believe you're an alcoholic.
You drink a little bit, but, you know . . ." The denial was phenomenal.
The fact that she'd been white-knuckling it may have had something
to do with that. She used to hide bottles all over the house. And my
dad drinks too.

While I was in treatment, Marjorie went through family counseling
with me. She told me one time while I was in there, in a session with
her, she said, "I want things to be like they were." And I simply looked
at her and I said, "Things will never be like they were. I am going
to change." And when I got out of treatment, I told her to leave.

I started going to AA the day I came out of St. Anne's and haven't
had a drink since. For that I'm real grateful. But when I sobered up,
I landed right in the middle of the reality of what had happened to
me, to my wife, and to my kids. It was a rude awakening. I had no
concept of what responsibility really was: I had never had to accept it.
Somebody always took care of me. My parents spoiled me rotten, and
then Priscilla took care of me. I never had to do anything, other than
go to work. Later on, I didn't even have to do that.

Within sixty days after I got out of St. Anne's, my son was being
booked for petty larceny. He stole some lawn mowers from a garage.
He was 16 at the time. He'd been drunk. I don't know how long he'd
been drinking, and I frankly never asked him.

I could see something had to happen. We had no discipline in the family, no direction. There was just nothing. My relationship with my kids had never been really excellent, but by now it had deteriorated. We all went into counseling together to try to open up some lines of communication between us, but Larry was unmanageable.

So I kicked his ass out of the house. I told him to change his attitude or to change his address. I wasn't willing to put up with his unacceptable behavior. He was continuing to smoke dope and had quit doing any schoolwork. He would go to school but quit doing the work. He would not do anything except exactly what he wanted to do. I couldn't live with that. We tried to work through it in counseling, we tried to work through it in our dealings with the probation officer.

Finally, he came home one day stoned out of his gourd. My mother called me and said, "He's here and he's stoned, and your dad is bringing him home." Before he got there, I called this emergency center down the street and asked if they did drug tests on the spur of the moment. They said yeah. So he got home and he's bumping around the kitchen stoned out of his tree. My dad comes in, and he's drunk. Quite a day.

I said, "Looks like you've been smoking some dope." "No man, no." I said, "Well then, you won't mind getting tested." And he blew up. I mean, he was crazy. Thank God I was calm. I said, "If you haven't been smoking, what's the objection?" This went on for ten minutes. He finally admitted that he'd been smoking, and right off the bat, I just told him, "You can't live at home and act like you act. You've got a choice to make." One of the choices was a boy's home, another was a juvenile jail, or he could make other arrangements. So we talked to Priscilla's sister and she agreed to give him a chance. I don't know what's happened with him. He doesn't call and I don't see him.

I think Larry's problem is drugs, number one, and behind that, that he's angry at me. For what, who knows? He won't talk about it. He does exactly what I did. I think that's one reason we don't get along, we're so damned much alike. It's like I spit and there he was. And what kills me is that I can see exactly where he's heading. Some of the things that happened to me are starting to happen to him.

But the situation is in God's hands. I can do nothing about it. If I try to push him the other way, it does more harm than good. The only thing I can do is to love him. And I can do that better from a distance at this stage of the game.

Some of the things I've had to do with these kids have been tough, okay? But the worst thing I could do is try to shelter them and protect them. That's the worst thing I could do. What I try to do is not drink and to be a decent person. To show them the love I can show them, to give them guidance and discipline. That's the best I can do. If they accept it, they accept it. It's a miracle that out of three kids, I still got two of them. It could have been all three of them.

My relationship with the other two is building, it's getting better again. We have our difficulties but we're beginning to talk about them. Those relationships have suffered some wounds, and I think the biggest wound was not talking about Priscilla, what they felt about it. We've just begun to do that. I wasn't willing to talk about it over the past couple years.

For the longest time, all I could do was go to these damned AA meetings. That's all I did, I just didn't drink. I went to two meetings a day for a year, sometimes three a day. I couldn't work anyway. I'd put in time but I couldn't work. I had this fear of people that I had never known before. I think it had been there all along, but it had been disguised. I was scared to death of people. I mean just scared to death of them. Looking at myself in the mirror was plenty hard enough, but having to look at someone else—I was petrified. And it finally got me—"incapacitated" is a good word. I just couldn't do it any more. The only thing I could do was not drink and go to AA meetings. So that's the only thing I did.

It took a period of about eight months to get over that fear. The way I got over it was, I just did the things that I was scared of. A fellow in The AA Program hired me when I was six months sober, and I did pretty good for about six months. But then I got so scared of people, I'd go out on a sales call . . . I'd walk up to a door and I'd get so terrified I couldn't knock. I just couldn't go in the door. I don't know what I was afraid of—it doesn't really matter—but I couldn't go through that door. So I quit that job. Then I went back and asked if I could try again, because I didn't know if I could stay sober the way I had acted.

So I went downtown to the Rowe Building, it's a high-rise building downtown, and I found the biggest account in the building. The biggest law firm on the East Coast. I knocked on their door. Sweating like a stuck pig. I was just scared to death. I walked in, I talked to the secretary, and saw the person I wanted to see. I didn't sell anything, but he didn't say no. I made fifteen cold calls that day, and every one of them was forced. And at the end of that week, I had made about fifty cold calls. That's how I worked through it. I just kept doing it. I couldn't run from it anymore. I just couldn't run from it. But I don't ever want to have to go through a week like that again.

When I sobered up, I had a whole lot of issues like that to face. And dealing with the death of my wife was a major one. It was real painful, and it didn't get cleared up overnight. I still get moments with it, but I don't let them last very long. I've resolved the fact that it wasn't my fault. That was one of the big issues. I felt guilty because she died, and I hadn't done all these things for her. Taking care of her, and like that. I *did* do a lot for her. We had a house that we built in the mountains, we had this and we had that. I wasn't the world's best husband, but I don't know many that are perfect. I had to ease up on myself, to see that it wasn't my fault. And I had to recognize I was a little bit angry at her for dying—even though it wasn't her fault—and I had to resolve that. It took time.

What worked for me was The AA Program. Getting honest with me. I'd met this grieving specialist while I was in treatment at St. Anne's, and I got in touch with him when I got out. I had heard he specialized in grieving, and I wanted to do my fifth step with him. See, there are twelve steps in AA, the twelve steps to sobriety. The fourth step is to write things down—about what you were like, about what you did, and what happened to you—and the fifth step is to tell somebody. It's a cleaning-house type of thing, taking an inventory of your past and then sharing it with someone.

You can share it with anybody you want. My AA sponsor drove to the beach and did it with a drunk. It doesn't matter who it is. You share it with yourself, with God, with another human being. The idea is that when you tell it, somehow it goes away. First off, when you write it down, you can't deny it anymore because there it is in black-and-white. And then when you share it, you don't have to worry about it anymore. All the stuff that is eating at you, you don't have it anymore. It's not like presto! it's gone. But the relief starts right away.

I chose this guy because I liked him. And once I started talking, pretty quickly things focused around Priscilla. I probably had eight or ten sessions with him. Some of them would last three hours, some would last half an hour. I cried a lot in the first few meetings. I hadn't done much of that in my life, but he began the process in me. It's okay to cry, to have these feelings. Because I didn't—you know—men don't cry. He forced me to see through a lot of that crap that I was holding inside. It's okay to talk about some of these things. How much I missed her. The way I'd acted. He told me that it was okay.

I had always fought those feelings. I had fought them as long as I could, with drinking. But they wouldn't start diminishing until I let them in. And when I finally opened those gates—man, those feelings came roaring in, Jack. And they overwhelmed me for a time. They really just overwhelmed me. I didn't know what they were. But when I could identify them and say, okay, I feel sad—when I admitted it—you know, the house did not fall down. A lightning bolt did not strike me. So I took it in little bitty steps. And I think the bottom line is that I just had to grow up and face what happened. And then say, okay, it happened. Now what are you going to do about it?

For me, being able to share what's going on inside of me—it's saved my life. It really has. Not only in respect to Priscilla, but in everything that goes on. I believe any difficulty I have, if I can get open and honest enough, if I can talk about it, something's going to happen. So I don't hold things inside anymore. I talk. And I either talk it to death—where I don't want to hear it anymore—or an answer comes from somewhere. And a lot of times I do get tired of hearing what I'm saying. But somehow the answer comes.

By the time I was done with those sessions, I had pretty much worked through my grief. I had opened up enough where I could talk about it when I wanted. I didn't talk to everybody about it, don't get me wrong, but I allowed myself the choice. If somebody brought it up, I could either choose to talk or not. I wasn't closed down anymore.

So when I say I'm done with grieving, I mean I can talk about it freely. You know, that awful maw in the stomach isn't there anymore. I'm sad, but that's okay with me. I don't live in it anymore. The memory is there, it'll always be there. And I'm okay with that. But it doesn't affect every minute of my life anymore.

I don't think I could have formed a healthy relationship with anybody until that process with Priscilla was pretty much finished. I don't see how it could have been healthy. You have to deal with the situation, with the death, not hide from it. You talk about these guys that get married a few months after their wives die. Shit, I couldn't decide to stand or sit to go to the bathroom at that time. I was incapable of making any rational decisions. But once that process was finished, that made room for somebody else.

I met Connie in The AA Program. I've known her for two years and we've been dating for a year. We've been in and out of this relationship three or four times. It's been a healthy relationship, it's been a sick relationship. Today it's real healthy. I think we're growing together. But we went through a lot to get to where we are. We'd get in, we'd get out, we'd get in, we'd get out. Right now, as we're talking, she's in the process of moving into our house. We have rented a house together. We moved boxes last night until 11:30. We're going to move some more tonight. Next Saturday, I'm moving in. And then, the Saturday after that, we are getting married. I'm amazed at how calm I am about it. I mean, I've been calmer, but I'm okay.

Things feel different with Connie. Number one, of course, I'm not drunk. But my attitude is completely different. When I got married to Priscilla, it was the thing to do. Have kids and buy a little house was the thing to do, and I did everything by the book. That's not to say I didn't love her, in the way that I understood love at that time. Wanting to take care of her, wanting to be with her, that stuff.

But with Connie, it's a nurturing thing. I want to see her grow, and she wants to see me grow. It's not a dependent relationship. I was dependent on Priscilla for my happiness, I think. I looked to her for approval and stuff. But I get that from myself now, and it makes a world of difference. I'm happy with myself today. I wasn't ever that way before. And I can't be happy with Connie until I'm happy with myself.

We had five hundred invitations printed and we've only got ten left. Most of the people we know are coupled, so there could be anywhere from no one to eight hundred people at the wedding, and the church only holds four hundred. If eight hundred people show up, I don't know where we're going to put them. But you know what's really funny? The first time I got married, we served four hundred people at the reception, and I knew maybe twenty-five. They were friends of her family and friends of my family—I didn't have many friends at the time. But I'll know everyone at this wedding. That's the difference two years has made.

I'm not a good advice-giver, but I know what worked for me. Get off that macho thing, that men don't feel things. It hurts. It hurt me for years. I hid from it and it just doesn't work. It doesn't go away.

And for God's sake, don't get wrapped up in another marriage right now. I believe it will kill you, I do. I can see the need to have a mate, to ease the pain, but that's not the answer. I believe if I'd gotten into another marriage right away, it would have been the same old stuffing, just stuffing it away, like before: *I don't want to look at it. I want to get married again. I want somebody to take care of me. I'm not going to change.* That's not the answer. The answer is in letting those feelings come through, so the next time the sadness comes up, it's not near as sad as it was before.

Change scares the shit out of me, it does. But it's necessary. If Priscilla hadn't died, things might have gone along just like they were going, forever and ever and ever. I could have just continued to be a low-level alcoholic, and the relationship that we had could have just gone on and on and on.

But her death precipitated a change in me. I am on the brink today of some major changes in my life, and I am excited about them. I mean, I do one day at a time, but I'm really looking forward to this. It's neat. It's wonderful. I spent a lot of time in my life being unhappy with myself. But I did what I did, I can't change that now. I did whatever I had to do to get where I had to go. And if Connie and I can get through what we got to get through to get where we're going, I guess we'll probably be all right. We'll probably live happily ever after.

Just as Sam turned to his religion and Jim turned to his work, just as Jan turned to his family and Mark and Hank turned to other women, when Randy was faced with the loss of his wife, he turned to the thing that had always managed to offer him comfort before. His drinking was not a constructive response, but it was a response that men are allowed in our society. And in some parts of our society, men are even encouraged to drink to excess, to avoid the experience and expression of all their feelings except their anger. Maybe the fact that anger is one of the few emotions they are allowed is part of what makes them turn to the bottle.

That may be part of the reason anger is a bigger issue in grieving for men than it is for women. While women's grieving is focused more on remorse—"If only I had done more . . ."—men may focus on anger more because their options are limited, and because they generally have more license in expressing it. Or they may experience more anger because they are used to having control, and faced with the immutability of death, they are furious to find themselves utterly out of control.

In any case, it is clear that Randy's attempts to avoid his pain by drinking only complicated the matter and made the pain greater in the long run. That brings up an important point: when you try to resist the pain, it makes the pain a lot worse, but if you relax and just allow it, it's easier to manage. It's a rule taught in natural childbirth, and it works for emotional pain as well. It is the resisting of it that hurts, as much or more than the pain itself. The more you try to be not in

pain, the more the pain has to pound at you to get the acknowledg-
ment it deserves.

If you are in the habit of anesthetizing yourself with drugs, it is very
likely you will be turning to them now. Men who drink *always* drink
more when they're widowed, and many also find themselves turning
to sleeping pills and Valium. That's entirely to be expected, and if you
find yourself having a few more drinks or popping a few more pills,
that is not necessarily cause for alarm. But you should also be aware
that alcoholism in widowers is significantly high—especially in those
over 75, who have the highest rate in the country—so if you have a
problem with drinking, this is a great opportunity for it to reach full
bloom. If you feel yourself slipping over the line, don't hesitate to get
help. Alcoholism is not a problem you can lick yourself. It is also not
a problem that is especially easy to admit, so if you're a friend of a
widower and you see that his drinking is getting serious, you might
want to get in touch with AA and learn about interventions.

As was noted in Jan's case, it is extremely difficult to be a parent
at a time like this, because it's a time when your children need you
the most and you have the least to give. But in this case, the problem
was greatly compounded by Randy's drinking. So long as he was drinking, he couldn't manage to be there for himself, never mind for his
children, and because of that, his children essentially lost both parents
at once. Instead of the parent they needed, they got another lost child,
and that difficulty was ladled on top of whatever difficulties they had
already as young children of an alcoholic father and whatever difficulty
they were having with the loss of their mother. The situation put them
in a turbulence of conflicting forces, which were further compounded
by the effect of Marjorie moving in and getting drunk with their father.
To a large extent, it appears the emotional needs of these children were
ignored entirely.

That's not entirely unusual. Often, when a mother dies, a father is
called upon to learn more about his children than he ever had to know
before and more than he probably ever would have had to learn had
she gone on living. And he needs to do it at a time when those children
are in crisis. All of that is not something that many men seem to have
an instinct for, and it is surely not something that they have been
educated for.

Many men in this situation simply hire a housekeeper and go on making money, assuming that in doing that they're fulfilling their paren-
tal role. Hiring a housekeeper is not irresponsible, but if you do that

in lieu of giving your children the nurturing they need, it simply may not be enough. Under the best of circumstances, children resent an absentee father, but under these circumstances, the effect can be much multiplied. If you are a widower with young children, eventually you're probably going to have to come to grips with the fact that you're not just a father anymore. You need to learn how to mother, too.

Unfortunately, Randy did not embrace the needs of his children. But he is absolutely right that he can't change what he did, and it is to his enormous credit that he signed himself into St. Anne's, that he extricated himself from Marjorie, that he joined AA, and that he went on those fifty cold calls in one week. He had to pick up all those stitches in the fabric of his own life before he could be of any use to his children or anybody else, and he showed great mettle in doing it.

If Priscilla hadn't died, it is conceivable that Randy could have continued muddling along as a low-level alcoholic. But it is a common occurrence that the crisis of losing a wife will bring other life issues to a head as well. For Randy, it not only brought his drinking to a crisis point, it ultimately brought to crisis his underlying fear of people, his dissatisfaction with himself, and his parenting style. The AA program not only gave him a chance to talk it out, it also helped him to structure a new reality for himself and it gave him many new techniques for coping with that reality.

Now there is a newly confident sense of self emerging in Randy, a self that has confidence built in. The irony in his tone when he predicts that he and Connie will live happily ever after reflects a new grasp of reality, a new recognition that life is a struggle and a new confidence that, taken one day at a time, he can handle it. He also seems to have found an appropriate place to carry his loss—he can share it when and with whom he wants, but he doesn't have to talk about it and he doesn't have to avoid it. He has many more options now than drinking and being angry.

Randy's story has a happy ending. In turning to an old, familiar way of dealing with problems and finding it not only didn't work anymore but that it was destructive, Randy was forced to find an altogether new way of coping, one superior to what went before. In many ways, Randy is better off than he was before Priscilla died, because the crisis forced him to grow.

Many other people, while they may not necessarily find their familiar ways of coping destructive, do discover that those familiar ways don't work anymore—or just aren't available anymore—and that they also have to look for altogether new resources. For Karl, the resource that helped him through, even though he had never turned to anyone for help before, was a widows' and widowers' bereavement group.

Karl

K ARL is 67. Until he retired four years ago, he worked in the
mail-order shoe business.

Born in Vienna, Karl came to the states when he was in his
early twenties, after he was released from a concentration camp on the
condition that he leave the country. It was the late 1930s. He met Lynn
about two years later at a friend's house and fell in love on sight. Her
family was against their marriage because Karl spoke very little English
and, as he says, "didn't have a buck in my pocket," but Lynn went
against their wishes, broke her engagement, and married him anyway.
In the course of thirty-eight years of marriage, they had two children
together—a daughter, now 36 and married and living in another city,
and a son, now 34, living alone close by.

A year and a half before she died, Lynn began to complain about
regular stomachaches. The doctor treated her for ulcers, but a second
doctor found cancer. He operated to remove the stomach and the spleen,
and administered chemotherapy, but it was too late. She suffered and
failed progressively. She finally died six months later at home. This interview was conducted one and a half years after her death.

She died on August 19. She died right here in the house. The nurse
at the time, who had the night shift, told me at about 8:00 that we
should call my daughter, that she feels the end is coming. At about
2:00 in the morning, we were in the den, in the other room, and the

nurse called us in and she said, "She's going." And she went fast. I was talking to her, I was holding her. It happened in about ten minutes. Then it was over. The nurse did the rest. She called the doctor. The doctor came over and signed the death certificate.

I actually broke down. We all were prepared, but you know, when the end comes, you're really not prepared. This wasn't the first time I saw people die. While I was in the camp, I saw many, many people die. But when Lynn died, it was different.

It was horrible. She didn't know anymore what was going on, she was so drugged all the time. Her mind was completely gone towards the end. She couldn't talk, couldn't move. She didn't eat anything at all. She came out with things that were frightening sometimes. She asked for her mother who had passed away about fourteen years ago. She was just out of it. It was a very difficult situation for me, being alone. Well, I had my son here. And my daughter came up a few times. But I had nobody, really. I had to handle it alone.

At first, I just felt life was over for me. I wanted to finish it too. I was thinking crazy, crazy thoughts. I wanted to end it all because I just felt that I couldn't go on without her. Whenever I made myself a cup of tea and I looked at the gas, I thought, "This would be one way." Then I got hooked on sleeping pills. I couldn't go to sleep without them. Then I finally cut them in half, then quarters. I finally got rid of them. I don't know who told me to do it that way, if it was a doctor, I don't know.

I was in touch with a lot of people during August, September, October—talking to a lot of people, getting advice from a lot of people. But it didn't mean anything. It's well-meant advice, but it doesn't . . . No one really knows. I didn't know until my wife died. I didn't realize what it is, what it really means. It is the rest of your *life*. You are *alone*. You open the door and walk into the house and there is *nobody there*. And in my particular case, there is really no one to turn to except friends.

I didn't get too much support from my son. He is a hell of a nice kid, but he was pretty much broken up too. He really loved his mother. So he really, you know, couldn't give me support. My daughter had gone back home—we don't get along—so my son was my only family. We see each other now about once or twice a week, which is more than we used to see each other. Before, he used to come home to eat, bring his laundry sometimes, stuff like that. But in and out, you know. So this did bring us closer. We see each other more often.

But we couldn't support each other. I was trying to shield him, to protect him, which I shouldn't have done. I mean, he was old enough to talk to and tell him how life really stinks now. But then he would have worried more, not only about the loss of his mother, but worrying now about me too, which I didn't want him to do. He felt bad enough already, losing his mother. So I didn't tell him that I was, that life didn't mean anything anymore. And he, he did the same thing to me. We both felt very, very bad but didn't tell each other. We talked about little things, about what it really meant to lose her. We really didn't talk too much. We still don't talk about it.

So I had nobody to talk to. Then two or three months later, I joined this group I heard about from the hospice. The hospice has been very good to me. About two months before she died, my wife fell off the bed and broke her arm, and I brought her to the hospital and there I found out about the hospice. They had social workers come to the house, talk to her, talk to me. Later on, they got nurses for me. I really don't know what I would have done without them. They were great.

While Lynn was still alive, the hospice ran a group for people whose spouses are terminally ill. And after she died, they had another group for the survivors. It started in the fall and I think it lasted for four or five or six months. They generally run for about six months. As a matter of fact, they have a dinner at the end of the six months that they invite the previous group to. They had one last night, so I went there.

Our group became very close. We were a small group of about ten people. There were four men and six women. And funny, there was no, you know, after meeting a couple of times, that one man is getting interested in a woman, or anything like that. Because maybe, I don't know, we need each other for something else.

The first time I went there, Pamela, the woman who was leading it, asked us all to tell our story. We went around and each told what had happened to us. And, you know, there was one man there whose story was practically the same as mine? His wife didn't suffer as long, but all in all, it was the same pattern. He lost his wife just about the same time, at almost the same date. He had two children, a son and a daughter. He had the hospice in his house. And he had suffered an awful lot. He knew how I felt. I knew how he felt. It was great. I mean, it was great to find somebody you can talk to. We cried together many times.

There were two other men whose spouses passed away also about the same time. We had a very strong feeling together. One of the four men was two weeks in the hospital—he had a bypass—and we went to see him. And he actually broke down there. Because, you know, he said that he wouldn't know what to do without us anymore, we are family. Really close. We know how, how the other one feels, suffers, and by getting together and talking about it, we are helping each other. And you know, we talk about everything. We don't talk just about our wives. Of course we talk about them, but I mean we talk about politics, we talk about plays, we talk about movies. And we cry when we want to. We support each other. We almost became a family.

We don't meet anymore officially, but we still meet about once a week, all the men. Then every fourth week, the women join us. They didn't keep meeting separately. The women dealt much better with it. They start doing whatever they like much faster than the men. Either going back to business or taking courses in school, or whatever. I think they're much stronger than men. So they didn't keep meeting separately. It was just us four guys who continued it, then sometimes the women join us, too. We talk with them and have dinner, it's great. This really worked out for us. We all made progress, you know. Quite a bit of progress. We still have a long way to go, but it's nice. It's like a family.

I see even more of Frank. Maybe the reason was the other two fellows were older than we are. So they are not interested in going out. You know, they're already 75. They don't expect much from life anymore. But Frank does. So we call each other once in a while and we go out on a Saturday night, for example, on a double date. We didn't start to do this until after the first six months. Even now, sometimes, we don't meet. But we can call each other on Saturday morning, for example, and say, "What are you doing tonight?"

Usually in a marriage, it is the wife who keeps the social life going. The wives call each other up, get together, do this, and do that. And then the women also, they call each other with "what are you doing for lunch?" "Let's play Mahjong," or whatever. Men don't do that. Men . . . I don't talk to men very often. If I call them, I call them for a reason. But just to talk on the phone for an hour about the sale downtown or something, men don't do that. Before Lynn died, I never had a close man friend, so this relationship with Frank is really new, unique.

I think he is much stronger than I am. What I went through when I was young—a terrible experience. When I came out of Dachau and found that my parents disappeared, I just couldn't understand it. Just simply on account of religion, just simply because you're Jewish? Later on, I found out that they were sent to a termination camp. Then going over to England and not knowing anybody there. And then I came here, again starting fresh. It was rough, and I survived it. But somehow, this situation I am not handling as well as Frank. I always felt he was handling things, he was doing things that I can't do.

But he thinks I'm better off than he is. He is floating around quite a bit. He can't find himself. He can date every night someone else, but he didn't find one in particular who he feels that he is comfortable with, who he wants to be together with. I am different. I dated and then, I didn't like running around. I just felt that it's much nicer to be with one person that you enjoy, that you feel comfortable with. Maybe he will meet someone. But he always calls me the lucky one because I met someone. And he feels she is terrific for me.

She *is* good company for me. She's "up," she makes me laugh. We go out just the two of us, or we double-date with Frank. We have a good time together. And we can talk freely about my wife and her husband. She lost her husband three years ago, so she knows the whole bit. She went through it herself. So I can talk with her about it. Sometimes I even cry when I'm with her, I can't hold it back sometimes. And she understands it perfectly. She says I will never forget Lynn. But that doesn't mean, you know, that you can't start a new life. This doesn't mean, because one gets married again, that he forgets the past.

Of course, you won't love anymore that great love. I can't love again like I loved Lynn. I had not been in love before I met Lynn. I had my share, oh yeah, I was a bastard when it came to that. But really, love, no. I never loved anyone like I loved Lynn. I don't know why, sometimes I really feel that there was no other married couple who felt like we did. We were the joke of a lot of our friends. After thirty-seven years of marriage, for example, we were holding hands or kissing each other at parties, which you don't find anymore today. Almost like you're on your honeymoon. It was something, I tell you. She was a very good type of person.

We never talked about it, but knowing what I went through before, Lynn wanted to make it up to me in whichever way was possible. And she really spoiled me rotten. I am sorry now she did it, 'cause I am lost here in the house. I mean, she didn't let me do *anything*. So I don't know how to run the house. How to do a load of laundry, or how to . . . You should see me, the way I do laundry. It's a real stitch. I mean, what can one do about spoiling, making two scrambled eggs? But you should see me the other day, making scrambled eggs. The kitchen was a mess, the eggs came out lousy. I really don't know how. It's so *simple*. I get mad at myself. It's . . . I eat out most of the time. I'm just not interested in cooking. I'd rather go out and eat.

But now I can be at Doris's house—sitting across from somebody, talking, eating—and it's great. I don't know if I'll get married again. But I tell you, I hate the way I live now. I mean being alone. I hate waking up in the morning alone. I hate going to bed alone. I hate eating alone. Mornings are very bad for me, very bad. That's the worst part of the day. I can go to bed tonight, for example, being fully content. Tomorrow morning, when I wake up, I just feel lousy. Going to the breakfast table, eating alone. So this is why I wonder if I would get married again. I guess I will if this one is the right one for me. I never loved anyone like I loved Lynn, and I really don't think that I ever will. But I guess there are different kinds of loves. I'm not who I used to be. I was 23 when I met her. I'm different than I was.

And I can see that I'm getting better. I go to the cemetery quite often—maybe four or five times last year—and the first few times I was really gone. I couldn't, you know, I never could have driven home without my son. I really broke down. But I can see it is getting better. I still cry, but more and more I can control myself pretty good. So maybe this shows me that as time goes by that it is getting better.

I think the main thing is you have to get out of the house. Sitting in the house and thinking doesn't help an awful lot. Even if you have to go out alone and go to the shopping mall, just walk and see people. This is the most important thing. Don't end up sitting home alone. I went back to work just to get out of the house. It's just a job, doesn't mean anything. It's just to get out of the house. On days where I don't work and the weather is bad, and I am staying in, it's tough. How much can one read? Or watch the stupid television?

Another way of helping yourself is by helping others. Like, Pamela called me a month ago. She is breaking in a new group of volunteers for the hospice, people who will go in when there is a dying person in the house—like I had a volunteer in my house—and do things for the people there. Go shopping. Or you can talk to the volunteer, or you can cry to her. She can sit at the bedside and talk, whatever. So Pamela was breaking in a group of volunteers and they have to learn all different things. One thing is that they have to know what is expected of them, and so on. So Pamela called me and asked if I would come up there and talk to them and tell them my experiences with one of those volunteers. And I said, "I really don't think I can do it.

95

I know that I'll break down." She said, "This is what we want you to do, we want them to see what it means for a spouse to have a volunteer come into the house and what they have to expect." I said okay.

So I went up there, it was three weeks ago, and they asked me all kinds of different questions. At first, I was a little nervous. Pamela put a box of Kleenexes right next to me and we laughed. I really didn't think I'd be able to talk to somebody about it. I really wouldn't have believed it. But I did it for one thing. That maybe if one of those volunteers will go in the future into a home where the wife has died and the husband sits there and doesn't know what the hell he is doing . . . What a great help she would be, what a wonderful thing she would be doing. So I answered them, their questions. And I tell you, I'm carrying on and crying. But when I left that meeting, I felt good. I felt very, very good. And last week when I saw Pamela, she said, "They're all going to enter the program."

So, you know, it made me feel good. And I got that sense of helping people from that group that I was in, too. I think so. Yes. It really means a lot when you know that there's someone there you can talk to who understands what you're going through. So this is what I mean, if you can help other people in the same situation, then you help yourself a lot, too. It makes you feel kind of good.

After I finished talking with Karl, I realized a curious fact. With him, more than anyone else I talked to, I had felt an inclination to want to minimize his pain, almost to make light of it somehow. I'm not sure where the impulse came from. It may have been my mood at the time, or it may have been a reaction to what I perceived as traces of a courtly European manner. But I felt the signal came from him, that that was what he wanted of me. Perhaps this had something to do with his experience in the camps.

Just as the death of a loved one can bring other aspects of your life into crisis—the way it brought Randy's drinking to crisis, the way it may have played a role in bringing Jan's son to crisis—it is also true that bereavement can resurrect old ghosts from the past. Traumas you thought were long since buried—or successfully swept under the rug— may rise from their grave to haunt you now.

Knowing what we do of how grief can raise those monsters from the deep, we have to wonder how Karl's experience in the concentration camp affects the grieving of his wife. Maybe the depth and breadth of that earlier loss was just so massive to hold that he somehow signaled me that we should skate the surface of his sadness, because once you dip into it, it just goes on and on and on. And to the extent that you can be aware that your bereavement is setting off other critical feelings in you, you may be able to exercise greater control over their effect on you.

In any case, it does not appear that the grieving of his wife, even compounded with the woe of his past, ever brought Karl to considering suicide seriously. The thoughts of killing himself seem to have been used intermittently as a narcotic, rather than viewed as some sort of real solution.

If you have had thoughts of suicide, it might be helpful for you to know that virtually every widower does, at one time or another. Some men, like Mark, even come to depend on the thought as a source of comfort, the way you might come to depend on sleeping pills or Valium. As with sleeping pills and Valium, thoughts of suicide may actually help to get you through the night, and if that's as far as it goes there is no cause to be alarmed by those thoughts.

But as with sleeping pills and Valium, you can also get overly dependent on thoughts of suicide, and that dependence could converge with dependence on pills and alcohol in a most unfortunate way. On this, we harken back to George's advice from the first chapter:

> Don't beat yourself up for running, for using defenses not to feel. But be aware that you're doing that. And be aware that hopefully that will be only temporary, that soon enough you will encourage yourself to remember, to feel, to cry. The way out is, where you want to end up is, with the preservation of the best of what you had in a permanent place where it can't be robbed or taken away from you.

Before you're finished with this book, you might want to go back and read George again. He had a lot of good things to say. Jan deserves a second look too.

Even though it seems as if he had many friends around to give him advice, it is clear that Karl felt alone and estranged from everyone but his son. The fact that he felt he could not share his grieving with his son left him entirely alone. It may have been true that Karl's son was so broken up that he literally could not have dealt with his father's sadness. Or it may have been that Karl couldn't bear the burden of his son's sadness. But it is also possible that if they were able to share their grieving, they would have each found the other's grief did not so much add to his own grief as it alleviated it.

It is an opportunity that is missed more often than not: fathers and sons are often not able to help each other much in grieving. The relationship is so complicated that the tendency to dependency in either direction seems dangerous, and in any case, even though they are grieving the loss of the same person, they are grieving very different losses. The loss of a wife and the loss of a mother are two very different things. There could conceivably even be a kind of competition for the claim on her memory. Add to that the fact that fathers and sons are often more accustomed to strutting and fighting with each other than they are to sharing their heartaches, and it is easy to see why a father and son may not grieve well together.

It is also very likely that Karl felt his son wouldn't understand him. Everybody talks about how no one can understand how it feels to be widowed unless they've been through it themselves. Of course no one can understand it entirely unless they have been through it. You have to communicate it to people. You have to help them understand.

To be sure, your loss is so great that it will take a great deal of effort to make someone else understand it, but that's no reason not to begin. Trying to explain your loss to someone in smaller parcels may allow you to parcel out the pain a bit for yourself, to deal with smaller parts at a time. Of course, there is always the problem of whether people will be able to listen, no matter how well you explain it. And you have to learn to discriminate between those family members and friends who can't or won't hear what you say and those who can and will.

But even if you can explain it, and even if people will listen to you, many men simply don't want to share their feelings with family and friends. Their feelings of anger and guilt and despair, and their thoughts of suicide, may carry too much stigma for them to feel comfortable talking of them to people who are part of their lives and who knew their wives. Sometimes it's just easier to talk to someone new. And since you are, in fact, in an altogether new situation, talking to someone altogether new makes a certain amount of sense.

In this case, Karl was able to find for himself a real soul mate, someone who understood his pain with a minimum of explanation, and succeeded in forming a friendship with him that was different from any friendship he had ever had before. He not only found new friends, he found new ways of being a friend—new ways of relating to people, new ways of interacting with them—which have expanded the boundaries of his personality. He makes his own social connections now, maintains his own social network, instead of having that largely done for him.

If you find you cannot get all the support and companionship and understanding you need from your family and friends, you might want to look for opportunities to meet new people. Later on in this book, we will suggest some ways to go about that and give you some phone numbers and addresses, in case you are not quite as lucky as Karl was in having a group come to him.

Karl was very fortunate that he was able to find new friends without having to go looking for them; the bereavement group just happened to be there when he needed it. It is a good example of how helping services work best. Too often, helping services are set up in such a way that they just wait for people to come and ask. They assume that just because they are making themselves available, they are fulfilling their social role. But widowers (and widows too) often find they have no guess as to what they need or where to find it, and men are disinclined to go looking for help in any case. So if you're seeking to offer helping services to a widower, you are likely to be more effective if you go to him.

Karl brings up an interesting detail when he talks about how difficult he finds the mornings. Every man talks about a particular time of the day that is most difficult for him. George and Jan agree with Karl that it is the morning. For others, it's coming home at night. Perhaps it is the transition times that are most difficult—from sleeping to waking, from office to home—when you are uprooted from one place and not yet rooted in another, perhaps it is then that your underlying rootlessness is most profoundly felt.

Coming home at the end of the day is an especially difficult time for men. Women are often accustomed to spending time alone at home, but men are more often accustomed to coming home and finding their families there. For men, coming back to an empty house at the end of the day can feel like walking into a mausoleum.

If you find that that is true for you, you might want to try to establish some transitional routine to get you somehow rooted in yourself before you go home and have to face your rootlessness there. The space between leaving work and going home is a good time to go to a gym, or to go for a swim, to work out the tensions of the day and refresh yourself for the evening. Or maybe that would be a good time to sit in a café and read. Sam sits down and plays the piano or organ as soon as he gets home, sometimes without even turning on the light, as a way of easing his transition back into the house. Whatever your most difficult time of the day is, it might be wise for you to identify it and anticipate it, and to develop some rituals for getting yourself through it.

Of all the things that Karl has learned about getting himself through this time of his life, perhaps the most important is the help he garners for himself by offering his help to others. That, in the end, may be the strongest argument in favor of joining a group such as the one he joined. Not only do your needs get tended possibly better than they are getting tended anywhere else, but you also come to realize that you have something to give, that while the person who relied on you more than anyone else ever did is gone, you can still be needed. And because you're just one in a group, you can be needed and utilized without being too much depended upon.

Unfortunately, as men, we are often averse to joining groups such as these. Surveys have shown that men are afraid of being induced to disclose their vulnerability before they're ready; they're afraid they'll be called upon to lead; they're afraid they'll be called upon to give before they discover that in fact they have something to give; they're afraid they'll be outnumbered by women; they're afraid they'll be rejected; and they're afraid of the unknown.

If the surveyors are to be believed, we are a morass of fears. But in their litany of our fears, they have missed one thing. We are also afraid of being touched. Many men mentioned to me that their perception of such groups was that they always want everybody to be hugging everybody.

In short, there are many reasons that men do not seek such a group, or take advantage of it even when it is offered to them. If you are trying to encourage a widower to join such a group, you might want to address those specific fears in a very direct way. And if you are a widower who thinks he might be able to use such a group, but you are experiencing some reservations, we thought we'd give you a chance to look in on a widowers' meeting—no hugging—just to give you an idea of what you might expect.

Jake, Fran, Mike, and Jerry

JAKE is 64, a salesman. His wife died six years ago, of cancer. Fran is 65, a retired plant superintendent. His wife died five months ago of diabetes, after a long illness.

Mike is 67, a retired truckdriver. His wife died two years ago of a massive coronary.

Jerry is 55, a foreman in a textile mill. His wife died two years, four months ago of diabetes and kidney disease after a very long illness.

They have come together this Tuesday night, as they come together every Tuesday, to spend a couple of hours talking about their experience with widowhood over a couple of cups of coffee. The setup is very casual. At times, their number swells to six; sometimes it shrinks to two or three. There are no rules or regulations. The group is led by Liz and Jim, the owners of the funeral home from which the wives were all buried.

As the men begin to straggle in, the conversation meanders through a typical array of topics—the flu that's currently going around, business problems, flooded basements, the best routes for getting to various places, weather, the whereabouts of the others, world events, and the problems of eating alone in a restaurant. At one point, Jake embarks on a story about a telephone call from his son who was asking him for money, and Liz takes that opportunity to begin to focus the conversation.

Liz: Have you talked to him about your plight?

Jake: Well, no. It's hard to talk to him. I mean, *he's* always talking, so it's hard to talk to him much. But I'll tell you, every time I see him, he walks up, in public or private, and he gives me a great big hug and a kiss.

Liz: Your son.

Jake: That's right. I don't care where it is. Just a big, big hug and a kiss, every time. A lot of people think that's stupid. They do. Not macho, whatever. But that's the way he expresses affection.

Liz: It means a lot.

Jake: You'd better believe it.

Liz: Would you tell him you're in a support group?

Jake: Oh yes.

Liz: You did?

Jake: Oh yes. I told him. He thought it was a good idea.

Liz: Would anyone like to share what was good or bad about this past week? Just kind of plunge right in?

Fran: Well, I had a pretty good week. I accomplished a couple of things that I hadn't been able to do before. One has to do with a recreational area in a nearby town. It's a place that my wife and I visited many, many times. I haven't really had the courage to go back again since she died. I knew it would be emotional. But the other evening, all of a sudden, I just kind of got a message that said "It's time to walk Bristol Lake." So I went. And I enjoyed it. I did. It *was* emotional. But I enjoyed it, and I will go back again.

Liz: Can you talk about what the emotions were?

Fran: Well, I walked down the trail—you know, we used to walk there hand-in-hand—and I felt a sort of . . . closeness. I stopped and watched the geese that are there. We used to do that together. At first it was pure emotion: "I miss you." But as I walked around, it was getting dark and cool, and I felt just kind of like a nice, warm glow. Really, really good. Good feeling.

Liz: Oh, that's nice.

Fran: Really good feeling.

Liz: Did it frighten you to *enjoy* that time? Did those feelings feel . . . ?

Fran: Well, it happens all of the time when I go to the cemetery, which is about every day. I like to go to the cemetery. Sometimes I sneak up the back way and say, "Aha, I bet you didn't think that I was comin' today." Ha, ha. And I always kind of reach down and rub the marker there a little bit, and we have a little chat. And of course I'm talking to two people, there. I'm also talking to my son Sam. He's been gone twenty-seven years. Ginnie never admitted that Sam was gone. So we never, from the day of the funeral, we never visited, not even once. So this is the first time I have been back, since Ginnie was buried over there. So that's emotional, too.

Liz: What do you say to Sam?

Fran: "Hi! How you doin' today?"

Liz: That's great.

Fran: Just like that. Why not? And my dad's right there too. And I kind of mention once in a while that I haven't forgotten him either. I like to go to the cemetery.

Liz: You have done a lot of "processing" as far as Sam is concerned, haven't you?

Fran: Oh, I have, sure.

Liz: You want to say something about that?

Fran: Well, you know, it upset Ginnie tremendously to talk about it.

Liz: Talk about "it." Sam's death?

Fran: Sam's death. And Sam, you know. I took her to get psychiatric help, but she never really admitted it.

Liz: Again, admitted "it." His death?

Fran: Yeah, admitted that he was gone.

Liz: But you have both pictures out now, and enjoy . . . ?

Fran: Yes.

Liz: And you're not afraid . . . I don't have any sense that you're afraid of your grief. What I hear is that you're comfortable to experience whatever is going to happen . . .

Fran: Yes.

Liz: To go with the tears . . .

Fran: Absolutely. Then the other thing I did—it may seem minor—but we sold our home and moved in August and we have a big storage place down in the cellar and I never really got it cleaned out. I was starting to, gave some things away, but I couldn't bring myself to really put in any time on it because I felt "What's the use?" But this week, I took a whack at it. And that was another kind of good feeling.

Jim: Accomplishment.

Fran: Yes.

Jim: Did something.

Fran: Yes.

Liz: My joy for you is that you are very comfortable, very positive about your grief process.

Fran: Well, I just tell it like it is.

Liz: Yes you do, and that's wonderful. The other thing I'm excited about for you is that you have a sense that it's important work. And more than that, that you have experienced a lot and walked through that place of pain. You have a real sense of peace. And I think that's so exciting.

Fran: One thing I want to mention, though. This gentleman over here mentioned it. Doesn't like to eat alone in a restaurant. Neither do I. I don't like to go out . . .

Liz: I heard you respond, when he said that.

Fran: Yeah. I go out to breakfast, but I go to the same place every day and I know that when I get there I'm going to see one, two, three, four people I know. And some of them will come over and join me.

Liz: What do you do about dinner?

Fran: Dinner? Oh, I usually eat at home.

Liz: And you will eat a good meal?

Fran: Oh, yes.

Liz: Do you exercise?

Fran: I walk. And now, of course, I'll be walking Bristol Lake.

Liz: Do you know that there are certain foods that help you stay out of depression?

Fran: No.

Liz: Foods that are low in fats and sugars and caffeine. Fats and sugars and caffeine are all things you should avoid.

Fran: Super. I do without all of that. Cause Ginnie was very good at this. Ginnie was excellent at it, foods.

Liz: High proteins, Vitamin C, lots of fruit, that's good. Lots of exercise.

Jim: Anybody want coffee?

Jerry: Yes.

Jim: The caffeine's good for you.

Liz: How are you doing, Jake?

Jake: I seem to be doing okay. I still have the problem of the nights.

Liz: Are you sleeping?

Jake: Yeah, I'm sleeping okay. I'm surprised that I slept so well just after she died, for almost two weeks. Maybe it was sheer exhaustion. But lately, I've been waking up in the middle of the night and having a tough time getting back to sleep.

Liz: What happens when you're awake at that hour? What do you think about?

Jake: Nothing, really. Nothing. I don't know what wakes me up. But if I can't get back to sleep, I'll take a sleeping pill—you know, prescription—that'll knock me out enough to get me back to sleep. I don't want to have to hang around at 2:00 in the morning.

Jim: You have things to do?

Jake: Next day, yeah. I'm very thankful that I am working. That's my saving grace. It is. If it weren't for that, I don't know what I'd do.

Liz: Have you been to the cemetery?

Jake: No. Nor do I have a desire to go there. That doesn't help me at all.

Liz: Is that okay for you not to do that?

Jake: Yeah. Yep. We went quite often, the two of us, when my daughter died. Uh, you know, two and a half years ago I lost my daughter, who was 30 years of age, to . . . uh, cancer . . . excuse me . . .

Liz: That's all right.

Jake: And, uh . . . That was, uh . . . That was, uh . . . That's all right . . . I do this too on the telephone sometimes and then I straighten up. That was a very stressful thing. But, uh, we were able to . . . cope with it. Because there were . . . two of us. But it's so different now. Because I don't have anybody to talk to. That's what makes it tough. There are lots of people to talk to from 8:00 to 5:00, but before I know it, it's 5:00 and I've got to go home. And I hate like hell going into that place.

Liz: What would you say to her when you got home?

Jake: "Hi."

Liz: Right now. If she were there, what kind of things would you say to her?

Jake: We'd talk about what had happened that day. I'd tell her, you know, if I had written a very good order that day. I get a very, very marvelous feeling when I write an order and put in my pocket. As I did do last Friday. I had an excellent day. I wrote I guess the biggest order I probably ever wrote. So that's the first thing I would have said. And she would tell me where she'd been or what she did that day. She always used to have a story. I don't think a day went by that she didn't have a funny story. She could have been on television. She had some winners. Always a story. And we would argue, real heavy, about political things. She was here and I was here. But we'd get together in bed. We enjoyed each other. I respected her tremendously, and she respected me.

Liz: When you hear Fran talk about being able to experience the width and depth and breadth of his grieving, what does that say to you?

Jake: Well, uh, I think we're a little different. I'll tell you . . . I'm not grieving that much. I still cry a great deal, at night. But I don't *grieve* as much now. That may sound very crass.

Liz: Oh, no.

Fran: No.

Jake: Let me see if I can answer this way. Within about three weeks after she died, I just went through the closets and threw everything out. I did it gradually. I started to throw away her sweaters, and that was enough for Saturday. And the next week I did a little more. I just felt this was what I had to do. I didn't want to open up the closet and see all her golf skirts hanging there, and all her sweaters, things like that. Shoes. So I threw them out. I don't know if it helped me or not. I really don't know. But I felt the sooner I do this, the better off I'm going to be. The sooner I'll get my head screwed on tightly and get on with my life. It seemed to help me.

Liz: How long has it been since you buried your wife?

Jake: Just a month and a half. Christmas Eve.

Liz: How long has it been since you buried Ginnie, Fran?

Fran: Five months. September 22.

Liz: Well, I think that what you're doing, Jake, is probably right for where you are. I mean, in terms of time.

Jake: I would like to ask a question. I suppose it's too early for me, but, uh . . . I enjoy female companionship. And what I'm trying to say is that this particular female called me up a couple of weeks ago— we have known her for twenty-five years or so, my wife and I, and she happened to be, she's been divorced for fourteen years—and, uh, she asked me if I wanted to go out to dinner. I turned her down. I just don't know if I'm going to be able to, I don't know, *converse*. I don't want to talk about my wife. Maybe it's too early for me to even think about it. I'm not, I'm not, what I'm talking about, let me just say one thing here, what I'm talking about is a strictly platonic female relationship. That's all I'm talking about. *Nothing else.* No romance, nothing at all. It's just that, that . . . Once in a while it comes to you, you would like to take someone to dinner, that's all.

Liz: What's your question?

Jake: Well, should I do something like that?

Liz: Well, let me ask you that.

Jake: I'm saying no. Because I'm afraid, I'm afraid I'm gonna, I'm gonna be talking about what has happened to me. And I don't want to do that. I want to talk about something else. I don't want to bore that, that female. And believe me, I mean, I mean strictly just, just . . . She's female . . .

Liz: She knew Laura?

Jake: Huh? Oh sure. They were dear friends.

Liz: Well, maybe she needs to talk about Laura.

Jake: Dear friends. She has suffered a great loss in Laura. But I'm just saying to myself, that's going to be very boring . . .

Liz: Mike is going to burst apart if he doesn't get a chance to speak.

Mike: I wanted to know if I should tell him of my experience . . . I had a chance to take this lady out . . . We were just going out to eat. You know, I felt like a 16-year-old. Honest to Pete. After all, it was over forty-five years since I'd had a date. I'm saying now, how do I act, what do I say? I'll make a fool of myself. I'll be stutterin'. I'll be doin' this, and be crazy.

Jake: Well that doesn't enter my mind at all. I can carry a conversation with her on the phone. And she's not looking to get married, looking for a husband, or something like that. It's just that I'm trying to figure out if it's too damned new for me, or should I wait, or what should I do?

Liz: Why don't you try it and find out?

Jerry: I was just going to say, you're never going to know the answer unless you call the lady up and say, "Look, would you like to have supper?"

Jake: Well, especially, I'm thinking . . . For instance, you know . . . You get home Friday night . . . I know I've got Saturday and Sunday to look forward to that are absolute blanks. I'd like to cut them out of the calendar. And once in a while, you feel—you know, I'm near a lot of restaurants—and you feel like, oh hell, I don't want to go out alone, I should call a female up. But I don't have that many females to call. I don't know that many . . .

Jerry: Don't call them up Friday afternoon and expect them to go out on Friday night.

Jake: I know, I know that. I just wondered, I thought people might have some thoughts . . .

Liz: Why don't you go?

Jerry: Go.

Fran: Go.

Mike: Aw, go.

Liz: But may I suggest something to you? And I could be 100 percent wrong and time will test it. What you're going to go through from now until whenever it takes, is building a bridge from the life you had with Laura to a life without her. And you're going to make a lot of mistakes and you're going to have a lot of successes. And the only way you're going to have either is to go out and experience it.

Jake: To try it.

Liz: And if you do start a relationship with this woman, or any woman, *go slowly.*

Jake: I have no interest . . .

Liz: I know you don't tonight.

Jake: I have no interest whatsoever in any kind of relationship except for companionship. Someone to talk to, that's all. On a given night, on a Saturday night, or a Sunday brunch, or something like that. That's all. I don't want . . .

Liz: You don't tonight, Jake. And that's fine. Because I think that in your heart it's true, you do not.

Jake: Well, I think that's pretty normal.

Liz: Absolutely. But what I'm saying is, what my experience has been, is that the widowed community starts seeing each other and it turns out to be so comfortable because it's something you want so much, you want that female companionship, and the next thing you know, two months down the road, you're saying what the heck have I got myself into? And I'm not saying that to scare you. I'm just saying if you need to go out to dinner and a movie, whatever, go ahead, experience it. The only way you'll know is to try. *But go slowly.*

Mike: It's great. I'll tell you. Just to have somebody sitting across the table. Like I went to this play with this lady. Just to have somebody next to me. Poking her in the arm or something. I don't mean any sexy stuff. But I mean, just for that companionship, just to be riding along someplace and have somebody sitting beside you, something like that, just that sense of companionship.

Jake: It's under the heading of loneliness. There's nobody to talk to in my . . . my house. I used to have a home. No more.

Liz: The only thing I would caution you with is that it's just six weeks. And I think that Mike and Fran and Jerry would agree that you've got a lot ahead, just so much ahead in terms of grieving. And what few moments you can get of relaxing and enjoying, you know, they're precious, because you're going to have pain.

Mike: She's not saying this to cause you alarm. This is something that we've all gone through. You're going through it now. Jerry has gone through the biggest part of it. You'll never, ever lose the pain. The pain will always be there. You'll learn to live with it. It will slowly get easier, easier and easier. I think if you asked Jim or Liz about me now and when I first joined, there is a big difference, isn't there?

Liz: Your pain then was just running rampant.

Jake: You weren't that much different from me?

Mike: No, no. All you had to do was say "Sandy" and the floodgates opened.

Jake: Well, I think I could keep the conversation going so it wouldn't always revert back to my loss . . .

Liz: Isn't it okay if it does?

Jerry: Maybe you oughta just let the conversation go wherever it goes.

I mean, if she wants off it, she'll change it. And you'll do fine with it. Don't worry.

Fran: I spend some time with a lady who has recently lost her husband. We'll talk about Ginnie sometimes, and we'll talk about her husband, and when she comes to a point where she doesn't want to talk about it, she'll say "I guess that's about enough of that," and we'll talk about something else. Just as simple as that.

Liz: I keep thinking I want to tell you, "Relax." I just feel you're so uptight tonight. Do you think so, Fran?

Fran: I feel that he has a lot of barriers up.

Liz: And it's okay if you do.

Jake: Maybe I'm fighting it too much.

Liz: I think you are. I think you're issuing so many orders. Did you always do that?

Jake: Yeah.

Liz: Well then, you're going to do it now.

Jake: I've always thought of myself as an extremely orderly person. I raise hell with the girl in the office because her desk looks like the wind, like someone opened the window. I have to have everything A, B, C, D. That's the way I am.

Liz: Grieving is going to drive you nuts. There's nothing orderly about it.

Jerry: That's for sure. Don't try to keep everything in perspective.

Liz: There is no order to grieving. You can't put it in a box.

Jerry: You can go along for a Monday or Tuesday, but it'll come at you on Wednesday. And then be gone for another day.

Fran: Do you feel guilty for those two days you haven't thought, haven't grieved?

Jerry: No.

Liz: That's a very good question.

Jake: I just feel that the more I grieve, the less good it's going to do me. I've got to live my life now, without her. I accept the finality of it. There's nothing that can be done with it.

Liz: Yes, there is. Have you been here when we've talked about the tasks of grieving?

Jake: What happens to you, you mean?

Liz: First, you have to absorb the fact that your wife is dead, and that she's never coming back. That takes an undefinable time. It's different for everybody. Second, you have to experience the pain. It's horrendous and also undefinable as to the time it takes. The third step is to adjust to the environment without Laura. Again, these things are subtle. They will be sneaking up on you over the course of the next year or two. And fourth, you will have to withdraw your energies and emotions from her. And all of those things are in and out of each other all the time. And it takes a long time for all that to happen. And all of it spells "out of control." And for a high-control person like you, who says I'm going to control this thing, dammit . . .

Jake: I can't control it alone. I accept that.

Liz: You can't control it with *help*, either.

Jake: I wouldn't be here if I thought I could control it alone. I need you, I need, I need your support. I do get support from you, you know, whether you realize it or not. I draw support from all of you. And I hope I can give some myself.

Mike: You see, you do give us support.

Jerry: We all handle these things a bit differently.

Mike: What a ball I had this weekend.

Liz: Where'd you go?

Mike: Ski-mobiling.

Liz: You did it?

Mike: Did I do it. I went cuckoo. Just like a little kid. Right across the lake, seventy miles an hour. It was something I've always wanted to learn. Oh, what a ball. Just so nice and smooth.

Jim: You had a good time?

Mike: What a ball.

Fran: So what's your secret, pal? 'Cause last week you were an inch off the floor. Something must have happened.

Liz: When you left here last week you were a mess. How did you get out of that?

Mike: I just said the hell with it. I'm not going to let this bother me.

Liz: So you did what I said.

Mike: What did you say?

Liz: Last Tuesday night, I said that you had done everything you possibly could, so just leave it here and go out fresh. So that's exactly what you did.

Mike: Yeah, but it took me a day or two. It's terrible to get down like that, isn't it? I thought I was losin' my mind. Honest and true, I thought I was losin' my mind. I couldn't remember anything, it got so bad . . .

Fran: Wouldn't want to see you stay like that.

Mike: I wouldn't want to be like that. I probably should have stayed home last week. Because that was, something like that is almost contagious, don't you think?

Liz: Mike, can I ask you a question?

Mike: Oh sure.

Liz: Next week when Jake feels like that, do you think he should stay home?

Mike: If . . . No. No. You're right.

Liz: Jerry, how are you doing?

Jerry: Me? I'm doing fine. Can't wait to see what tomorrow brings.

Fran: Really?

Jerry: Yeah. Every day is different. It's gettin' to be a pleasure to go to bed at night so I can wake up in the morning and see what the hell's going to happen.

Mike: You've got to be kidding.

Jerry: No, I'm not kidding.

Fran: This is a complete reversal.

Jerry: Yeah, but I like wakin' up in the morning so I can see what the hell's coming up. Cause every day is different. You know, about two weeks ago, I said, the hell with this. I said, that's it. So now, I just look forward to the next day to see what's going to happen.

Liz: Are you dating?

Jerry: I am going out with a few. Nothing serious. I call up a lady and see if she wants to go to supper with me. And if she wants to go, that's great. If she wants to go dancing after, all right. If she wants to go home, I take her home. Don't matter to me one way or the other what she wants to do.

Liz: Is it satisfactory?

Jerry: Yeah, it's good that way. That way nobody gets hurt. Nothing serious. Just gives me a night out and someone to talk to.

Liz: Have you done anything about your smoking?

Jerry: Yes. I have increased from one to a little over two packs a day.

Jim: Oh, you're getting there.

Jerry: Getting there. The more I try to quit, the more I smoke. The more I think of it. And the more I smoke, the more coffee I drink.

Fran: So between the caffeine and the nicotine . . .

Jerry: Between the caffeine and the nicotine and the emphysema . . .

Liz: You know, for somebody who professes love of life so much, you're really contradicting yourself.

Jerry: I know.

Liz: Do you have the desire to quit?

Jerry: Yeah, I wanna quit. I just have absolutely no willpower. I have willpower for 99 percent of everything else, but not for these goddam things.

Mike: Well, if a doctor said to you, "Hey, Jerry, you're either gonna quit smokin' or you're gonna lose your legs," what would you do?

Liz: He's as much as been told that.

Jerry: I was told five years ago that I'd be dead in ten. But I didn't quit smoking.

Mike: Well, what are you gonna do? Go the nine years, then quit?

Jerry: No, I'm going to go the ten years. See what happens.

Mike: That's cuckoo.

Jerry: I know. Tell me what I don't know. I tried, Mike. I was down to about three quarters of a pack. And I constantly thought, kept thinking, "Fuck, how do I get off these damned things?" Every time I try to quit, I smoke more. I never used to smoke before I had my coffee in the morning. But now, I get up in the morning and before I put my shoes on, I light a cigarette.

Mike: Well, if the doctor says you're gonna die in six months if you keep smokin, and you keep smokin' and you're dead in six months, it's your own stupid fault.

Jerry: I know. Mike, you know you were miserable last week. I wasn't feeling much better than you was.

Fran: You never said that.

Liz: What was going on?

Jerry: There was nothing going on with me, mentally. But Monday when I went to work—Monday was a little bit icy—I was going into the office and I hit a patch of ice. Just as the nurse was coming in. And I landed on my back again.

Jim: You mean, you didn't grab for the nurse?

Jerry: Nurse was too far away. So she took me into her office. She says, "Take your shirt off." I says, "The last girl who asked me that I asked her if she'd take her shirt off first."

Liz: Oh Jerry, that's so tacky . . .

Jerry: So I take my shirt off and she says, "What the hell did you do? Your chest is all black and blue." I says, "I fell down a flight of stairs." So she sent me to get it X-rayed, and my family doctor was there. So he says, "Emphysema actin' up again, Jerry?" I says, "No." So he has a look at my X-rays and says, "You cracked two ribs." He says, "I'll tape you up. Take a few days off, and you'll be fine." So I went back to work.

Jim: You told them all about it?

Jerry: At work? Hell no. I never said a word. Nurse asked me, "How'd you make out?" I says, "The X-rays looked pretty." It's fine, except when I cough.

Jim: I thought you were coughing softly tonight.

Liz: Are you strapped up tonight?

Jerry: No. I took the tape off this morning.

Jim: On whose orders?

Jerry: Mine. But I was lucky the nurse was there. If there'd been nobody around . . .

Jake: When my wife was in the hospital, I had a kidney stone attack. That's worse, I understand, than having five children at a time; I guess it's probably one of the most painful things you can go through. This was my second one. And I had to drive myself about ten miles to the hospital.

Jim: Don't they have ambulances over there?

Jake: Well, yeah, they do. But I suppose I didn't think of it. And besides it comes in waves. When the stone is moving is when you get pain. If it just sits there, it's fine. But that bothered me, that I was alone. The last time I'd had it, my wife drove me over. It bothers you, when you're alone.

Mike: I know. Sometimes I think, Geez, I could be in this house a week and nobody would know . . .

Liz: What is your greatest concern as a widower?

Mike: My greatest concern. I think, loneliness. Just being without her. Hey. Two thirds of my life I spent with her.

Liz: What has distressed you most, Fran?

Fran: The loneliness. Easy answer.

Liz: How about you, Jerry?

Jerry: What?

Liz: Oh Jerry, you make me so tired. What distresses you most about being a widower?

Jerry: Oh, right now, not too much. Well, gettin' up in the mornin' and gettin' that cup of coffee or somethin', and nothin' else to do. When Jo was alive, I had so many damned things to do in the mornin'. That's the hardest thing to get used to. Get up in the mornin', there's nothin' to do.

Jim: You ever see yourself married again?

Jerry: To be perfectly honest with you, I don't know. I really don't know. I don't know whether any woman would be dumb enough to put up with me.

Jim: Well, there's a lot of dumb ones around.

Jerry: Right now, I don't think I'd want to get married. Not right away. I've changed. I've changed a hell of a lot. I used to be, like, organized. But now I just do things sporadically. I'll take any challenge, any foolish damned thing. If something pops into my mind, I'll do it. If I wake up at 4:00 or 5:00 in the morning and want to go fishing, I'll go fishing.

Liz: So you are enjoying the freedom . . .

Jerry: I don't know if it's enjoying the freedom or trying to break the boredom.

Liz: Jake, did I ask you those questions? Would you like to answer them?

Jake: That you just asked them? I have no desire to marry again. It's just too new for me.

Jim: What's the worst problem you have right now?

Jake: Just loneliness. Everybody's the same. Loneliness. I just hate it.

The meeting did not end this abruptly. There was a winding down with small talk, with plans for the next meeting, with inquiries after those who had not come this time. But we ended our account where we did

because it underscores a point. When asked, each member of this group said the biggest problem he faced in widowhood was the loneliness. And indeed, most of the men I talked to said exactly the same thing. Among all the problems widowhood poses, loneliness seems to be the most difficult to deal with. As we have pointed out, it is also one of the most deadly.

Getting together with a group of other lonely guys every Tuesday night in the basement of a church is not a solution to that problem. In fact, it may appear at first to *underscore* the problem. But it does address the situation better than staying home every Tuesday night and watching television, or wandering aimlessly in a mall, or even reading this book. Given the fact that everyone claims that no one can understand him except another person who's been there himself, a group like this may be the only place in the world where you wouldn't feel lonely at this moment in your life.

If you are recently widowed and feeling lonely, and if you feel that no one can really understand you, it might be worth your while to give a group like this a chance, even if, like many men, you are staunchly not a joiner. You only have to go once, after all. And you may find, as these men apparently have, that there is something that happens in a group experience like this that answers some deep-seated need and keeps you coming back for more.

This particular group was started by the wife of a funeral director in a small suburban town. When she ran into men at the supermarket who had recently lost their wives and asked them how they were doing, they would actually tell her the truth. To everyone else in town, they said they were getting along all right. But to Liz, who had ministered to them at the time they lost their wives, they admitted they weren't getting on so well.

Apparently, they sensed that she was willing to hear the truth, rather than secretly wanting them to assure her that everything was okay. Most of us, frankly, want that assurance. Most of us would rather not hear that someone is not doing well, or else we want to hear of their pain as a way of legitimizing our own—an unfortunate form of empathy.

As time went by, Liz became aware that there were several men in her town who were not doing well in their widowhood, and it seemed only natural to her that they should be brought together so they could try to help each other out. She came to this conclusion without awareness of Dr. Silverman's work and implemented it without any training in group process. But, as you can see in this chapter, she is doing a

good job. She is good at asking leading questions, getting the men to verbalize what it is they've lost. She also gives out accurate information about what to expect in grieving—the disorderliness of it, for instance—and she does some mothering, in terms of diet and exercise, which is entirely appropriate.

If you are a professional who is interested in being of help to widowers, Liz and Jim's success points up the fact that you don't need a lot of special training to offer such help. You just need a little knowledge and a lot of compassion. We would have liked to see these men interacting a bit more with each other—most of the dialogue was with Liz rather than among the men—but there was quite a bit of silent communication going on around the table throughout the meeting.

When Jake began to cry, for instance, about the loss of his daughter, there was a quickening at the table, everyone came alert. Nobody rushed to make him stop or made a big fuss over him. Nobody said, go ahead and cry, which could have been patronizing. They just sat there and let him cry. Jerry nudged the Kleenex toward him. That kind of silent communication is sometimes far more potent than words of any volume and description. So while everyone talked directly to Liz more than they talked to each other, it wouldn't have worked the same way for each of them to talk with her alone. There was group communication going on, whether it was verbal or not.

If you're thinking of initiating a group for widowers, there are some people who can help you get started. The American Association of Retired Persons has a training program and a library of written materials. The National Self-Help Clearing House helps people to set up self-help groups of all descriptions. The addresses and phone numbers of these organizations are listed at the end of this book.

As for this particular group, we can see that Fran is doing well, arriving now at a point where he can allow his grief to flow without tensing up against it. It is questionable whether he would have come this far this quickly in his grieving if it weren't for this group, especially since he had spent the last twenty-seven years of his life being ''forbidden'' to grieve his son. This group at last is giving him the permission that has been withheld for so long—to grieve not only his son, but also now his wife—as well as guidance on how to grieve and a place to do part of it.

Giving permission is one of the most important things a group does. While most men are not forbidden to grieve for twenty-seven years, most do experience discouragement from our general cultural atmosphere about the grieving of their wives. People want them to get over it, fast. People want them to get married again and get on with their lives. People want them to be okay, partly because they are scared of their pain.

In an atmosphere like this, it can be a great relief to find a place where you can grieve openly and long, without any pressure to pack it away. It may seem odd, as an adult, to seek permission from your peers to do what is utterly natural, but on the other hand, it's pretty odd that as a culture we don't give men the right to be natural.

Jake's dilemma over whether to take a woman friend to dinner raises an interesting issue. One of the interesting things about it is the adolescent ring it has, as if he were standing among the boys on one side of the gymnasium wondering whether he should dare cross to the other side quite yet, while the chorus around him chants "Go, Go, Go." It's understandable how a man might feel thrown back into adolescence in a situation like this. Many of these men married when they were barely out of adolescence and have been married ever since. It makes sense that, single again, they might find themselves feeling adolescent again, and this time feeling more awkward with it than they even did before because this time, after all, they are adults and "ought to know how to behave."

But if widowhood casts you back into a quasi-adolescence, it also gives you an opportunity to learn what we seldom learn the first time through adolescence, or perhaps while we are married—that it is possible for a man and a woman just to be friends. Our society ill prepares men and women to see each other that way, and because of that, simple friendships between men and women are rare and usually suspect. But Karl talked of friendships between men and women blossoming in his bereavement group, as if the group gave its members permission not to have to relate to each other sexually. Later on, we will meet other men who have, in their widowhood, discovered whole new ways of relating to women.

Maybe Jake was ready to explore new ways of relating to women with the woman friend he mentioned. And he should certainly explore everything he can. But the fact that he protested so much that there wasn't anything sexual in it suggests he wasn't really convinced himself that he could take this woman to dinner without it turning into a "date." That's why he felt ambivalent.

Liz was absolutely right to encourage Jake to enjoy whatever pleasure he could find. But knowing what we do about men and women and widowhood, she was also absolutely right to warn him to go slow, even if his intentions were entirely platonic. Inasmuch as Jake seems in a hurry to get on with his grieving, one can imagine that his going out with a woman might very well become sexual.

That's not necessarily a problem. For some men, plunging into a hot affair right away can be a way of passionately embracing life, and as long as they have no interest in any long-term commitment, that's fine. But many men, once so involved, very easily slide back into marriage. Especially if they have been married for many years, it may be hard for some men to relate to a woman sexually in some way other than as a wife, which can lead to a hasty remarriage.

Again, the theme here is loneliness. If you are recently widowed, you may well be feeling an intense need for female companionship. If you are, and you can handle it without feeling too ambivalent, by all means go for it. Enjoy it. Luxuriate in it, if you can. But keep in mind that you can do it without getting sexually involved, if you're not ready to do that yet, and that you can get sexual without necessarily getting married. There are many different ways to relate to women, and maybe this is a chance for you to explore some of the variations.

For all the mutual support that is going on in this group, it is also important to note that the group in part withholds its support from Jerry. There were several moments the group cut him off, and when he was allowed to speak they gave him a pretty hard time about his health. This kind of reaction is another way a group like this can work. Jerry has been widowed two years, and in many ways it seems that he is somehow stuck in his grieving. He has a tendency to go over and over the same ground, without reaching new perspectives on it. Assuming the group has, in the past, attempted to give him new perspectives and found him unwilling to take them—just as they now give him health advice which he refuses to heed—it is appropriate that they should now refuse to listen to him unless he is going to make an effort to change his point of view. If you aren't really trying to cope with your troubles, all you're doing is complaining. Withdrawal of support can sometimes be an effective way of encouraging someone to behave differently.

Sometimes a problem may be so rooted in a person's character structure, however, that the relatively simple effects of reward and punishment may not be enough. Some men find they need more individual attention. Some men, like Bill, find the services of a psychiatrist useful.

Bill

BILL is 55, about to take an early retirement from his job as a drill-press operator in a machine shop. He met Helga when he was stationed in Germany after World War II. She was a local girl, the cook, and they were married after he was discharged. He was 21 when they married. Helga was 31. "She was one of the strongest people I have ever known in my life. I was the more insecure person, because of my childhood background, and I drew from her strength. I probably still do. As a matter of fact, I probably draw from it more now than I did before." In the course of thirty years together, they adopted one son, who is now 32, married, and living nearby.

About a year before she died, Helga was diagnosed with cancer. Eventually it metastasized to the lungs and then to the liver. "I knew that she was dying, but I didn't want her to know. She knew that she was dying, but she didn't want me to know. I guess some people call it love. I didn't want to hurt her, she didn't want to hurt me. I was advised that I should have embraced her, and told her that I knew, and hugged her, and all this sort of thing, but everyone does it their own way. I wouldn't have done it any different. I wouldn't know how."

This interview was conducted almost five years after Helga's death, and two years after Bill remarried.

I was with one of our dearest friends, Felicia, down at the hospital chapel. We had been with Helga for a time. We had seen that her condition had worsened and had gone to the chapel to pray that the good Lord take her. She needed peace. She needed not to suffer. When you love somebody enough to wish that—I can't really think of anything more to describe what I call love. I was really concerned that she sleep.

As we walked back into the room, she was gasping, she was in trouble. We went over to her and pressed the button and called the nurses and she gasped for air once or twice and was gone. Felicia reached her before I did. Helga died in her arms. I was holding her hand. There was nothing we could do for her, but we just . . . we wanted to hold on.

The doctor came in and asked us to leave, so he could do what he had to do, and I knew there was nothing else I could do. I took her clothes and her handbag home. And when I got home, I washed out her laundry and hung it out to dry. One of my neighbors was shocked by that. She told me later, she says, "You know, I couldn't understand what was goin' on. There was no need for that." But it was the order thing, I guess. One word to describe the German people—Helga was German—is order. *Ordnung* is the word. My life before I met Helga was completely *un*orderly. I learned a sense of order from her, so at her death there was also a need for a sense of order.

We had both decided we didn't want to go through this terrible thing called a wake, where people stand around and talk about their cars and their love affairs and the bills and the boss and all that crap—we had both decided we didn't want that. But I actually went against her wishes. I let the undertaker talk me into it—because he did a wonderful job on her, you know. So I said okay. Well, just for close friends.

And then at the wake, I asked the undertaker if I could do one thing. I got my tape recorder and I played a song I had written for her—I am a songwriter, after work. I wrote it on the occasion of our twenty-fifth anniversary, when I thought to myself, well, gee, it's still good after all these years. And while the song was playing, I held her hand. Not a dry eye in the room. Whether it was right or wrong, I really don't give a damn. It was something I had to do.

And I can only describe—and I've related this story to other people, to clerics, psychiatrists, to friends—there was a warmth that I can't describe. A very warm, alive, almost moist feeling to her hand. I know her hand was as hard as a rock. I know that because when I buried my mother she was as hard as a rock, and when I leaned over to kiss her goodbye I almost broke my front teeth. But I tell you now Helga's hand was warm. I know better, but that's what I felt. Anyone can say what they want, but I think that she reached out. I think it's love. I think it is. And I'll always have that memory.

And then comes a time . . . It's very hard . . . I would dread doing it again. I went from the funeral to my house alone, I slept in our bed alone, I got up and had breakfast alone. And that was it. That was as alone as I have ever been in my life. I did have a small reception at my house—my son, his wife, some friends from work, about a dozen people—but they left. And there I was.

I had never had a loss like this. Remember, I was someone who—like most men who go through what I've gone through—I was very dependent on my wife. It's almost chauvinistic, where you go home and you expect to find the hot meal and the laundry done, and the shopping. It's a difficult learning experience. When someone loses their loved one . . .

I lost my wife, okay? It's very simple to say I lost my wife, but that's not true. That's not true of anyone. In no significant sequence, in no particular order of importance, I say I lost a friend, I lost a lover, I lost a mother, I lost a sister, I lost a doctor, a nurse, a teacher, a finance expert, a fighter, I lost many, many people when I lost this one person. That's a lot. A lot of people think it's just . . . a wife, just a person, just one person. But unless you've walked that path, it's hard to imagine all the things you have to do for yourself all of a sudden.

Women I have known who have experienced this same situation survive much better because they cook, they wash, they shop, they do the bills, they rear the children, they know how to handle illness. And women are stronger by nature. They have more practice with being alone. And how to turn on the washing machine.

I got this friend named Mario, we car pool to work. He was widowed the year before I was. When his wife passed away, there was a need, you know, for making out checks. He didn't even know *how*. His wife had always made out the checks. Helga worked as a bookkeeper, and she tried to teach him how to do it, and he refused to learn.

That is devastating, that you can depend so much on one person. I think it's just your makeup. He needed someone all the time. He needed someone so desperately, he would have taken anyone. He's a guy that learned to be bigoted. He doesn't like black people at all. In my life, I've had a lot of black friends. Bigotry is not my line. But one time he even told me, he says, "You know, I don't even give a damn if I get a *nigger* in here, just as long as there's somebody here."

He finally married this woman. She told him she didn't love him, that it would be an asexual situation. She was marrying only for comfort. And he went into it. He was that desperate for someone. You get these frustrations from people. People do reach that stage where they will settle for anyone. It wound up in divorce.

Now he's married again. And he's falling into that same trap again of being with just one person and turning everyone else away. And the truth in that is the fact that when his new wife went to the hospital— cancer was suspected—the first one he called was me. But it turned out she didn't have cancer. And now that everything's okay, he doesn't need anyone else. I think that there should be someone else in your life.

I believe in friends. One piece of advice I would give is that you should have as many friends as you can, because I was left alone. No bowling buddies, no beer drinking buddies. If I'd had more friends . . .

You reach a point where you hate going home, when "Have a nice weekend" makes you cry. How can you have a nice weekend, you know? I hate my job, I hate going home. I'd go home and I'd open that door—that was the hardest part, going home at night and turning the key. You know, there is no *sound.* It's easier if there's family and friends. I didn't have that, there was no one to lean on, no support system. A support system is extremely important. I wish I'd had it.

I thought maybe Helga's death would bring me closer to my son. We have never been very close. He was abused and abandoned—we adopted him at age three—and whatever scars he had from those first three years, he blamed on Helga and me. Naturally, since he didn't know he'd had other parents those first three years. We never told him he was adopted—we were advised not to tell him—and when he found out, after Helga died, it increased the distance between us. I thought it would bring us closer, but he didn't show any real interest. So I was on my own.

And people, they turn their backs on you. Your friends, okay? I came out of the hospital one time—Helga was very ill—and on the way out the tears started flowing. I wasn't sobbing, but tears were flowing. And this friend, she looked at me and she said "Oh, poor baby," in a tone that said, you know, you shouldn't be crying. "Poor baby." This was one of my *friends.* Maybe that's just the way she is. Come on, poor baby. But hey, I was sad.

I remember one night I was in bad shape—I was crying and swearing at the gods and at Jesus and everything else—and the phone rang and you know, I'm in control, but it was noticeable. So, "What's the matter? You okay, Billy?" So I say, "I'm all right." But I'm *not,* you know. "Oh God! Oh gee whiz!" you know? They don't know how to handle it. They don't *want* to handle it. They wouldn't come over and talk to you. No, it's, "Well, Gee Whiz, I'm sorry, God, she, you know, pull yourself together, she wouldn't want you to be that way, oh my God," you know. And you don't get the phone calls, 'cause God forbid you should be cryin' again. People don't want you to be cryin'. I think it's a reminder that they too may be hit with that. And they don't want it. It's normal.

When you lose your wife, you also lose other couples as friends. I think there are two reasons for it. One is the threat syndrome. I think you become a threat to the male. The other is the thank-God-it's-not-me thing. You are a reminder of the road we all travel someday. Your aloneness is a constant reminder of people's vulnerability, that they too may suffer that loss. And I don't think they want you around. So you learn to be alone.

But those people who didn't bother calling you when you were alone, when you become a couple again, all of a sudden you're welcome. They want to meet your friend, go to your wedding . . . This couple that somehow didn't have too much occasion to call me when I was alone, now they're back in my life. But I know them for what they are now. I call them friends, but I know they're not. They're people I socialize with. I know the difference now. I forgive them for what went on, but I don't forget.

A couple of months after Helga died, I was on the way home from work on a Friday night and I got this numbness in my fingers, in my toes, numbness in my face. It was Friday night, I was doin' fine—or I *thought* I was doin' fine—but I was gettin' hot flashes, you now, and my face started gettin' numb, my jaw. It was hyperventilation. I wanted to go to the hospital, I was driving by, but I didn't. I give myself credit for that. One part of me wanted help, to be cared for, wanted to be mothered, protected. And the other part of me, I guess, wanted to do it on my own, wanted to tough it out and fight it. I went home and I stuck my head into a paper bag. Then I called Mario and I guess we went out for spaghetti or something. But it happened quite often after that. I needed help to handle my life. I was in physical pain. I had taught myself not to cry.

I finally reached a period there when I didn't really give a damn. Why should I work? I don't like my job. I don't like my boss. What goal do I have? There's no one in my life. So you contemplate saying, The hell with this. So what if your money runs out? Don't worry. You've lost everything that has meaning. What the hell does money mean?

What does your job mean? What does your boss mean? Doesn't mean a thing.

I was on the phone with Felicia one time, and I says, "You know," I says, "it's okay to die." I had no desire to die, but I wasn't afraid of dying. It was just, it was like I received a message from Helga that she was okay. It was like I understood that Helga was okay and I was okay. But I must have said it wrong, something got screwed up. Felicia heard something else and she called the doctors at the HMO clinic. I guess she must have heard this as probably I was suicidal. And Jesus, all hell broke loose. They called me up and they said, You know we can have you committed, talking like that. We could put you away for your own good, there's a state law. If I didn't come in, they were gonna come get me. They were gonna put me away, you know. I says, There's nothing wrong with me, but they wouldn't understand. Oh Christ, all hell broke loose.

So I went and talked to one of the doctors there about what I was going through, and she suggested I see someone. I knew about psychology, I knew what was going on. I didn't need anybody to tell me. *My wife was dead.* I kept repeating, *My wife is dead. My wife is dead.* And the doctor said, "I know she's dead. And it hurts, doesn't it?" You know how they pull this out of you. "And it hurts, doesn't it?"

And, uh, we'd get it out. I'd start crying. I guess I'd start reliving it and accepting the truth, the emotional part. The intellectual part I could deal with. She's dead. She's gone. She's not coming back. I've spoken to friends of mine who have experienced the same thing, and yet I think even to this day, five years later, they still look up at the window as they pull into the driveway hoping to find the wife looking out the window and waving. They know, intellectually, she's not there. But dammit, they still look up.

So I went into psychotherapy because I had to learn how to cry. Here I am 50-odd years old and I never really learned how to cry. You have to be strong, you know. The doctor says to me, he says, Well, what makes you think you're weak if you cry? To me it was a sign of weakness. See, I brought myself up. I worked full-time since I was 12. From 7:00 until 9:00 in the evening, seven days a week. I joined the merchant marines when I was 16 years old. Ran away from home. I was on my own, I took care of myself. But all my married life, I had someone to take care of me. You know, I wasn't a baby, but I was dependent on somebody else. Now I had only me. So obviously I couldn't cry. In front of me? That sort of thing. But I learned how to cry, I'll tell ya. That guy, he spent lots of money on tissues. For two or three months, something like that.

If I hadn't hooked up with the doctors, I probably would have quit my job. I have no way of knowing what would have happened. It's a question I ask myself sometimes when I'm on my way to work and my life is in order and I see people on the street whose lives are in disarray—you know, alcoholism or whatever, they're homeless—and, you know, you ask yourself "Whatever happened to them?" Perhaps I could have been one of them. It's possible. Your money runs out. How many times can you go for assistance, to a hospital for free care? Eventually you're in the street.

Obviously, I had been in a very deep depression. It's hard to say where I would be now if they hadn't identified that, and I am very grateful for that. I could never repay them, never. All of them were very supportive. I went out and bought them fruit baskets—just, you know, enjoy, I want to thank you. I'd like to break bread with them, to call them friend, but professionals, especially in health services, they separate their lives. You know, they have to, I understand that. But they were very kind to me. Even beyond their office hours, when I would call and cry out, "I don't give a damn!" and I would swear and everything else and yet they were there, twenty-four hours a day. Even the receptionists. I gave them all baskets too. They were so important. Because, you know, you're not talking to doctors *all* the time.

I can't speak highly enough about the people there. That was the first time I'd ever seen a psychiatrist. God forbid, but if I found myself in this situation again, I think I would seek professional help. I would know better next time.

I look at life differently now. You go on from one year to the next and everything is fine and bad things happen to everybody else—statistics are made for other people—then all of a sudden you are a statistic. You learn from that. You learn to accept. I used to worry all the time. I used to worry about worrying. "Why am I worrying so much? I know it's bad for me." Like that. But now I feel like I have this wisdom, I understand a lot more now. I still have a healthy worry, but I don't have an excessive worry.

But still I was alone. I used to walk in shopping malls, hoping to bump into somebody, catch somebody's eye. There was a strong need to have someone, but I kept fighting this need to be with someone, the need to be dependent, the need to get involved again, to suffer the pain again.

There was this German Club in town. Now, I'm not a German and I never studied German. But I learned GI German so I could converse with Helga's mother and father, who couldn't speak any English. So my first thing was to go to this German Club just to be with Germans. To be a member of the club, you had to speak the language, or you had to be German-born. I'm Cape Verdian, so I had to go before a board of people and they talked to me in German and I had to answer them back in German. And I don't have a grasp of formal German grammar, it's just by ear. But they let me in.

This was my first socializing. I was trying to meet another woman. I was probably looking for Helga. They were 99 percent couples. But I did go out with one German lady—my first sexual experience—stupidly, as I think of it now. At my house. In our bed. That was a bummer. I was up all night. Not crying, but just tense, wide-eyed. Opened, my eyes were opened all night. It was almost like I was doing a penance. Probably punishing myself, you know, for doing such a thing. I thought about writing a song about it called "Blame It On The Wine." I paid the price for that, I tell ya. I would not advise that. That is stupid. The next morning here I am at breakfast, crying with this woman I just made love to, and apologizing. You know, it's not an adult thing to do. I would know better than doin' something like that again.

I went to the German Club often, though. I went there informal, or in a tuxedo. I always went alone. And one time I went and I opened the door and there was this laughter and these voices and everybody was happy and they were all quite German. And I thought, "What the hell am I doing here? I'm not German. What am I doing here?" So it was a realization that Helga wasn't there. And I'm not going to find her there. I went home. And it was okay. I might have had a tear in my eye, I might have had a tear. But I went home and I had a good night's sleep. I was at peace. And that was the last time I went to the German Club.

But it was a step. It was a step. You've got to socialize, you've got to. If you stay at home, it's gonna be a remote possibility that someone will knock on your door and say Hi. You know, it's not going to happen. It's a hard move.

Women told me constantly that it's easier for a man. Well I can say it's *not* easier. It's as difficult. Women have a reverse-chauvanistic thing. It's difficult for a man to make that step, to go and . . . You feel awkward. You lose your sense of, you're not secure. You don't have the strength of somebody else. You remember, I talked about all the people involved in this one person? Well, you don't have that support system. You take an awful beating, physically and mentally. And you have to get your confidence back.

So I went a couple of times to the Holiday Inn. A local radio station has a hot line party at the Holiday Inn on Saturday mornings. It's a hot line for people who are single, widowed, divorced, who want to get in contact with other people in similar situations. And then I found out about a private group in the suburbs, where divorced people get together and talk. And that was where I met Mary Helen.

We were into little rap sessions, you know—the single life as opposed to the married life, the pros and cons, that sort of thing—and she was sitting across the room from me with another lady. And the hostess wanted to take a Polaroid picture of the group. I invited both of them to come over and join us in this picture. They protested for a while and then they decided to come over. I said, "Take my chair." She says, "Oh no, I'll sit right here."

So she sat on the floor right in front of me so we could all fit in this picture. And, you know, proximity is important in relationships. So now she was there, I was there, and we talked about why we were there. Is this your first time? You know, like that. She was widowed about the same time I was. We'd both been widowed about a year.

She was going away on a cruise with a schoolteacher girlfriend to the Caribbean. I gave her my address to write, and she toyed with the idea of should I send this guy a card? She did, and I called her when she got back. We went out and both our dinners got cold because we just talked, talked, talked, talked, talked. See, that terrible need to have someone just to talk to again. It's important to have a friend.

We dated about two years, then married. I fought with her tooth and nail about the marriage, the hoopla, the ceremony. I mean, I wanted to go quiet. The Justice of the Peace is fine. I tried to convince Mary Helen that the wedding isn't important, it's the marriage. I had a damned good marriage and a lousy wedding—no pictures, no gifts, no nothing. We had to pay for two witnesses. But you know, she wanted this ceremony . . . Oh boy. Well, I survived it. But I think a lot of men might be discouraged because of this whole thing. You know, the marriage, the suit, the whole thing.

I think a lot of people who are widowed don't marry again for the fear of having it happen again. But I am combat trained, and I'm almost combat ready. I keep myself in training, because it was so devastating that I never want to go through that again. I'm willing to suffer that pain again, to do what I'd have to do if Mary Helen were to suffer the same problem. I would do battle again. But I would be prepared this time.

For the most part now, I prefer to learn how to do this and how to do that. I'll do the dishes, I'll do the dryer—not all the time, I'm not obsessive. I *was* obsessive at one point, almost demanding to do it. *I'll* do it. *I'll* make the bed. *I'll* go here. No, *I'll* do it. I'm much better about that now, but I still prefer to do more than my share. Folding the laundry. I mean this doesn't sound like a thing of much consequence, but when you're alone there are only so many hours in a day. You have to take care of yourself. And going from a physical job, as I have, on the way home to shop and then cooking, cleaning up, getting ready, bathing—there's no time for socializing.

Mary Helen is more into socializing than Helga ever was. Helga was more into home. Sewing was her hobby, home was her life. And cleaning, to a fault. She passed up opportunities to go out with her co-workers because it was Tuesday, laundry day. I'd tell her, go ahead, enjoy. But no, no. That was it. She wasn't antisocial, but that's the way she was.

Mary Helen is very different. She has some of the same characteristics that Helga had—unselfishness, devotion, a sense of humor. But there are differences in bed, there are differences in character and temperament, there are differences in tolerances, understanding, all these things. One is not better than the other. They're different, they're different people.

Mary Helen entertains more than Helga ever would, and that's probably important. If one has a large social circle, your chances of surviving are much better. You have sources to draw from, invitations to accept and decline, chances to meet people.

I'm happy now, but there are times when I wish I had my other life back. I wouldn't confess this to Mary Helen, but there are moments. Not for any particular reason. I know that Helga is gone, in the physical sense. But she'll always be there. Because she was, and she is. But I'm happy. I've found someone I can live with, pick up my life where I left off. Mary Helen is no substitute, she wasn't meant to be, but she fills the void that Helga left.

Today, my life, everything's okay. You know what I mean? It's okay. How do you feel? I got this far. This is the way I am today. I don't think that I'll have any problem with retirement. I think it will be easy for me. If I could acclimate or accept what I did and live through that terrible time, I can adjust to anything. Life is a piece of cake at this point. It really is.

Bill is a pretty interesting man. In spite of the fact that he was left to a large extent without resources, and the fact that he was surrounded by people who didn't know how to help him, he showed good faith in his own instincts and took full advantage of the help that happened to come his way. The fact that he washed Helga's clothes, for instance, on coming home from the hospital, was utterly unnecessary, utterly instinctual. There was no need to wash her clothes, it was just a blind routine. But it was a way of keeping her alive a little bit, and of treating her remains with respect, and it was a way of incorporating her strengths into himself, already, in a small way. He had never done the laundry before, and here he was already teaching himself how to take care of things. It was a useful transition ritual.

Playing her song at the wake was also a nice transition ritual, also arrived at by instinct, and it showed a good understanding of the wake as theater. It *is* a theatrical event, an arena in which to enact your feelings, if you choose to use it that way. In some cultures, mourners beat themselves. In others, they hire someone else to do it. But whatever the form, we all have a need for rituals. When we don't have them handed to us through our religion or our culture—or if, for some reason, we don't find those rituals satisfying—we're likely to make up our own on the spot. Bill's playing the song was ritualistic, just as washing the clothes was. Mark's carrying Joanne's bone in his pocket and reading the obituaries were examples of rituals. Jim's ritualistic denial of ritual by diving ritualistically into his work was a ritual. Some people may find their need for ritual embarrassing, as if it were somehow too primitive, but Bill showed good faith in his instincts by following through with them.

If you are recently widowed and you feel an instinctive need to enact your grief in some ritualistic ways, don't let a sense of conformity inhibit you too much and don't let the world judge you too much. If people had known that Mark was carrying a fragment of his dead wife's body around with him in his pocket, they very possibly would have been horrified. And they might have thought him peculiar if they'd known that he was clipping obituaries every day and saving what was left of his wife's toothpaste. But those little rituals helped Mark get through a very difficult time, and it's nobody's business but your own if you want to do such things too. In the end, there's no one who knows better than you what you need to do.

Bill's faith in his instincts, however, did not protect him from social isolation. Typically, men are dependent on women for physical care, for housekeeping, and for social networking. In Bill's case, in which he was married to a "lone-wolf" kind of woman, he was even more drastically isolated than most other men in his situation. On top of that, what social network he did have was largely inept. It seems that most of the people around him had not the faintest idea of how to treat him, and didn't seem much to care. He was left with virtually no one and had to find his way out alone.

Eventually, Felicia helped him by "turning him over to the doctors," but it was up to Bill to take advantage of that kindness. Not everyone bothers to take advantage of the help that is offered them.

He didn't do it without some struggle. He provides a beautiful illustration of the dilemma men go through when it comes to getting help. He knew she was dead, he accepted it. Why did he need a psychiatrist? And in fact, he did know she was dead, he knew it intellectually. But there are other levels at which that knowledge is harder to deal with, and if a man isn't coming to terms with that knowledge at an emotional level, it's hard to get him to understand there is something more he's not grasping. "My wife is dead," he'll keep telling you. "I know that. My wife is dead."

Fortunately, Bill got hold of a good psychiatrist. The psychiatrist didn't confront him, he invited him to explore further. And it wasn't very long before Bill stumbled onto a whole new level of understanding and grappling. It's not so much that he learned to cry as that he learned to embrace it. Before, he seemed to look upon tears as a slip, as something to be covered up. Now he can cry without hesitation. He has let go of a false image of himself as a man who does not cry.

One should not place too much stress on crying. Some men cry a lot, some less so. The tears themselves are not so much the point as is the fact that Bill has allowed himself to accept emotionally that his wife is gone.

Most people say psychiatrists are of no use in grieving, and to the extent that grief is not an illness, that is true. But just because you're grieving doesn't mean that you might not also have intra- and inter-personal skills or problems that a psychiatrist might be able to help you with, problems which, once straightened out, might make your grieving easier. In Bill's case, it appears the psychiatrist was able to help him adjust his expectations of himself to make his grieving a little bit easier, and that he also was able to help Bill develop his own coping skills.

If you think you might be able to make good use of a psychiatrist, don't hesitate to call on one, even if you have a natural aversion to the profession and other related fields, such as psychology and social work. As with a widowers' group, you only have to go once. Some people don't dare go even once for fear the psychiatrist will tell them they're crazy, then put them through some process that will make them like everyone else. There are some psychiatrists who would prefer it if every-one were the same, but fortunately psychiatrists themselves are not all the same, and some of them are very good. Bill came away from that experience not with a bookish knowledge of human emotional response, and not with a set of emotional responses that were like everyone else's, but with his own practical wisdom, a wisdom that is based very much on his own experience.

But for all the psychiatrist did for him, Bill was still alone. And, one of the things that people often need to learn to do in grieving is how to re-people their lives. Often, as with Bill, that means acquiring a new set of social skills, skills that are generally better learned from peers than from psychiatrists. Bill's use of the German Club is an early recognition of that need, and his walking away from it is a dramatic turning point in his grief. All of a sudden, he understood that he was looking for Helga and that Helga wasn't there. That was the start of Bill's new life, and it wasn't very long after that that he met Mary Helen. If he'd still been looking for Helga, he never would have found Mary Helen. He would have looked at her and thought, no, no, that's not my Helga.

Many of the men I talked to, in describing meeting someone they like, described it in terms of how much they talked. That's often true when you meet someone you like, but the fact that these men men-tioned it over and over again suggests that talking is one of the things that men miss most in widowhood. Marriage is at some level a constant verbalizing. Unless it's a stone cold relationship, there is almost always a running commentary going on that becomes such a part of your life you don't even realize it until it's gone, and you may not know you're missing it until you get it back. Until all of a sudden there is some sound coming back from the void.

Even in a marriage that isn't a constant verbalizing, there is continual communication of some sort going on. At the very least, someone is there who will notice if you don't come home, someone who will bear witness to your life, in its day-to-day detail. Without such a witness, you can almost feel that you don't exist.

Because of that need for a witness, women often make a special friend they can call at any time to report on any kind of detail. At midnight, for instance, to tell of a date, or the lack of one. It's like an AA sponsor, someone who's been there and understands the need. Men are not accustomed to having those kinds of friendships with other men, and certainly not with women other than wives or romantic attachments. So, in order to get that witness, they often plunge right back into marriage.

It is a reflection of Bill's growth that when he did remarry, he married a different kind of woman. Most of the basics are the same—the sense of humor, the loyalty—but he was careful this time to pick a woman who values an active social life. Not that he appreciates Helga's loner qualities less, but that he better understands the need for social support systems.

Bill has also found a place in his life for his previous wife. He can talk of Helga to Mary Helen any time he pleases, and her presence in his consciousness is not a threat to their marriage. The importance of this "finding a place" comes up over and over again. If you don't give your first wife a place in your life, she may creep up from time to time and want to know where she belongs, like a ghost that wants to be remembered.

You can't turn your back on your history, it's true. But finding a place for your history and living in it are two different things. Some men, like Joe in the next chapter, never seem to let go.

Joe

JOE is 78 and retired from two careers, the first as a military officer, the second as an executive for an auto parts manufacturer. He met Mary at a party when he was 35 and she was 22 and fell in love with her on the spot. He had had some other infatuations—"severe ones, you know, pretty serious"—but this was the first one that stuck. They were married for 33 years and had three children, two girls and a boy. Margaret, now 42, is divorced and lives nearby with her three children. David, 31, is single and lives one hour away. Chris would now be 35, but she died at age 24, almost a year to the day before Mary died.

When Mary was 45, she was diagnosed with a viral infection of the lining around her heart; it caused an inflammation that literally would squeeze her heart out of business. At the time, it was projected that she would not live out the year, but she struggled on for eight years more, fighting not only that viral infection but also other ailments that developed as a result of that disease and of the medications. Over the course of those eight years, she was hospitalized and brought back home, until, during one of those hospital stays from which she was soon expected home, she died, at age 55.

This interview was conducted almost eleven years after her death.

They assured me she would be home by the weekend—this was at the start of the week—but this time I could tell she was reacting differently. She would faint while sitting up in bed. She had never done this before.

So I called the doctor in one night. He came, I explained it to him, and he put her in intensive care. She wasn't comfortable there, I could tell, so I sat with her all the time. It was my nature to be with her because she was so much a part of me. A very nice lady, really.

At some point in time, I felt there was something very radically wrong. She had just gotten up—the nurse insisted she exercise herself, you know—and she was very, very tired. Very tired. So I helped her back into the bed, and I noticed a very peculiar thing. I don't know if I should say this to you, but I will, if it has any meaning. Her head became almost transparent, as if I could see right through her. And yet I couldn't see inside her, just a light around her head.

I've never seen anything like this before. Of course, I just . . . It seemed as if . . . It's so vivid in my mind, I could almost see it now. Right around her head—here—as if there was a light. And inside, it came from within, not outside. From within, a glow around her head. I wondered if maybe it was some kind of mystical experience, but I never pinpointed it. I talked to one doctor about it, but he didn't give me any indication of why it would happen like that. I never pursued it any further, or asked people why this would happen. I just take it for granted, that it was a natural thing. But it was so vivid that up to this day I remember it. An internal light around her head, and all I could do was kiss her forehead.

I went back into the waiting room. Soon after, the nurse came in to me and said "Your wife passed on." I went in, I looked at her, kissed her. The two doctors who had assured me that she would be home for the weekend came in; they both apologized because they had made a wrong interpretation. And while they were there, my son came by. He was living at home at the time and had just gotten out of work. He stopped in the doorway. I said to him, "Dave, you lost your mother." He threw his gloves on the floor. We embraced. And that was when she passed away. It was late afternoon, 3:00 or 4:00.

I'm not the type that sheds many tears. I am just not that way. But I felt this loss very deeply. I lost something that was part of me. When you get to be as old as I am, perhaps you realize that there is at least a possibility of two people becoming one. I anticipated her needs, and she anticipated mine, before we even spoke about them. We never had any arguments, except for one, in the kitchen. She got upset at me for something I had done or didn't do, and she was pounding me on the chest, you know. And after a while, I just laughed, and finally she did too. Realized it was so silly. That was our only argument. It was the type of relationship—over the years, you become glued together. So to me, her loss was very deep.

At first, I was very, very alone, especially on the weekends. But it has been . . . ten years? Eleven? Eleven years, almost. And somehow I don't remember it now. I don't remember that initial period of loneliness. How did I overcome that? I don't know, I just did. I wasn't desperate, you know. Gnashing of teeth and pulling the hair, not like that. There was never any ache. I just felt empty. I felt very, very much alone.

The family drew closer together for a while after Mary died. Very much closer, for a while. Even my people back home, somehow or other, became more important to me. I was born and raised in Italy until I was 7 years old, so I was strongly motivated towards the warmth and the kind-hearted attitude of the old Italian types, and the close family relationships. There is a strength in the family that in another generation or two you might expect won't be there, knowing the way our culture is going.

So at the beginning, we were close. We sort of shared the loss and that made it easier to bear, knowing that we shared it. We would talk in terms of how pleasant it was, and keep it in our minds. But after that time, it disappeared. About three years or so later, the family began to go their own ways again. Margaret began to have her children, and developed her own life and life-style. And David developed his own way of life. They moved on from this closeness.

I get to the point sometimes now of thinking perhaps they should remember their mother and sister more than they do. Like I will say to Margaret, "Have you been to the cemetery?" On holy days, you know. And she'll say that probably she was too busy or something like that. Sometimes she does go, but I would want her to go and not forget. The same thing with David. But David doesn't come here too often now.

The passing of time has not diminished the feeling left by the death of my wife, nor by the death of my daughter. I think about them quite often. When I'm alone, I think about them more than I really should, perhaps. That's why I want to have people around. When I'm with people, I'm very active. It's only when I'm alone that I think.

So I got involved with activities. I was retired, perhaps, but there was a lot that I could do. I'd retired at 67 because I knew that Mary was very sick, and I wanted to be with her—I wanted to stay home with Mary. Then my daughter died the next year. And Mary died the year after that. What saved the situation was the fact that I managed to do things.

I ran a $35 million project at the hospital. I'm president of an organization whose operating income is $1.4 million. I'm active with the community council. I just retired from another board. I was active with the Boys' Club, worked with the Red Cross and the college. To a cetain measure, all those activities took the place of my loss. I was constantly doing these things so that the only time I would remember was when I was completely alone.

Sometimes at night, it was difficult. You know, I haven't had any sex since Mary became ill. And up to this point in time, I've been totally without it. Oh, I've thought about it. It's normal for a man to think about sex. But somehow or other, whatever energy I had for sex I released through activities. And at my age now, I don't miss it. But even in the earlier years, after Mary left, I didn't miss it.

It's a matter of schooling yourself. You have a feeling, well, yes, you've had a lifetime of sex with a wonderful person. As much as you could have wanted, as much as you could have. Then suddenly, you don't have it. And you school yourself to think in terms of, well, I don't really need it. I can be bigger than that. If there is a need, an unconscious need, I just don't satisfy it, that's all. I just drive it out of my mind. No matter what the need is, no matter how strong, you can overcome it simply by putting your mind to it. Occupy your mind with other things. It takes a lot of concentration. You have to make up your mind that this is the way it's going to be. It was a very conscious thing. I actually said to myself, "I am going to put this energy here."

And I put it into activities. Those are the things I substituted for the desire for sex. Or for anything else. Anything I needed, I was able to take it away and give. Rather than get, I gave. It seemed to satisfy the need. I would come home at night and understand that I had done something worthwhile, and it worked.

In all these activities, I've always had the company, the smile, the words and the affection of members of the opposite sex. They always seemed receptive to me, and I felt comfortable with that. But I never looked for one in particular. Everyone kept telling me, "Look for someone else. Later in life you would appreciate someone to be with you." Probably now I realize, yes, I would like a companion. Just to talk with, you know. But I never could get close to anyone for this sort of thing. Never could.

I did meet one very charming lady. She was young, much younger than I, and we met one night and went to dinner. She was a very attractive woman, but she spoiled it all by suggesting marriage on the first night. That really threw me off. I said, "No, this is not for me." And I've never seen her since.

I know my daughter Margaret gets the brunt of all this, because she's divorced. I feel an affection towards her that almost isn't right. She's got a life of her own. But I depend on her, I demand things from her that I know I shouldn't. An example: She went to Chicago two weeks ago, for an entire week, and I was upset about it because I felt we could have gone to Maine, the two of us, to visit my brother. But she went to Chicago to visit a friend. Not relatives, not even family.

She says she wishes that Chris had lived so she could take some of the load off her shoulders. It would have been nice if she had. I depend too much on her, and she does feel a little bit burdened. Even David will say the same thing, that I depend on Margaret too much. If I had remarried, that might not have been the case. But it's only, that will be, I think, in time—how much more time, I don't know—but to me, it's something that could be worked out.

My dependency on Margaret has increased over the years. Whenever there's a social function—and there are many—I always take her. Even when she was married. And now I'm beginning to have a daughter—little Julie, ten years old—and *she* wants to go with me. And I take her to social functions. And beginning next month, I'm building an apartment right here in the house. A separate apartment for me to be in, and Margaret will move into the house. So I'll be with my grandchildren.

After Mary died, some people suggested I sell this house, and there have been times when I thought of selling it. I got to the point I had it appraised, and had some salespeople look at it, maybe to put it on the market. But then I tried to picture myself living in the same city, somewhere else, and I couldn't see it. Because the things that we did here . . . There's a set of steps leading from the rear of the yard out to the street. We did it, together, one Saturday. And down in the cellar, we put in the asphalt, we worked on it together. And the tiles, we worked on the tiles. To think in terms of leaving here and going somewhere else . . . Probably I should do it. Probably I should do it. I could get a better environment, or a different environment.

But it's comfortable here. Her room is almost exactly as it was when she passed away, her bedroom. Except that my daughter sleeps there when she's here, and my nieces sleep there. I don't use it as my room because as soon as she got sick, Mary had her own room. Her bottles of perfume are still there. Her nightgowns are in the closet. I tell Margaret, I wish that she would get rid of some of this stuff, but she doesn't. "Oh," she says, she tells me that, "yes," she has gotten rid of some of the stuff. But it's simply that. . .I don't know, I don't know.

You know, this funny thing . . . Sometimes when I'm alone at night and I'm getting ready to go bed, I go by her room . . . I shouldn't say this . . . But I feel there's a . . . No, it isn't a presence. I feel . . . There's not a void. Mary and Chris are close to me, even though they're gone. They're very close to me. That feeling, I can't explain it. But I'm comfortable with it. I say, no matter what it is, it can't hurt me, because it's love. Whatever it is, it's all based on love. Even after all these years.

I can't explain it. I'm not a mystic. I simply understand things. We're never gone from this world. I think we're always there. If we have touched people, they'll always be with us. The people that are gone will be with us. Somehow or another, you never really shake them off. You don't want to. You want to hold on, hold on to the past, to the things that were so beautiful, and you know you can never have again.

I have religious beliefs. When I'm troubled, I say a little prayer. Sometimes it helps, sometimes it doesn't. But I'm not a fanatic. All religions are equal to me. Whether it's Catholic or whatever, I believe they reach God. They travel different roads, but they all go to the same place.

I say a prayer every night to Mary. And I say a special prayer every Tuesday, and I light a candle for her. I've done that for years. I never forget. When something happens, I say a prayer and ask for the intercession of Mary and Chris to help me out. When I'm near the cemetery, I drive in and say a prayer. Just for ten minutes or so, say a prayer. And once a year, we have a prayer at the church on the anniversary of the death of both my wife and Chris.

I do believe in the afterlife. It seems such a waste if there wasn't. What the hell are we doing? What are we doing, if there wasn't something beyond, the continuum . . . I often think about it—what could it be? How can we find out? But no one has ever come back and said, "This is what you're going to expect." Oh, I know some people have said, "I died on the operating table, and I saw this and I saw that."

What credence we put on that, I don't know. But I have a conviction that something continues. Some continuum. I believe that Mary and Chris, because they were loved in this life, never leave.

I have notes that Mary wrote. I keep one in my billfold. It's a poem she copied from somebody, and I keep it, it's in her writing. And these cards. At the funeral, they have a little prayer with a picture of a saint. Both Mary and Chris, I keep the little cards, small cards, in my billfold. These things are part of me and they'll always be a part of me as long as I live. The fact that Mary was with me, the fact that Chris is my daughter. This always will be with me. I'll have them as long as I breathe the air that we're living in. Maybe that has something to do with why I haven't sought a companion, that I feel companionship from them. I can't put my finger on it, but I have that satisfaction. Sure they're gone, but Mary was mine, Chris was mine. And they haven't really gone. There's a poem that said it. I've got it downstairs. Wait a minute, I've got it here, in my appointment book. It's by Helen Steiner Rice.

When I Must Leave You

When I must leave you for a little while
Please do not grieve and shed wild tears
And hug your sorrow to you through the years
But start out bravely with a gallant smile
And for my sake and in my name
Live on and do all the things the same
Feed not your loneliness on empty days
But fill each waking hour in useful ways
Reach out your hand in comfort and in cheer
And I in turn will comfort you and hold you near
And never, never be afraid to die
For I'm waiting for you in the sky.

That poem was in a card that I received after Mary died. A sympathy card. I made copies of it. I've kept it with me all these years. I pull it out and look at it sometimes. Once in a while, not very often.

This is what Chris had when she died. This was written by the doctor that took care of her—"Thrombotic Thrombocytopenic Purpura." This is his actual note, his actual note ten years ago. I don't know why I'm carrying this. Beats the hell out of me, I don't know. I just carry it. It has some connection, to me it has meaning. I could throw it away right now. But I decided to keep it.

If you have recently lost your wife, I would advise you to become active. Go out and do things. Draw that curtain as quick as you can. Occupy your mind so that you don't always think about her. Draw that curtain. Go out and do things. In another environment.

If you're young, I certainly suggest you go out and make a new life for yourself. In fact, there's a doctor here in town, a very good friend, he lost his wife. We were at a function together about a year after. I sat down with him and I talked with him. He was young and very sad looking, drinking. I said to him, "Remarry. You're young enough, go do it." He's about 40, I think, 45. Something like that.

Three months ago, I went out to dinner, and who was sitting at this booth but that doctor. "Come here, come here," he says. "I did exactly what you suggested." "What is this?" "I'm married. There's my wife at the counter." I couldn't believe it, she looked so young. I went up to the lady and said, "Is that man your husband?" And she said, "Yes." And they are very happy. He bought an airplane, he's flying the airplane. He made a new life for himself.

But I can't see that anyone would want me at my age. Oh sure, there are some women who would say yes the moment that I asked. But I cannot visualize myself in a new life at this point. I just couldn't do it. Is that selfish? I don't know. I had such a pleasant time with Mary that that has been enough to carry me through these empty years. I was completely satisfied. It was such a fun thing. And I cannot visualize myself with another woman now, doing the same thing, enjoying it. I can't. In a sense, I wish I could. I wish I could look for someone to be friendly with, and talk. I think there's a beauty in that, and I don't seek it nearly as much as I should.

It is true that some men, when they vow to love their wives "until death do us part," observe that promise meticulously, until their wives' last breath. It is also true that those same men, after a suitable period of mourning, often move on to another relationship without in any way feeling that that betrays their original vows. But there are some men in this life who marry just once for eternity, and even after their wives pass on remain married to them.

This seems to be true for Joe. He didn't marry until late in his life, apparently because he was waiting for the right woman to come along, and by the time he found her, he was ready to make a commitment to her literally for the rest of his days, whether she lived that long or not. In these times, when marriages are dissolved almost as often as they are begun, that kind of unalterable devotion can seem almost mythical. Indeed, it sounds as if Joe and Mary had an almost storybook marriage—very empathic, loving, and reciprocal. Joe's life with Mary was completely satisfying, and because of that, he has no intention of ever letting it go.

This may present a problem. There's a part of Joe that lives in the past. To be sure, there's also a part of him that lives very much in the present: if everyone focused their energies as he does on community service, this world would be a better place. But it appears the only way Joe has found to not let go of his marriage is to live in the past with it. He doesn't seem to have found a way to remember his wife and daughter in such a way that allows him or his surviving children the freedom to move on.

This partly has something to do with his concept of family. Joe has many friends on all his various committees, but it is only with his family that he seems to be really engaged. He doesn't appear to get much of a sense of connection to the human community through friends. He doesn't understand, for instance, his daughter's priority in visiting friends instead of family, perhaps because, to him, friends don't have the same kind of meaning as family. He only feels that sense of connection through blood ties, through his kin.

Of course, that's true for a lot of us. It is the family ties that bind. But sometimes, those family ties bind in the sense that they constrict. And, while it is appropriate that Joe should turn to his family for much of his gratification in terms of human relationships, it appears he is also trying to keep the family intact by keeping things the way they were when Mary and Chris were still alive and David and Margaret were still at home. He keeps Mary's bedroom the way it was. Her perfume bottles are still set out. Her nightgowns are still hanging in the closet. He holds to the past with sheer willpower, as with willpower he does without sex. And, as he says in discussing sex, that takes a lot of concentration.

When I looked at Joe, I couldn't say this choice had impaired him in any way. When he told me his age, I thought I heard him say he was 68, not 78. And when Joe talks about Mary, he sits back and lifts his face as if he were lifting his face to a spring rain. From the smile on his face, it is clear that her memory truly makes him happy. Somehow, even with her gone, he still gets emotional food from her.

The only real problem is the burden this situation may be placing on Joe's daughter. There is nothing inherently wrong with a 42-year-old woman sharing living quarters with her father. It gives him the opportunity to be near his grandchildren and to have some help as he ages, and it may very well help her out in terms of budgeting her schedule and financial resources. In fact, it is the loss of this extended-family kind of arrangement that we so much lament. But there is more going on here. Why is it Margaret's responsibility, for instance, to dismantle the "shrine," to travel with him when he travels, to go to the cemetery more often than she feels the need to?

Joe says he cannot visualize himself with another woman. But in fact he *is* with another woman. He has, in an abstract way, wed his daughter. She is his primary companion. And that is a problematic solution. If both of them were thoroughly happy, we would need to raise no questions about it. But Margaret complains about feeling burdened, and Joe says he knows he's burdening her. He says he thinks about Mary and Chris more than he really should, that he feels a certain amount of discomfort living quite so much in the past. So one has to wonder what it is that keeps these two people wed to a situation that they themselves perceive to be less than optimal for them, particularly since they have the freedom to change it. Margaret's role in this situation is something we cannot understand because we don't have any information, but with Joe, we can speculate about what might be going on.

One thing to keep in mind with Joe is that he had three major losses three years in a row—his second career, his daughter, his wife—and while he doesn't make anything of it, that doesn't mean we can't. We don't know to what degree he might have become battle weary with loss, unable to deal with all that disruption, and to what degree that might feed his need to hold onto the past now, to settle into a pattern that gives his life some familiar order. If you're dealing with one loss at a time, maybe it's easier to grapple with the meaning of that loss than if you are experiencing multiple losses.

It may also be important to note that this is a very Catholic story, full of religious references (i.e., the light around Mary's head, like a halo; the bedroom that has become a shrine; the notes and cards Joe carries around, like religious artifacts). It appears that the structure of the Church allows Joe to cleave to the past, even though he acknowledges that he is in no way fanatic about Catholicism. Perhaps, within this context, to get involved with another woman, or even just to rely to a greater extent on friends, would be, in Joe's mind, akin to divorcing Mary—which is not embraced by the Church.

Perhaps it's not a matter of divorce, but of abandonment. It may be that at some level Joe feels that if he moved on to a relationship with another woman, or changed his relationship with his daughter, or came to rely to a greater extent for emotional food on friends, he would be somehow abandoning or forsaking his relationships with his wife and daughter.

We can only speculate in Joe's case, but we do know these sorts of feelings present an enormous dilemma for many men. Having pledged themselves to one woman, how can they now move along to another? Or even, without getting reinvolved, how can they let go of the past and live again wholly in the present? When you've managed to find such happiness in a world that is so full of woe, when you've managed to protect it from all the forces that would put it asunder, when you've found someone who makes you rise to the best that is in you—how do you let go of that? How do you let go of the thing that means more to you than anything else? And if you do, what do you have left?

After getting through the initial shock and anger and despair, this problem of how to continue loving your wife while also living your life is perhaps the most difficult task of all in grieving the loss of a spouse. Some people never manage to do it. Some people live out their lives in a kind of emotional museum, wandering through the corridors of the past, fondling their memories at the expense of being fully engaged with living in the present. If you find yourself slipping into that pattern to a greater degree than you want to, be aware that you are at a pivotal point in your grieving. After the early stages of intense remorse and pain, the problem, to a large extent, becomes a matter of how to let go.

There are many men who simply choose *not* to let go, and continue, to one degree or another, living in the past. But there are other men, like Gordon, who do not move fully into the future not so much because they want to hold onto the past, but because somehow they can't seem to shake it.

Gordon

GORDON is 61. He is a retired career Navy officer. He met Lynn when they were stationed in Texas. She was a WAC and a nurse, and in spite of the fact she was nine years older, he started dating her right away, every single night. He married her five months later. In the course of twenty-three years of marriage, they raised four children together in at least ten different places throughout the United States and abroad. The oldest, Jean, is now 32 and lives with Gordon and his mother. Sue, 31, lives in the same town. Gordon, Jr., 29, lives two hours away and Lynette, 27, lives in a city several hours away.

Lynn was an alcoholic who worsened progressively over the years. "Three months after we got married, I shipped out to Japan, so the first two years I was married I didn't know what was going on. But after I came home, I figured out what the problem was. Of course, what you don't know, when you're involved, is how to deal with it. I was probably determined that we could will our way through the problem." Finally, Lynn had to be put in a hospital, where officially she died of respiratory failure, at age 55. But Gordon sums it up quite differently: "She drank herself to death."

This interview was conducted thirteen years after she died.

I wasn't there the morning she died. I had been there the evening before. I knew she was in bad shape, but she'd been in and out before, you know, and I thought that she'd survive. Other times, she'd had up and downs—she'd been in several accidents—but each time she'd kind of bounce back. But I think what happened is, she gave in. Thinking back to how she behaved in the days and weeks before that—I think she just gave up.

That evening before she died, when I went in and saw her after work, it was just like every other night. But around 3:30 in the morning, the phone rang. It was the doctor.

"Colonel Hardy?"

"Yes."

"Your wife just died."

Just like that. That frosted me.

"Do you want to come over?"

"Yes, of course I want to come over."

So I went over to the hospital and the resident chaplain was there. He wanted to know if I wanted to see her. I did, and I said a private goodbye. Then I went out, talked to them some more, and then I went home.

I was in shock for about five days. It's kind of hard to describe it. I don't think . . . Well, I'd seen her, so I knew the finality of it. But it didn't exactly sink in, any kinds of thoughts, any kinds of feelings. I didn't really participate in any of the arrangements. The kids went down and picked out the casket. I'd go into my room and lie down. You know the old macho stuff, "Do men cry?" Well, yes. Indeed they do. I did. Not a lot. And only privately.

I felt, as I did with my father, a terrible sense of wasted talent. That she was not able to do the work that she was so talented at, or to be, in fact, as good a mother as she was capable of being. She was not a good mother to the kids because she was an alcoholic. Sometimes it would be all beer, sometimes it would be something else. Sometimes it would be anything she could get hold of. There were often bottles lying around. But she'd been a Girl Scout leader, a Cub pack leader, and as a nurse, she was especially good with the kids. She was really excellent with them. It's a shame that a person of such talent . . . She didn't appreciate her own talent.

I think the biggest feeling I felt was like a weight being lifted, the weight of this alcoholic person. An alcoholic can create terrible frustrations for you. There were times when she could get very nasty. I mean, I never messed around, never fooled around, even in Japan. But she accused me of it. And there were a lot of other things. When we were going to move, you know, and there was a lot of packing to do. She'd take on a drinking bout and just lie around, and I'd come home and have to get everything ready for the movers. So when she died, I sort of had the feeling—well, free at last. And I never felt guilty for feeling that. There was never any question that I loved her, but when she died, there was this feeling that this weight had been lifted. I felt it right away.

Before Lynn died, my normal work week was usually sixty hours, and I didn't really turn it off when I finally got home. But being a workaholic was a redeeming factor when she died. After about a week or two, I just went back to work. And I just kept busy working for the next year and a half. I put it in the back of my mind, and it just sort of ran out in bits and pieces over a period of time. I wasn't afflicted—if that's the word—with a lot of problems in grieving, the way a lot of people are. I would say it was pretty well resolved, or put into the background, within a year and a half.

The most difficult part was trying to bring up four teenagers without her. It's hard enough to bring up kids. I think I was probably too self-centered. Perhaps I could have dealt better with them had I not been so work oriented. My work caused me to travel a lot, and that left them on their own. I didn't have a housekeeper. They'd come home and there'd be nobody there. I'd fly into Washington and back all on the same day, and I'd come in on a late-night flight and they'd be lying there on the floor watching an X-rated movie on cable. If I were to do it again, I'd probably be less intensive with work. I would have gotten just as much done if I hadn't been so busy at it.

I'd been out of the dating game a long time—I was 25 when I got married. I was married for twenty-three years, and I wasn't sure how to get back in. It's hard. You tend to think of yourself as back when you were that age, before you got married. You sort of think life is that way. But it isn't. The differences in generations—how you dance and stuff, and all the little rules that one has of dealing with another person—it all seemed kind of foreign to me. And I wasn't sure I wanted to get all involved in going to bars.

Being in the military, around the military wives, I guess I expected the wives would be trying to set me up with someone. I was only 47 years old, and I had a good job, and so on. But it didn't really happen. I did get a proposition from one of my employees. I think she'd been divorced, and she was announcing that she was back in circulation for whatever kind of arrangement I would be interested in. She used words like "white knight" and this sort of stuff. I wrote back and told her that I wasn't ready to think about anything like that, and that I never got involved with people under my command.

Very shortly after that, I constructed a shell around me. I constructed this shell quite consciously. I didn't want to let anybody get too close to me. When you get involved in a sexual or emotional relationship, there's a lot of opportunity for somebody to get hurt—when things don't work out the way you expect. And I think I built this wall around me because I didn't want to subject myself to that possibility.

Two years after Lynn died, I retired. And it was about that time it came to me that I should go home. Maybe it had to do with the fact that my mother was getting to the point where she needed help taking care of things, maybe it was something else. But I felt it was the right thing to do.

After I got home, I started drifting into the solitaire habit. I was out on the street one day, and one of my high school classmates came along and I told him how bored I was and he said, "I'll take care of that." By the time I got home, the executive director of the United Way was on the phone with me, and I got involved with that. Then one thing led to another, and before I knew it I was right back into the workaholic syndrome. I've been involved in an unbelievable number of activities since. Over the last several years, I've usually been on twenty or twenty-five boards or committees at a time. So that supersedes any dwelling I might do on my personal situation.

Then about five or six years ago, my second daughter came home for a while. And in that particular period, we had a lot of conversations. She was very much encouraging me to break out of this shell I had built. And I decided that I would make some kind of effort to do that, to kind of loosen up a bit.

So I did. And that's when I developed this attachment I've had for the past several years, a strong emotional attachment with a very young lady. It's one of the most peculiar kinds of arrangements you could imagine. She was a friend of my daughter's who would come to visit the house. She was about 30 at the time—30 years younger than me—a musician. I always fall in love with pretty young musicians, you see.

When I was at Annapolis, I met a girl, a musician, who may have been the romantic attachment of my life. She was with an all-girl orchestra, and I was a stage-door johnny, sort of. She played intermission piano and sang at the Ice Terrace in New York, the hotel. I used to know all the musicians. Music was a big thing with me. My mother wanted me to go to music school, but I went to Annapolis instead. Anyway, I wanted to marry this girl when I came back from Europe. But when I came back, I was told she got married. There have been times when I've speculated how life might have been different if I had I done this or that. But I always say well, I wouldn't have had the four kids that I had. So I have no regrets about my past.

Anyway, this "attachment" to my daughter's friend has been going on for about six years or so, in varying degrees. It is not an overt relationship; my daughter isn't aware of it. And it doesn't include sex. It's more of an intellectual compatibility and attachment. We don't spend a lot of time together. It's sort of a nineteenth-century romantic, kind of letter writing sort of thing. It's not entirely reciprocated. And over time it's changed. We don't get together much anymore. I don't expect it will ever really come to anything.

But it probably satisfies a lot of my ambivalence. I have ambivalence about marriage. In marriage, one gives away a piece of oneself for the good of the marriage. And I haven't been ready to give away a piece of myself again, because I enjoy the freedom. I miss the closeness that I had with my wife, or would have with anybody. I like the closeness you get in marriage, but I like the freedom of being single. This way, I guess, I can have a level of closeness and still have freedom. I don't know. I haven't analyzed myself as far as that's concerned. But I've sort of been wondering lately whether I'm ready to think about marriage again, to give up my freedom in a sense.

One thing, for sure. If I'm going to have a relationship with somebody—maybe it's ego—I want somebody to care about me. I know I can care about somebody else. I know if I were to marry again I would probably be the world's best husband, because I know how. But somebody must care about me. I think that this attachment I have is probably a dead end for me. So therefore, if I'm ready to consider something else, it will probably be with somebody else and maybe with someone who's older. I'm perhaps getting ready to loosen up. It's a long time getting around to that.

It's interesting that Gordon reports the same sense of relief at the death of his wife that we hear from men who have been nursing their wives through extended illness. It is not that they don't grieve their wives, but that the illness was such a burden to both that death comes as a deliverance. It makes a lot of sense that Gordon should have this reaction too, because his wife *was* sick for over twenty years, throughout their entire marriage. Whether he actually nursed her through it or not is a moot point. He had to witness her decline and to confront on a daily basis the fact that he could do nothing about it.

To see the woman you love slowly destroying all the qualities you love in her can also create enormous amounts of ambivalence. You wonder to what extent the act is directed at you. But you think, no, it's directed at her. But, no, it's directed at nobody; it's simply a disease isn't it? Why, if you are able to love her, is she unable to love herself? And on and on and on. The emotional convolutions become endlessly entwined, and when your wife dies, those convolutions do not automatically straighten out.

It is well documented that the grieving of a wife for whom one has had ambivalent feelings is much more complicated than grieving a wife one has thoroughly loved or hated. It appears that in the thirteen years since Lynn's death, Gordon has not yet been able to overcome his ambivalence about her, and therefore about marriage. He talks all about it, about her drinking, and the frustrations it caused him, and about the effects he can see it is still having on their children. But as much as he has come to grips with the facts of her drinking and her death, it is apparent, from the way he has lived in the years since she died, that he hasn't yet come to grips with his reactions to those facts.

There's a lot about Gordon's ambivalence that can be seen in the relationship he's formed with the young musician. Ambivalent as he was about investing in a relationship with another woman, but under pressure from his daughter to try, he chose a relationship that was absolutely and utterly safe. He could have romantic feelings about the young woman from now until the world ends, and his bluff would never get called. He also chose a situation that harkened back to an earlier time, when he had his "major romance" with the musician in New York, and it has a whiff of "what if . . . ?" in it. The whole affair—or lack of one—is a perfect expression of the lingering ambivalence he feels.

Gordon was widowed at 47. He had plenty of time left in his life to build a new existence. In fact, it could have been entirely new because he was coming on early retirement and he could have even started up a whole new career. Instead, he circled back to his past and went back home to live with his mother. That was not inappropriate at all. All of a sudden, all of the structure in his life was gone—his marriage, his job, his children.

It made a lot of sense for him to go back home to regroup his troups, but it is unfortunate that he turned to workaholism again. With his previous structure gone, he had a golden opportunity to really grow, to create a whole new way of living—to take up his music again, perhaps, or to live out some wholly impractical fantasy he had never dared realize. He really was free because he was financially secure and had no responsibilities, but he stayed with his old way of doing things while the opportunity to restructure his life was slipping by.

If you find yourself cut adrift like Gordon, if you find the entire structure of your life suddenly gone, it's very likely that you will want to loop back to an earlier structure, too, because sudden, unanticipated freedom at this stage of your life can be a terrifying thing. In fact, it can be terrifying at any stage of your life. Freedom is, by nature, frightening.

But freedom is also *freedom*—to do things you've only dreamed of before, to become a lobster fisherman, maybe, to live in Martinique, to write a book, to take up painting, to turn old barns into luxury houses, to water-ski, to climb a mountain, to coach a Little League team. Once you've passed the point of having intense, consistent pain, there is no reason not to explore some of the possibilities. You might find that you can build yourself a life that exceeds all your previous imaginings of what your life could be.

To a large extent, that is the answer to the question at the end of the last chapter—how do you let go of the life you loved so much? The answer is, by building yourself a new one. That's not as simplistic as it sounds, and it's not necessarily easy. But after the critically painful period of your bereavement subsides—and it will—that is unavoidably the challenge with which you are faced. The rest of this book is devoted to the ways in which some men have met that challenge.

Murray

MURRAY is 71. As a professional psychologist in a large psychiatric institute, he has for more than forty years been involved in the particular psychological problems of the dying and has conducted extensive research on facing terminal disease. He has also written prolifically on death and related subjects. If anyone was ever "prepared" for bereavement, it was Murray. But all his psychological knowledge, all his experience with death and dying, all his contacts with people who presumably knew how to help him did not prepare him for the loneliness and isolation of widowhood.

Murray met Ruth at a party. They married when he was 37 and she was 42. After twenty years together, Ruth developed cancer that made her an invalid for the rest of her life. Over the years, the pain increased, as did her incapacity, until, for the last five years of her life, she lived for the most part on the couch. During that entire span, eleven years in all, Murray took care of her. She finally died at age 74.

This interview was conducted about three years after her death.

I wept when she died, when her heart stopped beating. I was alone with her at the time. The nurse was out, and her doctor was just outside in the nurse's station. And I went out and said to him, "I think we're in trouble, Dave." Because she wasn't breathing. And he came back and he said, "That's right. There isn't any heartbeat." And he

154

made some generous comment about what a great lady she was. And then he left me alone with her.

I remember kissing her after her death until her body began to turn cold. It took about ten minutes, until I became aware of the changes in her circulation. There wasn't any more circulation. So I was, as I was kissing her, I could feel her getting cold. And then I came back to my office. And there was a long distance call for me to say I had won a prestigious award. And I cried again, because I had no one to share that with.

I can't say that I was grief-stricken. The main part of my grieving was actually done before she died. I'd call it anticipatory grief. It's different from just forewarning, where you know that someone is going to die. Here, you do some thinking on what it will be like to live alone, what you will do, what you'll have to learn. The practical details, in other words. I didn't feel guilty about it, planning my new existence before she died, because I had known that widowers and widows who cope best are already thinking of what life will be like in the world after their spouse is dead. If you pretend, if you try to ignore . . . I think that's a bad thing to do. You're not going to postpone death.

So I was prepared for her to die. In a sense I was glad she died. At least she was relieved of her pain. She told me that if it weren't for me, she would have killed herself for that pain. I never told anyone that before, but if it hadn't been for me, she would have killed herself. And I could not have blamed her for it. I don't know what I would do if I were in a similar position, having progressive pain on top of cancer and not finding anything that could relieve it except death. I might well opt for death.

So I not only had no regrets that she died, I had regrets that she didn't die sooner. Her last five years were agony for her. As she got sicker and sicker, it was more and more difficult for her to climb the stairs at night. And then she'd get up and was just barely able to make it down here for breakfast. I can picture her coming downstairs and almost collapsing on the couch right there, because it became increasingly hard for her to navigate. And then the very last night before she went into the hospital, about ten days before her death, I had to carry her upstairs.

I wanted to be angry at someone. I remember towards the end of her illness when the pain was unbearable, getting angry at the little cap on the ketchup bottle and throwing it against the wall. Just under the surface of my calm, of being able to cope, there was . . . My nerves were fairly fragile. And I was fatigued as hell, I must say. There was layer on layer of fatigue, like geological strata. And since I was so tired all the time, I didn't have the energy for anger, for cursing God and all that. I just wanted to get her some comfort. The ordinary person could have gotten some relief with Demerol, codeine, morphine, whatever. But she was sensitive to all of that. So she went through hell.

Someone recently asked me what good memories I had of my marriage. And I couldn't think . . . Her illness has obliterated any good memories. I remember vaguely when she was well, but that is far overshadowed by those eleven years—those years were a third of our married life—they've completely obliterated those other years, the happy years. So the disease not only took her, it also took the memory of her. It was sort of a double whammy.

She was buried in a cemetery which is on the way to the institute, and I would go in there on weekends, and sometimes during the week at first. I had the grave marker put in early. I'd go in and brush it off, keep it clean. I felt I wanted somehow to continue doing something for her.

I remember I went to the caretakers—ordinary blue-collar guys— and told them who I was and that my wife had died a few weeks ago and I noticed her grave wasn't in good shape. And I wondered what they were going to do. So they explained that they put in flowers in April and October, and that they were taking care of it. And I said, "Well, you know, this is about all I can do for her now." So one of these guys said, "We know how it is." He said he understood what I was going through. I don't know if I'm conveying it. It was almost as if he touched me and said, "That's all right. I know how you feel." It was quite an experience from an unexpected source.

I think the expressions of sympathy that stood out most in my mind were from people like that that I really didn't know very well. Condolence letters, for instance, from people who had taken five minutes just to sit down and say that they were saddened, that they were thinking of me, things like that. I've made a particular point, ever since, when I hear of somebody's death, to write a brief note. You don't have to write deathless prose. Write anything, anything at all. It doesn't have to be poetic or anything like that. Just let people know.

I'm a man who prides himself on being quite self-sufficient. I've always, almost to a fault, wanted to do things for myself. I find it hard to let people do things for me, which sometimes will make them angry because they *want* to do something. But I did enjoy the condolence letters. They were very important. They made me realize I'm not nearly as self-sufficient as I have prided myself on being. I enjoy the company of people.

After Ruth died, I saw more of her son than I had in years. He would come around, maybe for his own sake, too. But we never discussed his mother. We just talked about ordinary stuff—baseball, his kids, like that. But we never talked about Ruth. It feels good to talk about it now. Although I think I could have used talking about it more a year to two back. But no one asked me to talk about it. So I never talked about it.

There have been times when I could have used a good therapist to talk to, but I never sought one out. The reason I gave myself was that there was no one I could turn to. People turned to *me*, because of seniority. I would not have known how to deal with it. Nor would, I presume, the therapist, if I went to a younger therapist. People come to me. Even my contemporaries, when they have some problem. Maybe that's just an excuse.

Of course, I read books about grief. It didn't do me any harm. But most books about grief are so schematic that they don't get specific enough. They'll tell you that first you go through a phase of loneliness and searching, mistaking certain sounds for the sounds of the deceased coming home from work, or something like that. Semi-hallucinatory events. But that has no reality until you actually have the experience.

I did hear one thing that helped me, though. I read that when Gracie Allen died, George Burns said the thing that helped him most was moving into Gracie's bed. So I moved into Ruth's bed. Yeah. For the first week or so right after her death, I would wake up and see that empty bed in the middle of the night—that was a rough experience. So I moved into Ruth's bed. And my old bed was the empty one. Then it was all right. So I got help through George Burns. He was the one who helped me the most.

I imagine most widowers wring their hands and talk about loneliness. Well, I didn't miss her pain. And I had been without her companionship for a number of years. When Ruth died, this house became mine. It wasn't built around her pain anymore. And I enjoyed living here alone. There was a certain independence. And I became content, in a way. I'd have my dinner at night, at the end of the working day. I would sit and read. I'd listen to music. I bought myself a good stereo set—the noise had always bothered her—and I began to use that big living room we never used before. I went on trips. Trips she hadn't been interested in. I'd always wanted to go to Peru, so the second summer I went there. And then I went to Alaska. Things I felt, through being married, I couldn't have done before. We went every summer to the same little place at Russian River. A beautiful place, but after thirty years, you get kind of tired of it.

When I came back from Peru, I knew something more had to be done. I knew I had to do something more than just be the old widower. I knew I wasn't going anywhere, unless I cut out going to the cemetery, making pilgrimages. So I deliberately kept myself from going to the cemetery. Because I knew it was time to let go—I'd been going there two or three times a week—so I forced myself not to drop over there on Sunday afternoons. Especially on Sundays, empty Sundays when there was nothing for me to do except go to the cemetery. Sundays were the worst. Always. And I make it a point, even now, when I'm here by myself and haven't planned anything to go out somewhere on Sundays. There isn't anything worse than staying in the house on Friday nights, and going down and getting the papers and staying through Saturday and Sunday. I've done that a couple of times and it drives you stir crazy, so I make it a point to get out, even go to the movies by myself.

I had a problem with that at first. As if I was doing something bad. I didn't want any friend of mine to see me by myself at the movies. I even considered going to the movies in a different town, because I didn't want to be caught. As if there's something, some inadequacy that was being exposed. I didn't want to seem like I had become a social isolate. And yet I wouldn't call anyone and say, "Let's go to the movies." I didn't know anybody. All the widows who are supposed to be out there, I didn't meet. Those I met, I wasn't interested in. There were a lot of paradoxes. I pride myself on self-sufficiency but didn't want to be seen going into the movies by myself.

But when I decided "All right, it's really time to put this in the past, I'm not going to the cemetery as often," I had the problem of what to do instead. There wasn't a hell of a lot to do. I went on trips when I could. I would go if I was invited places. I'd even go if I felt like making excuses, because I knew I'd better. It's so easy to dig a hole and pull it in behind yourself. So I'd take it as kind of a medicine, a therapeutic exercise. Even though I didn't have a hell of a lot of fun sometimes, at least I was doing something. Once I even went alone to the cottage where we used to go. But that just stunk, that was a bad scene. It wasn't—I mean, it was empty. I went up there when August came, for a week, when we traditionally went. Just to see what it would be like. And oh, it was an awful drag.

So I went to parties. A few parties of my contemporaries. And I was bored to death. They talked about the weather. They talked about their trips. And they talked about their grandchildren. And I was just bored. I'd never seen much of them before, but they were good enough to ask me over to dinner and things like that. And there were other friends where I'd go along as the odd man and things like that. But I wasn't really interested in dating for several years. I thought that was all behind me. I didn't have any urge to meet any women other than Ruth. It wasn't because I was pining for her. I just didn't have the desire. Until last January.

I went to a meeting last January in Copenhagen and I met a woman. And for the first time in years, I felt a response—she moved me off dead center—and it was completely surprising. I thought that was all behind me. But I was, I must have been in the doldrums. What I considered a natural phase of existence was probably doldrums. 'Cause where did my reawakening come from? That is what I'm puzzling now. All of a sudden . . . romance! All of a sudden . . . sex! I hadn't had sex for several years. I had no sexual desire. And the widows I saw, so what? I'd gotten used to the life of a monk.

I don't know how it is with men who get remarried within the first year, but I had no sexual desire for almost three years. And before that even, for ten years. Because Ruth was in too much pain. So sex had gradually faded, and I thought it was gone forever. I had no active libido, like a man who has no appetite. In a sense, I missed it. I missed the yearning, the explosiveness, the driving impulse that used to agonize me as a younger man. But on the other hand, I was glad that I didn't need it, that I wasn't so controlled by it. Again, self-sufficiency.

I think that what had happened was that over this eleven-year span the doldrums had become a state of normalcy for me. So that by the time she died, the loss, I was already down at that level so it didn't even seem unusual. I was in an emotional vacuum. Where there was this distance between me and the next person. And while I was very cordial and knew the right things to say—I could be pleasant and witty, a nice guy to have around and all that—it didn't go any further.

I'd been kind of packing myself in cotton for years and years and years. And I never even realized it. I never missed the companionship until I began to get it again.

That's why it's been such a revelization. Revelization? What does that mean? A revelation, a resurrection, reincarnation, rejuvenation—it's all of those things at once. The only thing I'm scared of is that she might meet some other guy who would be more suitable for her. After all, I am 71 years old and she is only 50. But I maintain that's a problem only if you make it a problem. So 50 seems young; it *is* young. I admit that. But I wouldn't be interested in a woman my own age, I can see that now. They aren't active enough for me.

She is moving around all the time. She was here last weekend. She lives in Phoenix, but I see her a lot. She comes here and I go there and we have a jet-age romance. All at once, I'm a jet-setter. I don't know whether either of us will want to get remarried, but every time I see her . . . I don't kid myself anymore about the illusion of self-sufficiency. I was just lonely and couldn't admit it. I wanted to be self-sufficient and not need anybody. I'd rather be needed than need other people. It takes a certain amount of courage to admit you're lonely. At least it does for me. Because you're—you admit you're vulnerable. And I've always been a lone wolf.

I was prepared to live alone for the rest of my life. I thought I would have a relatively harmonious old age and just go on and make a few trips here and there and be a grand old man. A legend in my own time. Go to Mandalay or Rangoon or wherever it happened to be. The way I went to Machu Picchu. But that's not the way it's worked out.

If I were to give advice now to a newly widowed man, it would be to accept himself for his frailties. Not to expect any time schedule. And not to expect too much of himself. There are going to be plenty of times when you'll falter, but you'll cope if you *believe* you can cope. I've learned that from other widowers. If you agree at the outset that you're going to be able to cope, then you're going to be able to cope.

I have a pretty good life now. I have no complaints. No complaints whatsoever. And I'm learning how to relax. I never knew how to relax before. I worked like hell, you know, when I was in my younger years. Highly motivated. But now—oh, we go dancing. I never went dancing before. Never, not with Ruth. And piano bars. I never knew what a piano bar was. Things like that. A lot of things that people take for granted, I never knew about.

So maybe that's my new challenge. Every piano bar in the world.

Well, it's fun, actually. At the same time I want to keep doing some work. So maybe this is the end of bereavement. But it's more than just the end of bereavement. It's a whole new phase of life.

That's it. A whole new phase of life. And it is a happy ending. So far.

Before we turn to the ways in which Murray has started this whole new phase of his life, there are some other aspects of his story that deserve attention. The concept he brought up, for instance, of anticipatory grief is often surrounded with confusion. Some people believe that the phenomenon of anticipatory grief means that you can somehow get your grieving done in advance—that the longer you have to grieve the loss of your wife before she dies, the less you will have to grieve her later— and it is a false conception.

When your wife dies slowly, you do, in fact, grieve her loss incrementally, so that by the time she dies you are already near the basement of your grief, as opposed to plummeting to the bottom after a sudden death. It's like the difference between jumping out the window or walking downstairs; it's a matter of how far you are from the bottom when you take that last step.

But you still have to take that last step. And for all the grieving you do in advance for the little parts of her you're losing, you're still invested in her until she dies. Once the door is closed, the quality of your grief is different. You have different business to take care of. There is simply no such thing as getting your grieving done beforehand.

In fact, there is no such thing as getting your grieving done at all. Grief for the loss of someone you love is not a finite thing. It does not ever end. It becomes an ongoing part of your life which changes over time, but there is always going to be sadness. The sadness gets fainter and fainter, it is more and more replaced with new joys, but it is never gone.

It's interesting that for all Murray knows about the subject of bereavement, he could say that he thought he was done with it. It is an indication, perhaps, of how desperately you want it to end when it's happening to you. But it is important to know that bereavement doesn't really have an ending, because to understand that takes some of the pressure off to hurry up and get over it. You don't get over the loss of a love. You make a place for it in your life.

But however much Murray's story may tell us about the evolution of grief, the most telling thing about his tale may be the fact that he never told it. Here is a man whose life was devoted to the belief that articulating your feelings gives you a handle by which to get a grip on life, but when faced with the loss of his wife, he never talked about it to anyone. No one ever asked, he says.

We have said before that talking about it is not by any means a cure-all, and we stand by that comment. But that is not at all to say that it does not have its value. The airing of feelings releases pressure, like the lancing of boils. And obviously, communicating your feelings to someone else alleviates your sense of isolation. And if, in that communicating, the other person can offer you a perspective that helps to change your point of view for the better, then the effort to talk has really paid off.

Assuming that Murray knows this, why did he wait to be asked to talk? If he understood the value of talking, why did he not initiate it? To some extent, to be sure, it was a matter of personal style—Murray has always been a lone wolf—but along with that, it appears he didn't ask because he just didn't know how. He had spent the past forty years of his life developing an identity as a man who has the answers. "People come to me," he says. "I'd rather be needed than need other people."

Many men get caught in this bind. They find, having built up the self-reliance society encouraged in them, that it is something of a trap. Not only are they entirely unpracticed in seeking out others to whom to reveal their vulnerability, they have also developed a persona that does not encourage others to invite them to reveal themselves. They get caught between the need to talk and the male imperative not to reveal their vulnerability. At the same time, those around them tell themselves they are doing them a favor by not asking them to talk about it.

If you are a friend of a widower and want to help him talk, it may be useful to realize that you may have to ask some relatively probing questions and not necessarily settle for a deflective answer. It may take some sensitivity. Not everyone is capable of talking about their feelings well, and different people need to talk to different degrees at different times. Some people may grieve best in silence, at least at certain times, and a widower must be given the choice of whom he wants to talk to and when. If he isn't talking to you it may be he doesn't want to talk to *you,* for one reason or another, and to bludgeon him with questions would be inappropriate.

But it also may be true that in his inexperience in giving voice to difficult feelings, he may answer casual questions with deceptively casual answers, and to help him to talk you may have to be aggressive with your questions. When Murray told me he kissed his wife until she started to turn cold, I asked him how long it took. It was the kind of invasive question for which journalists are always criticized, but he answered me without hesitation. There is nothing in the world that will loosen the tongue more quickly than someone who really wants to listen.

It is important to realize that people can be asked to talk, that indeed they may want, may need to be asked. At the end of this interview—an interview that had lasted three hours, late into the evening—Murray said three different times: "Ask me anything at all. What else can I tell you? Ask anything." It had been three years since his wife of thirty years had finally died, and this was the first time anyone had asked him how he felt about it.

The previous chapter ended with a discussion of the importance of building a new life, and Murray's story gives us a look at an important aspect of that. At some point, Murray came to the realization that it was time to let go, that for him to continue going to the cemetery all the time would ultimately get him nowhere, and that to change his routine required a conscious act of will. It would not happen by itself. He had to take a hand.

It is true that men, for the most part, tend to have the expectation that they will be able to cope with bereavement as they have coped with other aspects of life—by taking action, taking charge. Sometimes, often, men attempt to apply that will too soon, to force themselves to "get over it" before they've gotten into it. But in the right dosage, at the right moment, the will to put your past behind you can be a great strength.

Murray did, in fact, succeed in putting his past behind him, to some extent, by forcing himself to stop going to the cemetery. By doing that, he forced himself to face the hole that was left in his life and opened himself up to the opportunity that that presented to fill his life with new things. He wasn't trying to force himself out of his bereavement, he was actively, consciously doing the work of letting go of Ruth.

In part because of that act of will—and because he wasn't saddled with ambivalence, as Gordon was—Murray has been able to take advantage of the freedom that his widowhood presented him with. Rather than just returning to his workaholic pattern, he started developing new pleasures. He bought himself a stereo. Instead of returning every year to the same little cottage, he started going to all the exotic places he'd never been before. Instead of becoming the grand old man, he engaged in a jet-set love affair and started going dancing.

Murray has a very different life than he had before. He is using different parts of himself, expanding his conceptions of who he is and what his life can be. It wasn't always easy. It's interesting that Murray admits to feeling somehow defective when he goes to a movie alone. It's a comment often heard from women, but in a world where men are allowed to travel by themselves, some people are surprised to find that men have this feeling too, especially those who have always taken pride in their self-sufficiency. But all the will and freedom to move about in society alone doesn't protect you from feeling like a leper alone on a Saturday night. The world moves in couples, and if you aren't part of one, you can feel defective.

Murray faced that discomfort, though, and in facing it allowed himself to grow to the point where he became a part of a couple again. It is a very different couple from the one he was part of before, with different rules and expectations, because he is a different man. It's a very different circumstance from jumping into another relationship to replace one that has been lost. This new relationship has given Murray a whole new look at life.

But however happy we are for Murray now, we can't help but regret those eleven years that he and Ruth went through. It was the cruelest form of death. As Murray said, the disease not only took her, it took his memory of her. Some people, faced with such a situation, refuse to let death do that to them. Some choose to check out on their own. And some of those people, like Derek, find that decision transforms their lives.

Derek

EREK is 56, a writer. When he was 23 and a cub reporter in Manchester, England, he was sent to interview a young woman about her leadership role in an organization of Manchester youth. Somewhat taken with her, he took her with him to a concert a few days later, and married her six weeks after that. During their 22 years together, Jean and Derek raised three sons. The eldest, Edgar, is 32, divorced and living in England. Clive is 30, married, two children, and lives in the north of England. Their adopted son, also 30, has not been in touch for quite some time.

When Jean was 40, she was diagnosed with cancer of the breast, which very quickly metastasized to cancer of the marrow. It got to the point that virtually every time she moved, she broke a bone. She was essentially collapsing from within, disintegrating. After a year of progressive pain, she came to the brink of death, and a few days later, when Derek went to see her at the hospital, she told him she wanted to end her own life when she felt it was time. She asked if he would help her. Derek remembers, "It was a complete surprise to me—it had never, never occurred to me—but I said, immediately, yes. It was an instinctive answer. Here was my best friend, my closest companion, the person I owed more to than anybody else. If that was what she wanted of me, that was what I would give her. She said, 'I want you to get an absolutely lethal dose of drugs . . .' "

Jean lived for another nine months after that and they never spoke of it again. Her condition continued to worsen, though, and on the

Wednesday just before Easter, the doctor said nothing more could be done. On Friday night, unbeknownst to Derek, she called the boys to her side, gave them a lecture, and said goodbye. And on Saturday morning, she spoke to him. This interview was conducted almost eleven years after her death.

I went to the window and opened the curtains. As I turned, she said, "Is this the day?" Just like that.

She came from the north country—a Lancashire woman—and they speak in a very blunt, straightforward fashion. She had a plan worked out, but she was running a check by me to be sure that she was right. It's a terrible thing to take your own life, even in those circumstances. You want to be sure you're right, that it's true that you are close to death. That's why she put it as a question.

It was quite a question. I knew that I was going to say yes, but I found it hard to get out the words, to get a grip on myself. It was like passing a death sentence. But eventually I said, "If this is the day you want to die, I can't put up arguments. If this is what you want, okay." And immediately she said, "Then I'll die at 1:00. Have you got the drugs?" I said, "Yes." And she said, "Then shut the door. I don't want to see anyone else."

We sat talking together all that morning. We went over things that had happened to us, and settled the few quarrels we'd had in our life. There were only three or four. One was over whether we should buy a certain house or not, and we agreed that in that case she was right, we should have bought the house. Another time, I was determined to go to London to seek greater newspaper experience and she didn't want to go. She said, "You were right then; you did make more of yourself when we went to London." So we sort of settled our quarrels. And we played our favorite music, a piece by César Franck that was played at that very first concert. It was an amazing morning. It was very rich, very sharing. I cried endlessly. She didn't. She kept on saying, "Stop crying. There's nothing else we can do. I am going to die."

Then the time got toward 1:00—I made no move—and she said, "You'd better go get it." I went out and made two cups of coffee, and in hers I put the drugs. I told the boys she was close to death. And then I brought it back in to her. She said, "Is that it?" I said, "Yes." We had a hug and a kiss, and held each other. And then she picked up the coffee and drank it, all of it, very determinedly. And she said

"Good-bye, my love." And then she went unconscious.

I sat with her—she was deeply unconscious—and then after twenty minutes or so, she vomited very slightly. I thought, what if it all comes out and she wakes up? I hadn't been told what to expect in terms of how she would die. I think it would have been helpful. So at that point I resolved to kill her if she came around. I looked at the pillows that were beside her—there were a lot of pillows—and I thought, I am not going to let her down. I promised her she would not wake up. If she comes around, I will suffocate her. I know now that that's not unusual, that people do these things for their loved ones—I hear of many such stories—but fifty minutes later, she stopped breathing, so I didn't have to end her life myself.

My daugher-in-law came in and she closed Jean's eyes. I said, "We'd better get the doctor to certify the death." And when I saw his car come down the drive, I walked out of the house. I didn't want to lie or deceive him, so I went out the back garden and over the meadows for a walk. I thought, "If I'm not here, there's no deceit." When I walked back, his car wasn't there, so I came inside again. The death certificate was filled out "Death by carcinomatosis." And to any logical person, that was what she *had* died of.

The undertaker sent his men around and they took the body away, and that was the end of it. There was no funeral service and no memorial service. That was what she wanted. Over the years, I've wondered whether there should have been a memorial meeting—other people might have had a need to grieve for her—but I felt that her funeral had been that morning, that that had been her memorial meeting. I saw her off on her own, while she was alive. It was a remarkable experience. If she had died differently, if I hadn't had that opportunity to say goodbye to her, I might have handled the rituals and ceremonies differently. If it had been a sudden death . . .

My brother died three weeks ago in the operating theater and his death was an absolute blow. He went in for an earache—he would have come out that afternoon—but the doctor gave him an anesthetic which brought on cardiac arrest, and they pulled him off the operating table 90 percent brain dead. I watched the nurse shine a torch in his eyes, and there was no pupil movement. They were the eyes of a dead person.

We had a family conference. I said, If we're going to switch him off, we must switch him off everything at once—food, water, oxygen. If we switch him off only one, he will only linger on the other. His daughters were very fond of him. They said, no, we can't starve Daddy to death. But I told them he wouldn't feel it. And that to have the courage to help him, we had to do it all at once. We talked about it and finally agreed. And then, as the head of the family—now the head of the family; he was my older brother—I went to the doctors and said that he should be allowed to die quietly. They disconnected him at 5:00—tea time—and he died about 10:00.

For my brother, there was a funeral service, and later a memorial meeting at home where we talked and shared and cried, and I did get something out of that. I couldn't help but feel the family warmth and unity, and how much he was loved. But he was a beautiful, healthy man in the prime of good health. His death was enormously sudden. With Jean's death, there had been so much sharing of the dying before it happened, there had already been a lot of tears and a lot of commiserating and talking. So I told the undertaker just to scatter her ashes in the field. I thanked him, and then I took off.

I went back to work immediately. I had been working on and off— the *Sunday Times* was most generous, I could either work or not work, as I pleased—and the editor came to me and said, we need a man in Florida to do some travel articles. So I took off to Florida—I was there about three weeks—and then went down to Jamaica. I lived in Jamaica about a month, researching material for a book I was writing on Michael X, a civil rights leader in England, and I just stayed away.

I wanted to be off on my own. During Jean's death, I had been overwhelmed with love and support from people, and now I just wanted to be with people I didn't have to talk to about it. They thought I was just some journalist gathering information. I didn't have to talk about death. In England everyone knew—it had been in the papers, that she was dead—and I had to share it with everyone, whether that person was close or not. I found it overbearing, harrassing, to share it with everybody. So I ran away to escape it all. It may not have been the right thing to do, you know. But that's what I did. I wasn't abandoning anybody. My sons had their own love relationships. Edgar was 20, Clive was 18. One was married, the other engaged. They were tied up in their own lives. And they had to cope their own way anyway. So I went off by myself.

I returned to London after two months, to a little apartment that I had taken with another writer. He was suffering from a divorce, I was suffering from bereavement. So we just wrote all day. And every evening, we'd stop at five and have a couple of drinks, and then we'd go out on the town. London's a great place in the evenings, and every night we went to escape. Just escape, massively. We'd never get back 'til eleven or midnight, fall straight to sleep, and at nine the next morning, we'd be back to the typewriters. It was like a fever dance.

I found I had a tremendous desire to be with women in every way, an almost obsessive desire. On the morning Jean died, she made me promise to get married again, and she mentioned the names of some people who would be good candidates. But at this point, I was just womanizing, rather than seeking another life partner. It was pretty much a new girl every week. I was 45 at the time.

That summer, I had a mad affair with a schoolteacher. It was enormously carthartic. It made me feel a whole man again. I felt relieved. I felt I could cope. I felt I could handle a relationship with a woman again. It was laughter and sex that did it. She was in her early 30s, but she looked about 18 or 19, and we had a lot of fun. One day we were walking down a London street hand-in-hand, laughing and joking, and a guy stopped his car, wound down the window and shouted at me, "I don't know how you old guys get the birds like that!" He says, "I can't get birds like that!" And he wound the window back up and drove off. Satisfaction!

By the fall, I'd resolved to get married. I started answering ads in the personal columns of the *New Statesman*, and one week there was this ad that said something like, "American student seeks friendship with man willing to put feet on table." I was fascinated by it, so I replied, and when we met, we fell in love. She was a lovely woman— the right age and type, intelligent. We walked down Drury Lane and had a drink or two in a pub, then went for another walk, then had another drink in Covent Garden . . .

I had to go to northern Ireland that week to cover the bombs and shooting there, so I wired Ann a dozen red roses. She was doing her thesis on Eliot, so I rushed into a bookshop in Belfast, looked through a T. S. Eliot book and sent a quotation with the roses, just to show I was on the same wavelength. And we married seven months later. About a year after Jean died.

A year after that, I started the book about Jean's life and death. Ann was the only person who knew the full details, she knew the whole thing. And she said to me one day, "Instead of another book on racial problems, you should write a book about Jean." I said, "No, I don't want to write about Jean." But she pressed, "You must, it's a marvelous story. You have so much to tell people.''

And so I started to write the story. It was very difficult, extremely disheartening. Ann had to help me because I was blocking out a lot of the painful experiences that I'd told her about. The writing opened all the wounds again. But I got the experience in better perspective by writing about it like that. I can see my story much better now than when it was locked up in my own mind, just a jumble of thoughts. Once you bring it out, your friends start to ask these odd but pertinent questions—like, well, weren't you thinking of sex at the time? And then—well, yes, I guess I was. It helps you, these probing little questions, to be more honest with yourself. We all shut out to a certain extent.

I decided to publish the book for two reasons. One, Ann convinced me that it was a story of human life that appeared not to have been told before, and that's what writers are all about, exploring the human condition. And secondly, as I went through the newspaper archives, I was struck by the stories of people who had been charged with the crime of assisting suicide. Their private lives were dragged out, warts and all, into banner headlines, and then at the end, the judge simply said, ''You've been punished enough by your conscience.'' I said to myself, That law is wrong. I'm going to strike a blow for this. Helping a loved one to die is a moral obligation that transcends the law.

And so we published the book. It was a sensation, it was so controversial. We had three movie offers within a week from Hollywood. I was heaped with praise and with criticism. People called me a murderer and others almost called me a saint.

My family didn't like the fact that I published a book about it. One aunt told me, ''Oh, they're talking about me in the supermarket. They say, that lady over there is the aunt of the man who helped his wife die.'' And she was embarrassed that they'd talk about her in the supermarket. The two boys weren't pleased, either. They were assaulted with questions, held up in the drive by journalists looking for the follow-up story—''Family Condemns Mercy Killer!'' So that was difficult, caused a lot of pain.

By the end of the week, the police came around and said, ''This is a crime. You can get fourteen years in prison.'' I said, ''I'm guilty, no question,'' and I gave them a signed confession of guilt. I had checked the newspaper clips and could see that I was unlikely to go to prison.

They interviewed doctors and family. My son's wife told them, yes, she knew that Jean was intending suicide, that she had talked about it frequently. And they interviewed several of Jean's girlfriends and they all said, yes, this was Jean's idea. She spoke about it on occasion. She never used the word suicide. She didn't see it as suicide in the conventional sense of the word—she saw it as accelerated death—so she had let it quietly be known. That's what the detectives wanted to establish: whether I had murderd her or persuaded her to suicide. And the evidence they collected was that it was all her idea.

Still, by assisting suicide, I had broken the law. But I was not prosecuted because of insufficient evidence. They *had* sufficient evidence—they had a signed confession—but there is a rule of thumb in England that if the person is terminally ill and they are assisted by a spouse, the courts don't want to deal with it.

By this time, I had moved to L.A. to work for the *Los Angeles Times*. And because of the book, *Jean's Way*, I became something of a spokesman for euthanasia. The book drew enormous attention to the movement because in euthanasia you're usually talking of elderly people—you know, old deteriorating people—and this was a book about younger people who were deteriorating. People realized, this could happen to *us*.

So I began to get requests to speak about euthanasia, to be on radio and TV debating, and I was fascinated with how varied the audiences were. There were people of all sorts at these meetings. And it began to dawn on me that I had a major issue here that hardly anyone else was tackling. There are organizations in New York that deal with passive euthanasia, like my brother's case, but nobody in America tackled the issue of active euthanasia: helping another to die. I decided to do it. I formed the Hemlock Society in 1980 to argue for the right to die and the right to assistance in death. It just grew and grew. Now we're a national organization with thirteen thousand members.

My goal is to change public opinion and to change laws. We have come to the conclusion that the ideal form of euthanasia is not necessarily what I did. You ought to be able to turn to the doctor and say, please help my wife, she wants to die. The doctor would talk it over with her and make sure everything is in order, that this was her desire. And she would sign a legal form to say I want my life ended and I take both the legal and the moral responsibility for it. The doctor can then give a lethal injection, free of prosecution. We've come to the conclusion that that is the ideal way it should be allowed to happen. Once that legislation is changed, I will consider my task completed. The Hemlock Society might at that point become a referral and counseling service, but I don't think I'd be much involved.

When Jean first asked me to help her die that day in the hospital, she said, "I've decided I don't want to die in here. I don't want to die in a drugged-out state, having lost control of my bowels and my mind. I want to die at home, with you." I felt pretty sure that if the situation were reversed and it was me in the hospital bed, I would have been asking her the same thing. And I'm convinced that the fact that she knew she could die anytime was a great safety valve to her; it gave her a feeling of confidence. She pressed on with daily life very confidently. She was not suicidal, yet she was planning suicide, if you get my meaning. She was very positive during that time.

My critics say that I run the Hemlock Society, and built it the way I did, to get redemption for my action. But that's utter nonsense. If anything, it's the opposite—I have done it in honor of Jean, because she died so beautifully. Her mother had died of cancer, in rending agony, ten years earlier, and Jean had been shocked by the sight of her mother screaming for help. Everybody was ethically thrown; nobody knew what to do. Her father just went into a trance. Jean had obviously resolved that she would not go to her own death that way. So everything about her death was thoughtful, caring, and planned. Her dying was a celebration of life.

Derek's story is like Murray's because it involves the phenomenon of anticipatory grief. He went through an extended period of anticipating Jean's death and grieved her loss in increments even as he cleaved more tightly to the parts of her that remained. But once she died, even though he had been thoroughly "prepared" for it, he still went into a tailspin. It is another example of the fact that anticipatory grief does not mean that you get your grieving done before the funeral.

In fact, Derek's recoiling from Jean's death came upon him much faster; his period of shock and numbness was shorter than it is for many men. And the way it came on him provides an interesting contrast to what we've seen before. Within two months after Jean died, Derek was having a hot affair, while two months after Carol died, George was impotent.

Perhaps the most interesting aspect of that contrast is the fact that both these responses are wholly predictable. George and Derek mark off the two ends of the sexual spectrum within which any widower can expect to find himself. It is, of course, the same spectrum in which you will find yourself at any other time, but as a widower, you may find yourself in a different part of the spectrum from where you were before.

While it's sure to raise a lot of eyebrows, to go womanizing as Derek did can be a very good thing. It could be looked at as escape, and in some ways it was. In some ways, Derek used sex the same way Randy used alcohol, as a way of escaping the painful feelings. But his sexual adventuring was also a recommitment to life, an escape from the clutches of death by passionately embracing the living.

Having found this passionate embrace, another man might have found himself getting married to the schoolteacher with whom Derek had his fling. And it is to Derek's great advantage that he knew that would have been a mistake. Unlike Mark, perhaps, who tried to cement a new relationship, Derek understood that he needed some laughter and sex and freedom from care, and that that was an entirely different concern from getting married again. If he had married that schoolteacher, he might very well have been locking himself into a relationship in which there would have been no room for his grief. It worked wonders for him to have a relationship in which he did not bring along his emotional baggage, but he was wise to realize that any permanent alliance would have to allow for it.

Derek's sexual dalliances provide another interesting contrast. While it was only a matter of months before Derek had a fling which gave him the confidence that he could handle a love affair with a woman again, Gordon, thirteen years later, has still not regained that confidence. People have different time frames which have to be respected.

If you are recently widowed, you are likely to be getting signals from people around you about what you should be doing. Within only days of George's loss, for example, he had a friend who was trying to fix him up with sixty different women at the same time that his daughter was trying to get him to say that he would get an electric blanket with single controls. He wisely ignored them both.

The only one who really knows what your biological needs are is you. But it may be worth taking a moment to say that if you are impotent, there is no need to be afraid of it. It is a normal reaction, and it will pass in time. It's just that your psyche is busy using its energy for other things. On the other hand, if you suddenly feel it's the middle of "rutting season," that also need not come as a surprise. If you do go womanizing, it probably won't last too long. By the end of the summer, Derek had decided to look for another wife, and was married within the year.

Once he did get married again, it is interesting to see the role Derek's second wife played in his grieving. It was Ann who encouraged him, even pushed him, to grapple with Jean's loss, to do the work that was required to find her a final resting place. Whether Ann saw it that way or not, that is what ultimately happened: by writing his book, Derek sifted through and found a place for all his feelings. He had to name them and own them and figure out where they fit in the scheme of things, and then figure out how to put them there. This is the process we're talking about when we talk about "doing grief work." While Derek's skill as a writer gave him the chance to do it by writing a book, some other men find other ways to do it that don't require professional skills.

Ann's role in this process demonstrates the way in which a relatively quick remarriage can work: when the second wife is able to facilitate the widower's accommodation to grief. Some people, in fact, believe that widowers should always marry widows because no one could be more helpful in doing your grief work than someone who's already done it for herself. In this case, Ann had been divorced, so at least she knew a bit about accommodating loss. She became intrinsically involved in his accommodation, working side by side with him in his new career. This marriage is clearly not an attempt to escape the loss of the first. It is a successful new alliance.

Derek, however, avoids all questions about his sons, claiming that they should be allowed to speak up for themselves. Perhaps they should. But they seem to have been left out of all this, to a large extent—left out of Jean's decision, until the last minute, and left out of a communal grieving of her loss. Derek claims that the hours before Jean's death were her memorial service, and it does sound as if that was a very lovely memorial service. But the sons didn't get to partake of it, and perhaps they were robbed of the chance to share their grief with their father, possibly with each other, and apparently with family friends.

Derek, in fact, admits that he may have been wrong about this. And given what we know from others about the sense of impingement that results when children are not allowed, for one reason or another, to grieve the loss of a parent fully, perhaps Derek's second thoughts are right. As he pointed out in discussing his brother, communal grieving rituals at a time like this can be very important.

But in any case, he has found for himself a successful adaptation. His life hasn't changed quite the same as has Murray's—he isn't really exploring whole new areas of himself and the world—but he is applying himself and his skills in very different ways. He was always a writer with a cause, but now he has a cause that is profoundly linked to his own experience. And in taking up that cause, he has given Jean's death, and thereby her life, wider impact than it might otherwise have had.

It is an appropriate way for Derek to continue to care for Jean, an appropriate way of remembering her, of keeping the past alive in the present without living in the past. And it gives his life added direction. Many people do this in less dramatic ways. Survivors of suicide often get ve.y involved in the Samaritans. People who lose someone to a particular disease will often get very much involved in fund raising for research. All of this is an appropriate way of remembering and giving significance to death.

Derek's critics say he is seeking recompense for what he did. He says he is honoring her. But the point, as far as we're concerned, is that her death has created this transformation in his life. It has caused this growth. It has given his life new meaning.

Not everyone loses his wife in such a way that her death itself becomes the seed of a new career. But some men find the loss of their wives so disrupts their lives and so dramatically alters their view of life that not only do they find themselves in altogether new careers but they find that their entire system of values is irrevocably altered.

Roger

ROGER is 59. He is a retired insurance man. He met Angie when he was 21 at a summer resort his parents owned and operated in the Midwest, and proposed to her a year later. During their thirty-four years of marriage, they raised two sons together: Roger Jr., 34, who now lives in Santa Barbara, and Matthew John, 31, who lives in Los Angeles.

When Angie was 47, she developed cancer of the breast. She underwent a mastectomy and was put on chemotherapy, and some months later, while vacationing on a houseboat in Michigan, she suffered a stroke which was induced in part by the chemotherapy. Roger hired a plane and flew her back home, then took an early retirement to take care of her. During the next three years, whenever he would hear of some new treatment, he would hire a hospital plane and take her to different places around the world, but in the end it did no good. She finally died at age 50 in a Cleveland hospital.

This interview was conducted four years after her death.

We brought her in on Friday and on Sunday night she stopped breathing. She was revived and all day Monday they had her on a respirator, and Monday afternoon, about 5:00, the doctors had a meeting. The chairman asked each of them their opinion, and each of them ended their statement by saying they felt they had to let her down. I said, "What do you mean, let her down?" And the chairman said, "Let her die. But yours is the only vote that counts." He left it to me to pull the trigger. And so I told him, "All right."

They removed her from the machines, hooked her up to a morphine drip, and put her in a private room. I tended to her alone. Later that night, my son came in and we sat through the night with her. At 6:30 the next morning, she struggled to sit up in bed, she hugged me, and then she laid down again. Then she turned her head to one side and took a little breath, like a little girl . . . and died.

I made arrangements to have the body delivered to the funeral home and walked out of the hospital. I remember it was a bright, sunny day and I felt a huge relief. I've often thought about that feeling. I know what it was about—I didn't have to worry twenty-four hours a day anymore, literally twenty-four hours a day. I didn't have to do that now. It got me through the funeral. But then the boys went home, and it dawned on me that I didn't have anyone to care for anymore, either. That's when my slide to depression began.

I did absolutely, positively the worst thing you could do. I gave away all her clothes in two weeks. I sold the house very quickly and moved. I packed up and moved to Santa Barbara, just two months after she died, so I could be near my son.

When I got here, I was very depressed. I had actually quit eating and didn't even know it. I had lost more than seventy pounds. I thought I was sick. I went to the doctor and he told me I was emaciated. I didn't even realize it. He told me I had to start eating, so I started eating again. But I was so weak and so depressed, I could hardly walk ten feet. And the weaker I got, the more depressed, and the more depressed, the weaker I got. I could hardly operate anymore. I was 56.

I thought I was going crazy. For a month or so, nothing had bothered me, during that numb period. But then, all of a sudden, this devastation overcame me, and I never did know exactly when or why except that it was there. I felt like a stranger in a strange land. I didn't belong anywhere. I went to a psychologist and then to a psychiatrist. They tried some things like, Bring in pictures of your wife and tell the story. But I could not tell the story to them. I don't know why. I had the feeling they didn't know what I was talking about. Neither of them had been widowed. So I went a couple of times and quit.

It was about that time that I decided to kill myself. I bought a .357 Magnum, the biggest gun I could find. I figured, if you take pills, you don't really mean to kill yourself. But if you stick a gun in your mouth and blow out your brains . . . I had it planned out. I even put a tarpaulin on the bed, so I wouldn't make a mess. I had the tarpaulin on the bed, the gun was loaded, and I was just about to stick it in my mouth, when suddenly something dawned on me. I had my wife's dog to take care of. Ginger. She was living in the backyard. I hadn't been thinking about Ginger. But suddenly I realized I couldn't leave that dog to starve. I'd have to kill the dog. And that I could not do. So I put the gun down. I decided if Ginger died, *then* I would kill myself. But she didn't die; she's still alive. And it turned out that having that dog to care for was a helpful thing. You have to feed them, give them water, walk them, stuff like that. And it has to be done regularly. It kept me surviving for a while.

Years before, I had clipped a story out of the newspaper called "How To Survive the Death of Your Spouse." At that time, I didn't know if Angie was going to die for sure, but I saved it so either she or I would be able to use it. And now I was desperate for help. So I called the Widowed Persons Service in Washington, D.C.—their number was in that article—and they were kind enough to give me the number of someone out here. That person was no longer involved, but they found somebody who was, and they in turn put me in contact with a volunteer aid. And that person saved my life. We talked, and for the first time . . .

See, I literally had no friends. When my wife got sick, I became more or less isolated because she needed twenty-four-hour-a-day care. And when I came out here, of course, I was a complete stranger. It turned out my son was out of town for a good part of the year, so I hardly ever saw him. I tried to talk to him once, early on, but it didn't work very well. Later, I found a cartoon and I told him, This is what your help was like. The cartoon was a picture of a man on a psychiatrist's couch and the psychiatrist is flailing his arms and saying, "Pack up your troubles in your old kit bag and Smile! Smile! Smile!" My son didn't know how to react to it. He laughed. I think he realized that that was all he could do, he didn't know what I was going through. And I didn't know what was happening with him, you know, grieving for his mother. We were just a pair of human beings trying to find our way. But after that one attempt with him, I talked to no one, really.

What this volunteer aid did for me was to allow me to tell somebody what I was going through, and that was the beginning of identifying what I'd lost. You can't just say that you lost a spouse, that's not saying enough. You've lost a lot of things. You've lost a companion, an ego builder, you've lost a counsellor who will tell you when you're right or when you're wrong. You've lost all of that. And you have to name what you've lost. I was also retired, and retirement is a loss to grieve too. When I first retired, I was so busy caring for my wife that it didn't really sink in. But when I got to Santa Barbara, it did sink in that I had also lost part of my identity. I was just a bum with money. At least I was a bum with money. Thank goodness I had enough of that.

We met in a public place, on the street, this volunteer aid and I. I was afraid of meeting someone like that, to tell you the truth. I didn't really know what this organization was all about. But we met and had lunch, and that was when my recovery started. Eventually, we had several conversations, always alone, nine or ten times, over a period of six months. We talked about problems of widowhood, such as, what do you do with this feeling that if I had done just one more thing . . .? And it worked just like the Widowed Persons Service wants it to work. You're with them, they help you for a while, and then they up and leave you. I always call it—these days, when I do it—I say, I love them and leave them. You don't want to stay around and develop a dependency state.

This experience got me interested in the Widowed Persons Service, and I took the training class so I could be a volunteer aid myself. Telling your story is part of the class, so I had to tell my story to people so they could tell their story to me. And that's how I started to talk to people. And it was just astonishing, the way my attitude changed. My depression just went away. It was a miracle. And it all came from telling the story, and talking with other people in the same boat.

Over time, I became more and more involved in the Widowed Persons Service, and we've grown into an extremely active organization here. We have thirty-one volunteer aids, of whom thirteen or fourteen are really active. Some will do it a little while, some find for various reasons they can't and drop out after the training. But to those who can do it, it is a great help in their own grief work. If they can have the satisfaction of seeing someone else get better, it helps them to heal themselves. And then they become role models for others, because they have lived through it themselves.

What you find in talking to a newly widowed person is that they have to have permission to tell you their story. You have to tell yours first, so then they can tell you theirs. We generally try to contact them two to three months after their loss. That's when we can help them best, at the bottom of their depression.

If you've seen a diagram of grief I'll try to explain it. On a pair of axes, you draw a line above and parallel to the horizontal axis and call that a normal state. "Normal" here means the degree of emotional stress you are under. Now, if at the time of death, a person was on the normal line, they will continue on that line for a while. That's the time of the funeral, of getting the estate settled, writing the thank-you notes, stuff like that. That is the numb period.

Then a strange thing seems to happen. For a short time, as that numb is ending, a person may feel somewhat better—for a very short period of time. But then suddenly something like anger will surface. Anger at the doctors, you know, the hospital, the nurses. Anger at yourself for something you should have done, or didn't do. And that's where the slide begins.

From there on, it just goes down, down, down. It goes down to a valley which has a relatively long base on it—long in terms of time. Then suddenly—and I mean *suddenly*—a person will start to feel better again and will go back up. They won't approach normal, usually, but they'll go up to some plateau. And that plateau may last as long as the bottom.

Then they will go back down again, but they won't go down quite as far, and the base line will be a little bit shorter than the first one was. Then they'll go back up again, and the up plateau will be a little higher and a little longer than it was before, and so on. It'll get that way until the valleys begin to be hard to find.

But. And this is a big but. Almost universally, at almost any point in time, a person may drop all the way back to point zero and stay there for a while. Eventually, they'll come back from it, and eventually they will gain control of their lives again. But that is the point where we can help them, near the bottom of that depression.

I'm working with forty-nine widowers now. That's impossible to do on a one-to-one basis, so I work one-on-one with nine of them, and then I have forty who meet in three or four separate groups each month. In the beginning, I found it almost impossible to get these widowers to talk to me. I would go and seek them out, but I couldn't get them to talk. I would get to the point where I could have a telephone conversation, but when we got around to the point of arranging a face-to-face meeting—which is absolutely essential—well, I was having trouble with it. So I thought if a widow went with me, it might seem more convivial.

So I started taking a widow with me, but it didn't work. The men thought I was trying to set them up, to trap them in marriage or something. And most men in that period just don't have any libido at all. It wasn't for sex, you understand, that I brought a woman there.

But the fact of her *being* a woman *meant* sex, and that did not work at all.

Then it occurred to me that one of the problems these guys were having was that they didn't want to have to tell their friends that they were going to cry on some other guy's shoulder. 'Cause it makes him sound like a sissy. Unfortunately that's the way it is, especially in my generation. It's a heck of a lot more acceptable if they can say they're doing something that *is* acceptable, such as going to a poker game.

So I started a poker game. First you had to come to supper. Then we had a two-hour discussion, where I acted as a volunteer aid. And then we had a poker game. Well, that went over fantastically. You see, what actually happens is . . .The poker game isn't what they really come there for, but it's sort of a sacrament, in a way. It's something that they play a little and then they can say they played poker. Everybody realizes that it's just a device, but we don't tell anybody our secret. We don't tell each other, either.

We also have cooking lessons. Many of these widowers—really I shouldn't say many of them . . . There were five of them at the beginning who didn't know *anything* about cooking. These five guys couldn't boil water without burning it. So I organized a cooking class. I had to learn when my wife got sick—I had to keep her eating—and I learned to love to cook. So I started a little schedule of classes. We would go from one house to another, and each guy in the class would have to fix dinner for the rest of us, using his own tools, his own pots and pans. I would help each time they did it, to show them what some of the tools were for. These men, you know, the food had always appeared on the table somehow, by magic. They didn't know beans about how it got there. I remember one man, early in the game, I had *told* him how to fry eggs, but I hadn't actually *shown* him how. And one morning he called me up and he had managed to get the eggs in the pan but he didn't know what to do with them next. So I told him, well, hold the phone down by the eggs so I can tell how they're doing. Sometimes it gets pretty funny.

So we have had some success here. We have forty guys involved. But I'll tell you, these widowers' groups are hard. The very first session, they question you, you get the third degree. "Why are you doing this? What are your motivations?" They have to believe that you want to help them, and you have to tell them why, what you're getting out of it. It's just a characteristic of men. They're the ones who have to make the deals, to read the contracts in life—if they're businessmen or lawyers, especially. I'm talking of my generation now, and of traditional marriages, where the man was the one who was up against the world and his wife stayed home and cooked.

And then, because I don't want it to turn into a session for telling jokes, I have to make it very clear that I am going to be the boss. Not so much by saying it, but by never letting my guard down, ever. I say, "This is the way it's going to run. You can do whatever you want when you leave, but while you're here these are our rules." I have to establish myself as a leader. You might think a group of women would be more susceptible to that, but no, it's with the men that you have to do that, from the very beginning.

But even once all that's established, still it's difficult. Men are *very* reluctant to talk of emotions, especially with one another. There's a generational shift going on—I've got one guy 34 years old, and he's been very easy with it right from the very beginning—but there are still a lot of men of my generation around. And that's one of the first things we have to overcome in our early meetings, to get people to admit to their feelings.

That is the most common mistake I see widowers make, is denying the death of their wife. There's no two ways about it. Absolutely the most common problem. You can say clever things about denial—you can say that denial is acceptance, because if you didn't accept the death of your spouse you couldn't deny it. But saying that does nothing for you. The kind of denial I'm talking about is, sure they saw the body, they know she's dead, but they'll still say everything's fine. It's not a denial of the death so much as of their reaction to it. They have an answer for every question and it's always the same answer. They don't explore their reaction at all. And they're not allowed to explore it, in many instances.

I had an experience with one man that really tugs on the heartstrings. This man—we'll call him José Martinez. After I had been here a while, word got around what we were doing, and one day this man called me up. This was unusual, for somebody to call me. But he was clearly in very bad shape, crying and distraught. He asked me if he could come in and see me the next day. I said fine.

Along about 1:15 that morning, lo and behold, here's José at my door. Now José doesn't have enough money to have a car. He *walked seven miles* to get to my house in the middle of the night, because he heard he could get help. He worked as a brakeman for the railroad, and he was having a very hard time. Of course, he was finding no help anywhere. The people he worked with were roughnecks and stuff, and he found no solace from them. But he had heard my voice on the phone.

So I told him, come on in. I was sleepy, but I woke up pretty quick. And he just wanted to talk to me. He was crying and it came to a point where . . . I got up, I raised him up by the shoulders—he was smaller than me—and I hugged him. I'd never held a man before. But pretty soon he stopped crying. And we sat down and talked some more. And then I took him home. That man has since become a devotee of Widowed Persons Service.

I guess I would have to say that I have found a new focus for my life, running the Widowed Persons Service and being involved in my church. I have sort of found a new vocation, ministering to people's needs. My values have completely changed. Before my wife became ill, I lived a life of acquisition. But after I came here, and after I started to recover, I joined a church and became involved in the Widowed Persons Service and now what I want to do in my life is just to help other people. This is a kind of activity I would never have *thought* of before; I was always thinking about making money. If Angie had lived, I would have gone on doing that until I died; none of this would have happened. But now it's human concerns that are at the top of my priority list.

When I talk to a newly widowed man, I don't give him advice. The first thing I do is ask him what his wife's name was and when she died. And then we start talking about it. And during the conversation, I look for common experiences in grief, and I recite my reactions to that experience, what happened with my reaction, and he can either confirm or deny that those are his reactions. And we proceed like that. He'll say, what do you do about this? But I try not to tell him what to do. He will solve his problems himself. What I do do is tell him what I did, and it may or may not have been right, and it may or may not be right for him.

Maybe the second time we talk, I do tell him one thing for sure. Just sit still. Don't make a move. Don't sell your house. Hang onto the clothes. If she just died, I tell him to be sure to see the body. But after that, it is an interchange of experience. It's an empathetic understanding and listening and responding. You let the person know they are in the presence of someone who's been there before. This is what helps. If he cries, you tell him that's fine to cry. If he sees his wife, if he saw her last night when he was going to bed—one man saw his wife in the middle of the road, while he was driving—you tell him that that's normal, that it happens all the time. He's not mentally ill. Of course, he *may* be mentally ill, he may be a lot of things. This is a slice of life. The only common thing is that all of us are widowed. I've run into drug addicts, alcoholics, ex-convicts, you name it. That has nothing to do with it. The healing effect is that by talking to somebody who has been there, he gets to see that he's not crazy, that somebody else has felt the same way. And that they lived through it.

With Roger we get to see more clearly than we have with anyone else the spiral of depression that leads many men to suicide, whether it be a quick version, like Roger's sticking a gun in his mouth, a slower version, like Jerry's increasing his cigarette habit to two packs a day, or an inadvertent version, like the insurance man that Peter talks about in the last chapter who so repressed his grief that he had a heart attack.

We also see with Roger the value that having a pet to take care of can be at a time like this. It was Ginger, in the end, that gave Roger an excuse to go on living—not a reason, an excuse. If he had really wanted to die, he would have gone ahead and done it; Ginger gave him the out. While no one else's experience with his pet was quite so dramatic, a number of other men in this book talked about the survival value of taking care of a pet. Hank, in particular, found the care and feeding of his dog gave him an interim structure to his life. And the medical advantages of having a pet to love and stroke are well documented.

With Roger, we also see a different way of breaking the silence. Unlike Murray, who never found a way of seeking a chance to talk, and unlike Karl and Bill who had their chances essentially handed to them, Roger took an active part in seeking the support he needed. It is very unusual—although it is becoming less so—to see a man actively seeking help. And the clandestine quality of his meeting with the volunteer aid on the street underscores the hazard he felt he was running in seeking such help. In a way, he was doing something that as a man he was not supposed to do—admitting his frailty, asking for help from someone other than a wife. Luckily, he asked the right people.

Roger's experience with the volunteer aid harkens back to George's predictions in the first chapter. He said he thought that grieving would largely be a matter of making reality out of what didn't feel real. And he said he thought that that would largely be a matter of coming to an understanding of what he did and did not get from his wife, in order that he would know what he'd lost and be able to find a place for it. That was exactly the process that Roger's volunteer aid helped him with. Roger started to name what it was he had lost and that was the beginning of his healing. So George's prediction is proved out. Here we have a man at the other end of the grieving process, confirming the predictions of a man who was just starting out on his journey.

If you are recently widowed, it might be helpful for you to realize that this grieving process is a journey that others have made before, that it is not uncharted territory, and that those who have traveled through it can confirm or adjust your expectations of what you're going to encounter. There are many people around who can help you if you will only make yourself available to them.

Roger's discussion of his work in helping other widowers may be of greater interest to you if you are in a position of trying to offer help to widowers than it is to you if you are a recently widowed man yourself. But if you are a widower who is contemplating seeking help from the American Association of Retired Persons' (AARP) Widowed Person's Service, or from some other source, it does give you some idea of what the person you might be talking with has gone through before he talks to you. Roger's description of how he talks to a newly widowed person can give you a sense of what sort of interaction you might expect from a volunteer aid: if you get a good one, he won't just give you the same old saws; he will give you very specific attention to your particular situation. Finally, Roger's discussion of his new work can also give you a sense of the ways in which helping other widowers can help you help yourself. Roger has a whole new life, a whole new set of activities, a whole new value system, because he started helping others.

And he's doing very good work. If he brought this much creativity to the way he did business, it's easy to see how he managed to be so successful in the business world. As an organizer of widowers' groups, he has created environments in which reluctant peers can be successful in overcoming their reluctance and helping each other. The poker game, for instance, gives the reluctant participants a good "cover." But it is the cooking lessons that are especially inspired. The cooking lessons not only give the widowers a good cover, they also address the problems widowers face on an entirely different level, at the same time, by teaching them practical skills.

The difficulties Roger has faced in trying to organize this help are also very enlightening—the need, for instance, to establish oneself without question as the boss. Most men, at least in some part of their lives, have taken on the role of leader. As husbands, fathers, businessmen, and as community organizers, that is the masculine role in life. In a roomful of men, the jockeying for dominance and leadership can be fierce.

Other men who have organized widowers' groups have had the same problem. One man, who has organized groups for everything from weight loss to battered women to grieving, told me he found that widowers were the most difficult group he ever dealt with. His experience was that they were incredibly cranky and malcontented, that nothing one did was ever enough, and that they tried to turn the whole enterprise into a business proposition.

As interesting as those problems are, it is also extremely interesting that Liz, the funeral director's wife who runs the group, discussed previously, did *not* experience them. She reported no difficulty in getting her men together. Perhaps a woman can lead such a group more easily, because these issues don't come up. A woman can play Mom—which Liz did, to some extent, in that group—and the men won't jockey to lead. It may be also that men find it easier to talk about their feelings if there is a woman running the group.

Roger's personal transformation is a fascinating thing. He is still a mover and shaker, as he has been all his life, but now he is using the skills he'd developed over the course of his business life to entirely different ends. The scope of the transformation is even greater than Derek's was, because Derek had always had a cause and Roger's previous cause was just to make money. But some people go still further than this. Some people not only learn to use their skills in different ways, and find their system of values has changed, some people find new resources in themselves they never knew they had.

Lou

LOU is 68. He is a retired production manager. He picked
Madelaine up on a streetcorner when they were both 18. He was
cruising around with his cousin when they saw four girls at a bus
stop and stopped. And he married her three years later. During their
forty-one years of marriage, they had three children together: a son,
now 44, and a daughter, 41, both married with children and living
in the same midwestern city; and a daughter, 36 and divorced, living
in the West.

When she was 63, Madelaine underwent surgery for cancer. They had
been planning to retire and build a home out in the West, but when
the doctors announced they were not able to get all the cancer, and
that Madelaine was going to die, Lou and Madelaine moved to the city
so she could be near the children. "The one thing I ever prayed for
was that I'd get her to the city and get her settled so she'd be near
the kids for a time before she died. That was her one desire, what she
wanted more than anything." She got her wish. She was in and out
of the hospital during those last six months, but she was able to see
a lot of her children and grandchildren. Finally, in the last three days,
she slipped into unconsciousness.

This interview was conducted five and one-half years after she died.

On the last day, I was there, and my son was there, and my daughter
from out West was there, and her sister was there, but my daughter

with small children was not there. I said to Madelaine, "Give up. No more. You've been fighting too hard." Her sister, who was standing behind me, swears she saw a reaction to that. And Madelaine died within an hour. Some people just need permission to die.

I had always thought there would be some kind of a struggle or something. But she was just breathing, you know—inhaling, exhaling, inhaling, exhaling

Silence.

That's the way it was. There wasn't anything else. She just failed to inhale again. At that moment I felt like somebody had lifted a large stone off my shoulders. Then the next morning, it came crashing down on me from a great height—the enormity and the realization of what it was all about.

My kids tell me they couldn't believe me. As soon as their mother was dead, I said the benediction over her and repeated it many times.

> The Lord bless you and keep you
> The Lord make His countenance to shine upon you
> And give you peace
> And give you peace
> And give you peace
> And give you peace . . .

And then I started to gather stuff up. Like, you know, we better get out of here. They'll want this room. A funny reaction.

The next morning, I got up—I didn't set the alarm or anything, but I woke up before it was light—and got dressed and walked a few blocks til I found a spot high enough to see the horizon. I was thinking, I'm going to see if the sun *really* comes up today.

I'd gone through this once before, see, when my father died. I was 18 at the time. And I remember I stepped outside and the kids were playing and cars were going by and people were going to the store and I thought, Hey, stop, Stop, STOP! Don't you realize what's happened? I've lost . . . But the world goes on.

The sun did come up that morning, and it was ragingly beautiful. It was November on the plains—a gorgeous, crisp fall day, around 70 degrees.

I thought that I had understood what it was to lose your spouse, because a good friend of mine lost his wife. But you just can't understand it unless you go through it. It's just . . . Well, you've seen the stress schedule. I mean, the loss of a spouse is the thing they measure everything else against. That is the saturation point, whether your marriage was good or not. Just flat out, there's nothing like it. You just don't realize what it is for it all to be over. All the things that run through your mind that are completely *over*. We had a very happy marriage. The kids were grown and gone, and we were looking forward to moving out West . . . And then thinking, All those things we planned are not going to happen now.

She was buried in the city. We had a funeral service and a lot of our children's friends showed up, so there were quite a few people there. And then on the Friday following, we had a memorial service in the town where we had lived, where I got to see all my friends.

And then I started running. My daughter was here from out West, and I said, "I'll take you back, instead of you flying back on the plane." So Saturday morning, we took off. We stayed our first night in a place that Madelaine and I had always stayed when we went out West. I went to the same hotel, the same restaurant—I thought I was a real hotshot. Going right in, not dodging the bullet, really machoing it through. Two years later, I'd cry when I went by an eating place where we used to eat. That was after I learned that it was okay, that I didn't have to show off.

When we got out West, Sharon went to work and I bummed around. I went for day hikes in the mountains, bummed around downtown. Then all of a sudden, I got the thought, okay, if I'm going to be alone, by God, I'm going to be *alone*. And I went into a sporting goods store and bought $600 worth of backpacking equipment. That was one thing Madelaine never wanted to do, was backpack. She'd go out for a day hike but she didn't want to sleep in a tent. So I said, that's what I'll do. I was 62 at the time.

Then, when I got back to the Midwest, I thought, well, here I am. I don't know a soul, there's a lot of lakes. I have all kinds of time to fish. So I went to the boat show and bought a boat and a motor and a trailer. This was right while my finances were still in a total uproar, so I didn't have the slightest idea whether I could afford it or not. But I wanted to have all this *stuff*. Maybe I was trying to stuff all the stuff into the void, you know. But I thought if I got rational, I might not do anything at all.

I used the boat a couple of times, but it never became what I thought it would be. It turns out I don't have time for it, because my life is so full now. But I did go up in the mountains. I would hike up for a couple of days and stay a day and come down. It was neat. I really . . . I think I grew. I learned a lot about being alone. I didn't ever really feel lonely. I wasn't as lonely as I might have been in a group of married people, of couples. *Then* I felt lonely. Up in the mountains, I wasn't lonely, I was just alone.

I kept journals. I've got three or four books at home, where I'd sit at night and write what I thought. I had never done that before. But when it gets dark and you're in a tent, you think, Why don't I just write? It's a way of conversing with yourself. It has a completely different effect, whether you just think a thought, or speak it, or write it down. It makes a difference. You see what you've written and think, my God, that's the way I *feel*!

I had some nice experiences, some quietness, super quietness. I remember one time I was hiking up in Porcupine Mountain in Michigan, on the shores of Lake Superior, and as I went through this forest, all of a sudden I came on an area that was all hemlock trees. And, my God, they were big, they went towering up until finally all the leaves came together and made a kind of a roof. It all was free of underbrush, because it was so shaded, but there was a lush, green growth on the ground. There must have been thirty acres of this. It was so cathedral-like, I was just overcome. I thought, This is how it is for Madelaine. This is her peace.

Another time I was on Isle Royale. It's a national park, uninhabited now, except for a little resort at one end and a general store at the other. They dropped me off alone at one end and I hiked six days to the other end. Three days in, I thought to myself, This is not the smartest thing you have ever done. Because I've got a heart problem, see; I had a heart attack right in the middle of Madelaine's struggle with cancer.

But I knew the risks I was taking, I knew the risks and was willing to take them. And the kids were willing to accept that. If I had had another heart attack while I was out there alone, I would have died a happy man. It's like this quote I just came across, a quote from Jack London. He says, "When I end up, I want it to be as ashes and not as dust. I want to burn out," he says, "not dry up." It was in a cycling journal I read. I get around on a bike.

I sort of feel that life needs to be lived. I have a real strong feeling that widowed people have a greater appreciation and a greater awareness of every moment of life. Because the death of your spouse—someone so close to you, such a part of you—forces you to come to terms with your own mortality. So you try to live every moment, and not let anything slip away.

Of course, some people get stuck in grief and feel that any enjoyment is disloyal to their dead spouse. But those people are trying to hang onto their identity as part of a couple. They're struggling with unreality. Single is different than half a couple. If you're half a couple, then maybe enjoying life *is* disloyal to your spouse. But if you're a single person, it's not. And if you're widowed, you're single. You may not *want* to be, but that's the reality of the situation.

It does take a while to accept it, though, the fact that you are single again. In the first year after Madelaine died, I still acted as her husband sometimes. I remember one thing specifically. She had a thing about leaving the closet door open after we were in bed, and more than one time in my life I'd got out of bed and closed the door. And after she died, I'd still get up and close the closet door. But one night—I think it was close to a year after Madelaine died—I looked over, the door was open, and I said, "Hell, I don't care. Sorry, Madelaine." And I went to sleep. A lot of people tell me that was the day that I got off it. That I accepted being single again.

As I said, she didn't take to camping, so we didn't do it. It was one of those compromises you make, lovingly and caringly. But you find yourself single again, and all of a sudden you don't have to compromise. Now you can let it out, whatever that desire was that you were sitting on. So now I do all kinds of things. I've got a group of friends—we go horseback riding, we go on canoe trips, we go on bicycle rides. We get together and have a ball.

Madelaine told me before she died, she said, "Lou, I want you to have a fun life." I told my daughter-in-law, I don't know if Madelaine meant me to have *this* much fun. But you know I'd give it all up if I could have her back again. Roxie says, I know you mean that from the bottom of your heart. But if Madelaine came back today, I'm not sure she'd recognize you. You are a completely different person. And I am. I'm a lot more risk-taking. And a little less shy.

What helped me a lot with that was this support group that formed called LADOS—Life After the Death of a Spouse. They had their first meeting in January, two months after Madelaine died. And I went, and I tell you, that was something. I didn't know a soul, but I felt an instant rapport. And I went to those meetings every month.

I remember the one in February. It was my birthday, I was at my daughter's. We were all there for a birthday dinner, around six o'clock.

My meeting was at 7:00. I got up, I says, I'm sorry, you guys, I got somewhere to go. And up to this time, I'd been going wherever they wanted me to go, you know. But I said, I got things to do that don't involve you. And I chuckled, because that felt good. That was neat.

I had another good moment like that. We hadn't joined a church in the city because Madelaine got so sick right away, but when she died I found myself a Lutheran church to go to. We'd gone to the Lutheran church at home. And about the third time I was there, I was shaking hands with the pastor, and he said, Are you Mr. Madison? I was completely taken aback. I said, I sure am, but how do you know? He said, Well, your pastor back home said I'd probably see you one of these days, and I've noticed you here a few Sundays now. That part of it was terrific. But the part that I remember now is, "Are you Mr. Madison?" For the first time I wasn't Karen's dad, I wasn't Stevie's grandfather, I wasn't Roxie's father-in-law. I was Mr. Madison. By God, I actually *was* somebody. And it really had an effect on me. It was okay to be somebody on your own, instead of connected.

By the time I reached the anniversary of Madelaine's death, I had a whole new life for myself. I belonged to this widowed persons group, I'd become a member of this church, and I had gotten involved as a volunteer aid in the Widowed Persons Service of the AARP. So I had a whole new social circle, a new focus for my energies, and a whole new way of being alone. Accepting, even enjoying it.

I'm still kind of taken aback when I think of all I did that first year. It just sort of bowls me over. My experience with other grieving people through the Widowed Persons Service—I'd be surprised to see somebody moving along that quick. But I wasn't running from my grief, because I was expressing it through this monthly support group meeting. That made me aware of the need to express it and to look into it—the term we use is "lean into the pain."

I'd go home and drag out all the pictures, and go over them and cry my eyes out. On my own, I would have avoided the pictures. I would have said, "That'll make me cry, I'm not going to do that." But they led me to getting right into it. They use the term "grief work," you know. When you've got so much grief work to do, get at it. So I got at it. And I credit both those activities—the Widowed Persons Service and LADOS—for steering me in the right direction, just helping me beyond measure.

They helped me feel comfortable with my reactions. I didn't do anything about Madelaine's clothes for a while, and that worried me. But they said, Hey, there is nothing right or wrong to do about the clothes. Some people spend eight or nine years at it. So that gave me relief. I didn't get rid of her clothes for two years, and when I finally did, it was because I needed the room. There was not an emotional problem with it one way or the other.

If you were recently widowed, I'd urge you to get involved with some groups like that. Just put your head down and do it. Do it. From what I've seen as a volunteer aid, the biggest problem that widowed men face is the emptiness, the loneliness, especially in the first year. And the biggest mistake I see is that they don't get any help with it. Because it's true, these reports you see about men not having close friends to talk to. Men have guys they go fishing with, guys they play golf with, guys they hunt with, but no one they ever sit with and talk about their feelings with. And that's what you need to do in grieving. A widow's group gets right into it, but a widower's group? It's harder. Men are afraid to express their feelings. They have a fear of being soft.

Things are easier for a man in some ways, though. I mean, it *is* a man's world. Going where you want to go and doing what you want to do, you don't have any restrictions, the way that women do. The things that I do, if I were a woman, it wouldn't be easy to do. Like, I go hiking anyplace. But there are parks in our town where a woman wouldn't dare go walking alone. So I think the first year is harder for men because they aren't equipped to go through and express the range of feelings, but from then on it's harder for women because they don't have access to the same range of possibilities.

Another piece of advice I'd offer is not to get married in the first year. There's so much you need to know about a person you're going to marry. You need to see each other under so many circumstances—it takes at least a year for all those circumstances to crop up.

How do you act at Christmas, for instance. How are you on the anniversary of your spouses' death? How are you on their birthdays? What do you do on your children's birthdays? What do you do about family gatherings? Not that you marry the family, but it's a point of consideration. And how does she react to you in your family setting? How does her presence there affect you? How does it affect your family? I know you can say, to hell with the rest of the world, we'll just go do our own thing. Well, that's great for a novel, but that isn't the way life works. You sort of get the whole package.

For myself, I have decided I don't ever want to get married again. Madelaine was very possessive of me. She had a rough childhood and I was the first secure thing that she ever got onto. It was fine with me to be possessed—it was not a negative thing, at all—but it would take an unusual circumstance for me to get married again. And after 14 months of what I went through with Madelaine dying of cancer, I have made that decision for all time.

Of course, that presents the question of sex. And after Madelaine died, I went through a stage of seeing call girls. But I don't do that anymore. I get more sexual satisfaction out of the friendships I have with women than I ever got out of call girls. I have lots of women in my life. These two women that started the LADOS group, they are absolutely my two closest friends. There are other women I meet and walk with in the park once a week. I have women I call up and say, hey, let's go have some coffee and pie. And I get more sexual satisfaction out of those platonic friendships than I ever got out of call girls.

I also get some sexual satisfaction out of being with Nancy. I met Nancy three years after Madelaine died. I was at a weekend retreat for widows and widowers, and our speaker was exhorting us to take risks. So I walked over to this young lady—she was twenty years younger than me—and I said, can we go out for dinner? She smiled at me and said yes. (Oh my God!) That was the middle of June. I didn't call until the end of July, but when I did, we talked and talked and talked and talked and talked.

We have a terrific relationship. It's a romance, but there is no sex. Just kissing and hugging, talking on the phone. It is a neat relationship. Sometimes I don't see her for a month, sometimes I see her three weeks in a row. She has a job, so between her job and her family, and living in different towns, we can't always see as much of each other as I might like. But an in-town relationship doesn't really appeal to me right now.

I did get involved, very briefly, with a woman who lives in town, but I broke that off right away. I could see she wanted more out of the relationship than I did, and I found that I was not comfortable in a sexual relationship without some kind of commitment. Not necessarily marriage, but some kind of commitment. And I wasn't committed to her. It was a guilt that I couldn't erase, so I just broke it off.

But with Nancy, it was funny. It was evident from the start it wasn't going to involve jumping into bed, so we said it, right out loud. Now half of our fun is kidding about it. We have a good time. Recently

I talked her into taking a weekend trip with me. We went to San Francisco—she'd never been there—and we shared a hotel room for three nights. That's always been in my head, that I could travel with a woman and share a room without getting into bed, and have a damn good time. And that's exactly what happened.

I'd be content to have everything stay just like this for the rest of my life. But I told Nancy, if you find someone to marry, you go ahead and get married. Because, I told her, I recognize the futility of a marriage between us. My life expectancy is something like twenty-five years less than hers.

One time she almost did get married. About a year ago, she told me, This man has asked me to marry him and I told him Yes. That was when I found out how much I really care for her. I had been pretty frothy about it, and I was telling my daughter-in-law—I said, Roxie, "If I'm so happy for Nancy because she is going to get married, how come I feel like somebody left their bowling ball parked in my stomach?" She said, "I wondered when you were going to get around to the truth of the matter."

But it didn't take long to get over that. I went home that Saturday night and said, tomorrow I'm wallowing in my grief. I'm not getting dressed, not going to church. So I got up the next morning. Sat around. Read the paper. Sat around. God, I was bored. So I went to church and got back into the stream of things.

Later on, Nancy backed out of that marriage and we resumed seeing each other. But now I know that it's okay with me if she gets married. I can handle that. So everything is fine.

In fact, I was musing one day, just kind of looking out in the back yard, and I heard myself say, God I'm happy. And I thought, what do you mean you're happy? What does that mean about the time you spent with Madelaine? I said that out loud to myself. There was this guilty feeling with it. And I literally got into a two-sided argument with myself—I was taking both sides.

But I argued myself out of the guilt. Because you've got to go with what's real. And what's real is that Madelaine isn't here. There is nothing I can do about that. Absolutely nothing I can do. And what's happened to me since she died, all these terrific people I know and what I'm doing—God, I'm really happy.

I still have moments, even now. I even have moments of tears. But now they're more for Madelaine than they are for me. When Nancy and I were in San Francisco, we were in a taxi and it was kind of misty and foggy outside. It reminded me of a picture I took on my last trip with Madelaine. We were down at the shore and she was standing out on a pier looking into the fog, looking into the nothingness. It was so expressive of her end, looking into the nothingness. And there, in the cab, I started to cry. Later on I said, "That surprised me." Nancy said, "I'm surprised it surprised you." So it does still happen, now and again. But basically I am happy. It doesn't hurt anymore. It took about five years.

It's actually amazing what a positive thing being widowed can finally become in your life. And I say that not just for myself, but from seeing other widowed people. I talked to a woman the other day and she said, My husband's been dead two years and I never believed I would feel so good. My life is just so good right now. In fact, she's got all kinds of problems. But happiness doesn't really depend on your situation. You can get two people who are under exactly the same conditions, and one will say they're miserable and the other will say they're happy. I've seen it, I've seen it many times. People are about as happy as they decide to be.

Having said what he just said about happiness being a matter of choice, Lou went on to say that a man who had recently lost his wife would not appreciate that thought at all. In fact, he said when he is talking to someone who is newly bereaved, he tells them quite the opposite: if they think it's bad right now, just wait, it's going to get a whole lot worse.

Those people often come back to Lou later and tell him how refreshing it was to hear that it was going to get worse. Because everyone else was telling them that it was going to get better, and all they kept experiencing was that it kept getting worse. We often withhold the truth from people because we want to spare them pain, but unrealistic expectations can cause more pain than the truth. In the beginning, the truth of the matter is that it *will* get worse. In the end, the truth of the matter is that it really is up to you to decide how happy you want to be. It is a challenge you can't escape.

Lou's way of meeting that challenge was imaginative and fearless. Instead of running from his aloneness, he turned around and confronted it. Not only did he confront it, he decided to embrace it, and in doing that, he found the distinction between alone and lonely. That is a crucial distinction. If you mean to be happy again, it is a distinction that bears repeating over and over and over again: being alone and being lonely are not necessarily the same thing.

Keeping a journal is something you do when you're alone, but not when you're lonely. It is a recognition that even though no one else is there, you are, and something worthwhile is happening. It is also an expression of self-esteem—that your thoughts are worth recording, and worth going back to read. Whether you ever go back to read them or not.

There is a fearlessness in it, too. Many people are skittish about writing down what they think because of what they might learn about themselves. If it's true that you never really know what you think until you hear yourself say it, or until you write it down, remaining inarticulate can be a form of self-fear. And assuming he was using lined paper, Lou was very literally not afraid to put himself on the line.

His willingness to articulate his feelings helped him enormously. If you articulate your feelings—to someone else in conversation, or to yourself in a journal—you bring them into consciousness so you can see what they are. Then you can help them along or crimp them, depending on what you consciously want. As Lou said, you have a choice. But until you know your alternatives, how can you make the decision?

We have been deemphasizing talking as a way of dealing with grief because it is so often touted as a magic cure-all. It is not the magical cure people claim, but it is a valuable tool. For example, Lou talked about how hard it was to recognize that he was actually happy without Madelaine, because it raised the question of whether he had been happy with her. He asked that question out loud of himself, even though he was alone. If he hadn't been bringing his thoughts and feelings up into consciousness like that, by articulating them, he might never have realized that there was that unresolved conflict within him. And never recognizing it, he might never have resolved it. He might have gotten stuck in not allowing himself to be happy, without knowing why he was doing it or that he was doing it at all.

Another thing that helped Lou meet this challenge so well was that he was not afraid to be irrational. He went out and bought himself $600 worth of backpacking equipment, and a boat, a motor, and a trailer which he almost never used. It was a good way to let off steam. Lou's decisions were not major life decisions such as marriage or moving to another town. They were also not decisions that would hurt him financially. He wasn't closing any doors by indulging himself in those pleasures—in fact he was opening doors onto some new kinds of possibilities—but they were possibilities that could be taken lightly. Getting married and moving are not things that you can do lightly.

Like the distinction Lou discovered between being alone and being lonely, the distinction between being single and being half a couple is important. Everyone remains half of a couple for a while. But after a while, most men cease to think of themselves as husbands to the wives they have lost, whether they take a new wife or not. It is not true for everyone. Joe is an exception; he has solidified a permanent position as half a couple. Mark was also still half a couple, but the other half of the couple had changed; he hadn't yet gone through a reckoning with being single again.

But Lou recognized pretty quickly that he was living for himself now and that he had to start organizing his life around his own needs. And because he went out and looked for them, he found there were a lot of people who were in the same boat he was—people of his age who were in exactly his situation, all of whom were looking to put together new lives for themselves. Now he's got all kinds of new friends, and they do all kinds of things together. He's got friends he goes cycling with, friends he goes backpacking with, friends he goes on retreats with, friends to walk with, friends to talk with, friends to have coffee and pie with. Instead of looking to one person to satisfy most of his needs, he has employed what has become a popular corporate technique—he has diversified his dependencies. All of his needs are getting filled—in fact, more of his needs are getting filled than were getting filled before—but they're getting filled by different people who bring out different things in him. In some ways, Lou has a fuller, richer life than he had before.

As much as Lou loved Madelaine, and as much as he loved his life with her, he has found a certain sense of liberation in widowhood. Widows often discover this because they find their roles as wives and mothers really limited them. But many men are also surprised to find that they are free of limitations—limitations which they embraced within their marriages—and that that freedom allows them to develop in new ways.

Some men even find, in being widowed, that they are not only free to develop parts of themselves that they had consciously not developed before, but that they also develop in ways they had never even dreamed of before. Without forsaking the wives they have lost, they are able to build new lives that far surpass their previous understanding of what life could be.

Peter

ETER is 36. He is currently in graduate school as a part of a career transition from industrial technology to social work. When he was 24, he was introduced to Sherry by his twin brother, as sort of a recompense for "stealing" another girl from him, and they hit it off immediately. Two years later, she proposed, and during their five years of marriage, they had two children together: Petie, now 10, and Marsha, 8.

During their first three years together, Sherry had recurring headaches two or three times a year and was told they were probably psychosomatic. But about a month after Marsha was born, Sherry had a blackout. A few months later, she woke up one afternoon and didn't know who she was. A few weeks after that, she couldn't speak coherently. The doctors did every test known to man—including one in which they bored holes in her head while she was still conscious, ran catheters through her brain for injecting dye, and then put her in a chair that rotated 360 degrees to move the dye through her brain—and finally explored surgically. They found highly malignant and completely untreatable cancer.

Peter set up a hospital room in his parents' house where he and his mother tended Sherry until she died. In early December, as a respite from nearly five months of full-time nursing, Peter went away for a couple of days to visit a friend, and while he was gone, Sherry slipped out, into unconsciousness. She died the night he got back.

This interview was conducted six-and-a-half years after her death.

When I got back, I went to her room and she was breathing, but still unconscious. I put my son to bed, but he got up-and-down and up-and-down several times to check on his Mom. Finally about 11:00, he said—a 3-year-old, now—he said, "I'm ready to let Mommy go to Heaven because I don't want her to hurt anymore." Then he went back to bed and stayed.

And she died at 2:33 that morning. Her mom was there—she said, "Something's changed," and Sherry had taken her last breath. I was standing across the room, but I had the distinct feeling that she had not been there for some time. We got my mom up, she whispered something in Sherry's ear, and closed her eyes.

Then I left. I went outside. There was a big, full moon. I thought to myself, "It's a straight shot tonight. Wherever you're going, it's a beautiful night to be going there." Then I went down and slept with my kids. The body was left where it was because it was the middle of the night, there was no need to do anything.

The kids woke up at seven. The first question Petie asked was, "Did my Mommy die?" And at that point, it hit me again. Oh, I thought. She's dead.

I said, "Let's go upstairs and find out." So we went upstairs. I was holding Marsha in my arms, standing at the foot of the bed, and she was staring at Sherry's body for the longest time. Petie was by her pillow, watching. I was just letting the thing unfold. My daughter stared for the longest time—this is an 18-month-old girl—and then she turned to me and held up her hands and she said, "All gone." She didn't have the language, but she understood, she knew. And it was then that I realized that in keeping the family together through it all, I had done the right thing. And I made the decision right then that I was going to follow through with that. I would not abandon my children. Just because they'd lost one parent, they didn't have to lose another. I would not go back to work.

Petie and Marsha had been kept very close to the situation. They were there in every hospital room that Sherry was in. When she was in intensive care all bandaged up, they had to ask "Is that my Mommy?" but they were still there. I felt that they had to know what was going on so they wouldn't dream up something worse.

Petie and I had been to the funeral home—we called it Louie's Big

House—and talked with the funeral director. We'd written the obituary and picked out a picture for the paper. He'd picked out a dress for her to wear. And when we picked out the coffin, he wanted to know everything about it. To see the casket opened and closed and where the feet would go, and, is she going to wear shoes? Every question imaginable. He had been well prepared.

I had been given a book, *About Dying*, by Sara Bonnett Stein, and we'd gone through that book together, too. It was a children's book, you know, but it ended up being the best thing that I could have done for myself. It was about a bird that dies and gets buried by the children, and a grandpa who dies and is buried. It is a wonderful book, it's neat. It had large print that you'd read to the kids, and small print for you to read to yourself, explaining what this would do for the child. I'd read that book to Petie when he woke up from his nap. He'd stop me when he'd had enough. He'd come up and close the book, take it with him, and go off with it somewhere. Then in a day or two, he'd come back with the book and say, Read me some more.

Towards the end, he said, "Is my Mommy dying?" And I said, "Yes, I think she is."

He asked, "Why?" I said, "When we're done with our work down here and Jesus calls, we go back. That's where we came from and that's where we're going. And we don't know when our work is done, but when He calls, we go."

"But why does she have to hurt?"

"I don't know."

"Why can't the doctors fix her?"

"Don't know."

He would come at me from every different direction about the loss of his mom.

And he quickly figured that what I was saying didn't match what I was feeling. He would say things like, "You said that it was a happy thing to go back to Jesus. Why are you crying, then?" I mean, there is an answer to that: I was crying because I was going to miss her. But see, I hadn't aligned my thinking with my feelings yet. I was saying all the good and acceptable things that were going to happen, and wasn't admitting to feeling angry that she was being taken from us, that God could do such an awful thing. He picked up on that and helped me to recognize my feelings. He made it okay for me to be at home with those feelings and thoughts. He did more for me than I was ever able to do for him.

When he figured out that Sherry had died, Petie went out and got his shovel. He had a shovel picked out and he said, "Let's go down and dig the grave." And I said, "Well, a lot of people want to help us with that. We're going to go to Louie's Big House so all the people can come, and we're going to take some time to do this."

So we did. I had pictures of Sherry printed and had her baby book at the wake, from when she was a little child, so the family could go through the book and remember . . . We had her scrapbook there from her teenage years. People came and shared stories about Sherry that I had never known, about how they had known her. We had a happy time.

Petie and Marsha were there the whole time, running and playing, and all the cousins . . . They would run up to the coffin and kiss Sherry's body, then laugh and run away. I didn't know what was going on and didn't find out for several years. But years later, I was reading a story to Petie and he said, "Oh, look, there's my Mommy." The story was *Sleeping Beauty*. And here was Sleeping Beauty laid out with flowers all around. I had read that story to him as a child, and he remembered it. And he thought, and his cousins thought, and all the other little kids thought, that they could wake her up just by kissing her. That totally escaped the adults.

There were hardly any tears on my part. I was real—I don't know— in shock, I guess. Real numb. And yet I took a great deal of pride in being on top of things. I thought, we've still got a body here, and we're going to take good care of it. I'm going to make Sherry proud of me. So there were no tears on my part until the actual funeral mass. Then they came, when the coffin was closed, and I realized this was going to be it.

I took Petie out before the mass to see the hole in the ground— before they put the grass over it, and the canopy and all this junk. When the bird died, they buried him in a shoe box and put it in the ground, and I didn't want to upset the good information he'd already gotten. So we went out there with his shovel to see the ground and the hole, to see the place.

Then after the funeral mass, the old men in coveralls came up and lowered the coffin into the ground while everybody stood around. The priest tried to lead people off, but they didn't go. They didn't go. They stood around and watched as the coffin was lowered into the ground, and the concrete cover was slipped over it. Then Petie shoveled in some dirt with his special shovel. He still has his special shovel, the shovel he buried his Mommy with.

I got a lot of comment on that.

"I would not have done it that way."

"I could not have done it that way."

"That was wrong to do it that way."

People couldn't believe you'd do anything at a funeral but the normal stuff. But no one left the funeral grounds while we were burying the body. It was like they were experiencing something new for the first time, and didn't quite know what to make of it, didn't know if they liked it or not.

When we left that day, the coffin was buried. I remembered as a child, leaving a cemetery and looking back and seeing that coffin above the ground and the job not done. What a lonely feeling that was, thinking, God, you're *alone* out there. So when we left that day, the dirt was packed down and done. The job was complete.

The house where the funeral lunch was held was a mile from the cemetery. I was with my dad in his car, with my kids and my sister and my Mom. And I looked at the cemetery through the car window going by, and it was home to me. Sherry was there. That was home. And as I turned to look forward, it was like looking into total darkness. There was no forward to look to. It was a void, sucking me forward. The whole of me was in the past.

I was totally immersed in that impression for some days afterwards, as if there was no future. That this was it, there was no more. There literally was no more. No more me, no more kids, no more nothing. Just emptiness. That stayed with me for a long time.

There were two of me from then on.

I wrote about this time years later, my recollections of it. I knew when they were 13 or 14, my kids would want to meet their mom, to hear the story of her living and dying, and the part they had played in it. So I started to write it all down. I had never done any journal writing, but I think I wrote three hundred pages. And as I wrote, I remembered those first six months as void of activity. I was totally preoccupied with her loss, and with sadness and crying.

But years later, I shared that story with my mom and she said, "Not so, not so. You were on the road, you were driving." And sure enough, I looked in my mileage log and during that time I had put thousands of miles on the car. I looked at my calendar and it was full of activity. One of Sherry's friends had seduced me within a week of the funeral,

I was dating within three months, all kinds of things were happening. But in my head, I was home alone.

I do remember going to a store one time to get stuff for lunch. It was a very familiar store from my childhood, and I had to get bread and milk and cheese and one other thing. And I got the bread and milk and the cheese and I went to reach for the last thing and it was just too much. I had what someone later described as a panic attack. I had to put the items down. I backed up against the counter and watched as everybody watched me. And I thought to myself, do these people realize how naked I am? I really felt as if I didn't have a stitch of clothing on. I had to leave the store. I went home and in my mind I didn't leave the house for the next six months.

But in fact I was dating the whole time, more than I ever had before. I had never dated in high school, didn't date in college. Sherry had to ask *me*, or I would have never gotten married. But I looked at my calendar at one point and I said, my God, I've had seven dates with six women in six days. I'd never had that many different dates in my whole life. But I felt a pressure to find myself another wife right away. I wasn't going to be real fussy. I told people three weeks later, If I find a Catholic who doesn't smoke and doesn't drink and loves me and my kids, I'll be married within the year.

I got into a lot of relationships that were very needy. I found very quickly the people that were willing to listen to my story had had some sort of loss themselves, or were very needy. You can pick them out, the needy ones, and they're very appealing when you're lost. They're real. They have character. But they still have a lot of unmet needs. And the relationships that ensue . . .

The friend of Sherry's that seduced me had a poor marriage of her own and saw what she felt was a good marriage going down the drain, and she felt this terrible yearning to help, on top of her own neediness, and that was her expression of it. Another woman I dated had been divorced; she knew what loss was. But she brought all these other needs that I couldn't handle. The third person that I dated had never lost anybody. She was young, very sensitive, very caring, but she could not understand my loss, since she had never lost anybody. She got upset that I needed to repeat and repeat the story like that, like I had no room in my life for her. She sensed that Sherry was still my whole life.

I did tell my story over and over, every chance I got. I found it was very powerful. And I found it was an aphrodisiac for women, in a way.

Once you share a psychological intimacy like that, physical intimacy doesn't seem such a big deal.

About six months after I was widowed, I moved out of my parents' house. It took three months to complete the move and actually occupy the house, because every time I'd go to our old house, all these feelings would come back and I'd end up moving very little. Her clothes were all hanging in the closets, her pots and pans were in the kitchen, as if she had just gone out for a walk. Coming back to all those things caused so much pain and so much crying that I couldn't take very much at a time.

But even after it all was moved, I didn't occupy the new house until I got a high school gal to come in forty hours a week, to do the cooking and show me how to do stuff around the kitchen. It took me five different tries to boil the water for egg salad. We had green egg salad, runny egg salad, we had every kind of egg salad that didn't taste good that you could imagine. It was months before I could make egg salad. Finally, one day I put out a meal in five minutes and the kids were actually eating it without bitching. I thought to myself, Hey, I think I can make it as a homemaker. The meal was sliced apples with peanut butter.

I ended up being a full-time homemaker/mother to these kids. I took them to nursery school and on field trips at the nursery school. I helped at the hot lunches. All the things they needed to do, I was there doing them. I was totally surrounded by women. And when Mother's Day came around, I wanted a little recognition. When I didn't get it, I was pissed. So this year, when everybody was saying "Happy Mother's Day," I said to the group—my family was gathered—I said, "You know, no one has ever said Happy Mother's Day to me." So somebody finally did. I said, "Thank you."

While the kids were in school, I had six hours a day where I could do some work. Electrical, plumbing, carpentry work. A lot of the people I got involved with were single parents needing help, so I'd do a little work for them and they'd support me in some way. But what made it financially feasible was that we were getting survivors' benefits from Social Security. It used to be, when a woman died, the surviving spouse would have had to prove that she was financial head of the household in order to get benefits. But after the women's movement, they decided it didn't matter. If one spouse died, the other could draw. So Social Security was giving us over $1,000 a month.

But no one was totally supportive of the way I was handling things.

Shortly after the funeral, Sherry's mother said to me, I don't understand why you don't just go live your life, and let us raise your kids. Even my own mother couldn't understand why I was dating, why I was running, why I did this and that. Even my own mother couldn't say, "Pete, you're the only one who really knows what you need to do, go do it." That was when I realized that I was on my own. That the only one who could give me permission to do what I needed to do was myself. That was the hardest part, in a way. Trying to figure out for myself what it was that I needed to do. Once I figured out the advice I was getting was no good for me, I had nothing to go on.

Of course, I could have put my kids in day care, I could have gone back to work, they wouldn't have been in any worse shape. They would have just had different problems. But I found out that I needed them more than they needed me. They facilitated my grief by needing me to facilitate theirs. Marsha, being very young, had her own understanding of death, but as she matured, her understanding and recognition changed, and she needed to grieve some more. They continue, seven years later, to grieve their mother in various ways. And giving them permission to grieve over and over again made it easier for me to recognize when I needed to cry, or to be alone or to be with them.

I had been told it would take a year and I would be over it. That was such bullshit, I couldn't believe it. I kept waiting for that anniversary and when it came, things got worse. I went into a deep depression that didn't let up for seven months. The Christmas season was just awful. I just could not get out of the sadness. I slept a lot and cried a lot. Days would go by where I would do only what I had to do for the kids, then I'd sit in a chair or lie in bed. I simply could not function.

By the summer of that second year, things seemed to be going really well—I didn't have too many feelings—but in the fall I was right back into it. Around my birthday it got bad, and then I got a little break, and then Thanksgiving and Christmas were bad, then I didn't get a break until New Year's. Then I got a pretty good break, then Easter was bad again, and then her birthday was bad again, and then I was off for the summer again. Each year, I seemed to have bad days or bad weeks around those special times. But I never came to a point where I could know that I wasn't going to be disabled by these feelings—never enough to say, "Go back to work" or "Begin a new career." I got real sick of homemaking, though.

About two years after Sherry died, I got a call from a gal named Pat. She was starting a group of widowed people and asked me if I would come. The group that formed consisted of eight widowed ladies, and I became part of that group, founding this widowed persons service in my hometown. I wasn't really uncomfortable that I was the only man, because that was the first time I'd actually gotten hold of a widowed person who knew what I was talking about. Who wouldn't say, yes, but . . . Or, yeah, but . . . And who wasn't needy. My best widowed friend I met there—she was widowed three days after I was.

I'm still a part of that group, and we have since hooked up with the Widowed Persons Service of the AARP. I became a volunteer aid. And when the AARP formed a task force to find out why most men would not participate in the widowed persons groups, I became a part of that. So I've seen a lot of widowers and I've seen how they handle it. And it's absolutely clear that men are more threatened by widowhood than women. They die quicker, remarry quicker, their health is worse—it seems like men will do anything to get out of grief, even die.

It's funny how people don't know that. A gal from the university called me and wanted to talk to our widows' group. She was doing a research paper in the Women's Studies Department, and apparently the professor was directing her to find out why women who exhibit masculine coping skills do better in grief. And her data was just the opposite, that women who score very high on the feminine scale handle grief much better. I said, well, of course they will. Women are far more independent. And independence is a great predictor of good grief handling.

But we have a whole set of expectations about how to handle grief. You tend to feel better about a person who works her way through grief, who doesn't sit around and cry, who gets the business affairs taken care of, who stays in contact with church, who goes out shopping and doing things. You know, the masculine coping skills.

But sometimes the opposite is called for. This woman called our program once and said, you got to come help this poor woman. She's sleeping with her kids, she's got locks on all the doors, she won't fix a meal, she isn't going to work. All she does is cry all day long. I said, "How long has it been?" She said, "It's been a whole week." Hah. People think a week is significant. Or that a month is significant. Or six months. Or a year. It's not. For a man or a woman. And I think that woman's response to her grief was entirely appropriate.

Some people don't show much grief at all and some are incapacitated. But if you're hurting 100 percent of your capacity to hurt, whether it be a low capacity or a very high capacity, you're hurting 100 percent.

What more can they take from you? Everybody grieves differently. I've never heard or seen two men that approached grief in the same way. Their grieving is as personal as their relationships with their wives were. I mean, there's so much of loss that is peculiar to the relationship, that is different from anybody else's.

One fellow I knew got lost for a year. He sold his things, closed up his house, and just took off. He said he was so lonely that he would go on any new adventure. Someone would come along who was going to Canada and he went to Canada. Finally he woke up one night, and he said, "Ah, I've got to get on with my life." And then he came back to work.

Another guy I met at a conference just dated nonstop for years. Fifty relationships a year, almost one a week. No kidding. Caffeine, alcohol, smoking, and dating. He changed jobs, changed localities, changed his sexual orientation and entered the gay community, and finally his dog died. And it brought him to his knees. He was on the verge of suicide, grieving over this dog, over his wife, over his dad, his mother—he unloaded the whole thing. He found a good psychotherapist and had a nearly spontaneous recovery. He had been criticized for crying at his father's funeral, and then had never cried at his mother's and never cried at his wife's. But then this dog, that had been with him through all these other things—that was the killing blow.

And then, I know of an insurance man who was widowed, and people were worried about him because they heard him crying in his apartment at night. They would hear him at night through the walls. By day, he was exactly like he had always been before; he seemed to be totally normal within a week of the funeral. But here he was sobbing every night. He wouldn't talk about his wife but he would call widowed men to find out—how is he doing? The same as I'm doing? But the minute someone talked of his loss, he would cut it off. He ended up having a heart attack. It happened within the year.

Men are handicapped in grief. I think the socialization we have given men in the past is still very much of a ball-and-chain for them. And I don't think they've really grasped the opportunity that the women's movement has given them to be themselves. Especially older men. They are still chained to traditions that don't encourage them or allow them a variety of coping techniques, a variety of behaviors, a variety of expressions of grief. Something like half the widowed men get remarried within eighteen months. That is the one behavior that is universally blessed—people want you to get over it and get on with it. But from any other point of view, that behavior is unreasonable—in terms of making a wise decision, meeting and knowing someone usually takes more time than that.

As men, we aren't taught to express ourselves and to be who we really want to be, and that is a real hurdle. One of the biggest problems men face is figuring out what they need to do. For themselves. What *their* needs are. People will tell them, do this or do that. Lots of advice, maybe. But sorting all that out, what's right for them, is a big problem. Because as men, we're not socialized to tune into our own instincts. So when you tell a man to follow his instincts, that's a new skill that's very hard to learn at this point.

Consequently, men have a tendency to want to replace their wives. Especially if she took care of them, if they were dependent on her for laundry and cooking and cleaning, a social life—in other words, if they were dependent on her to keep their world going. Some men have never written a check. I was very angry at Sherry for leaving me with this recipe box. I would get out a favorite recipe and not be able to read it, you know. I didn't know that there was a difference between "tbsp" and "tsp." And when it comes to salt, there is a hell of a lot of difference. I found that out right away.

So I'm raising Petie differently. I'm paying particular attention to see that he can take care of himself. When I was growing up, our chores were the yardwork and the trash. That's as close as we ever got to taking care of ourselves. But Petie knows how to do laundry. Next year that's going to be his job, to do all the household laundry. This year, it's the dishes after supper. Maybe the next thing will be fixing meals. He already knows how to cook pretty well. I think it's important he knows these things. I think it's important that he be whole. That he be independent.

After a few years, I realized that I could be a parent and raise my kids alone—that I would do an adequate job—and that not only could I do it but I was comfortable doing it. I didn't need to have a relationship going all the time. As a matter of fact, I went for quite a while without a relationship, and I was very comfortable. I had a lot of friends. I had a real rich life. This was the fourth year, I think, when my life really reached full bloom as a single father.

I even learned to meet some of my sexual needs alone. I got this book of erotic stories—it was full of really interesting stories—and through those, and through exploring aloneness, I got very good at masturbation. I didn't even know about it until after I got married. I'd had no sex education at all. So I've become a better lover because I know more about myself, what I need. And it's not threatening to me to be alone, without sex. It's very nice to be married, but I don't have to be.

I have really gone through a transformation since I lost my wife, and it's hard to admit, but I wouldn't give up what I am today to have her back. I'm a much bigger person now. If Sherry came back today as she was, we wouldn't get along at all. I have grown. We wouldn't be happy. I always felt that my worth was dependent on what I could do for someone, what I could accomplish. It was always in terms of what other people thought, or in terms of doing things. But now I see my worth not being dependent on what I can do, but just on who I am.

And if I hadn't lost my wife, I probably wouldn't be in the process of going through this career change. I probably would have done what most people do—try to overcome my problems by trying harder, by pushing through. That's what I'd always done before; I was always in charge. But after my wife died, I found out I wasn't in charge of anything anyway, anything important, and that's when I started letting events and circumstances shape my life. And I've been much happier since. The things that have happened to me by chance have been more important to me than anything I've ever planned.

I see myself now as able to experience life more fully than I ever did before. I've experienced a great deal of loneliness that just rips your soul apart. But I've been able to sit with it, and go all the way to the bottom with it, and know the texture of it. I mean really *know* what it's like to get down to the point where you don't want to live anymore. There's a strength that comes from experiencing that that I never had before.

I was always afraid to be lonely. I would work, I'd get interested in something, I'd read—I wouldn't ever let myself be alone with myself. Just sit and experience all my stuff. But once you experience all that stuff—all the things you're proud of, all the things you're good at, along with all the shit you don't want to claim, all the possessiveness, all the crap in your life—once you own all that stuff and just allow those feelings to be—there comes a sense of, Oh. I don't have to be afraid anymore. I *don't* like my kids sometimes, I *didn't* like Sherry sometimes, I *don't* like some of the things my family has done. But I don't have to be afraid that people won't like me, because *I* like me. I mean, I might not like *all* of me, but it's all mine, and I accept it. I'm whole.

I pretty much know myself now—I know what I'm good at and what I'm not good at and I accept the fact that I'm going to fail again and be good again. If I get into another relationship, that is okay. But if I don't, that's okay too.

As it happens, I have gotten married again. I met Penny last New Year's Eve on a blind date in Michigan. I got this invitation to go six hundred miles to meet a strange gal and spend four days with her. And I said, Why not? New Year's is a bummer. Why not? So I went to Michigan and Penny traveled from Florida to meet. A friend was fixing us up, see.

And we clicked. I proposed to her three weeks later. We saw each other for four days, then traveled together to my house and spent another four days. The next week I went to see her, and the next week she came to see me. It was like that until we got married. We're just coming on our first anniversary.

There was something I recognized in Penny—she is an independent person. She is a whole person. There is no bringing her into my life, as much as joining her in a life that we build *between* us. It is totally different. Sherry and I were more dependent. Of course, we were very young at the time; we might have grown into this. But Penny and I don't need each other. We *choose* to be together. We *choose* to share our lives. We're certainly free to offer—and *do* offer—a lot of things to each other. I like to do things for her, and it's nice to have things done for me. But I *can* do it all. That's the difference.

You know, it's an interesting sidelight. Every couple has a private language—I had one with Sherry—and as I got involved with Penny, of course, a private language developed. And you know what? It's identical. I offered nicknames for things, just kind of because they were familiar to me, and she offered Sherry's response back to me. How that happened, I have no idea. But it was just spoken and spoken back, boom. It was my private language with Sherry, and Penny understood it.

The kids love Penny dearly, but Marsha has some anger at being left. I mean, she drew blood on Penny once. Penny is the mother, embodied, and Marsha is angry at being abandoned. At eighteen months, the sense of abandonment must have been just horrendous. Sherry was nursing her, and unbeknownst to Sherry and me, she lost her milk because of this illness. So Marsha was literally starving to death because she wasn't getting milk. There's a lot of stuff left for her to work out. And there will be, until she's an adult and finally gets her adult's recognition and understanding of death.

But it's striking, the difference in these children in one year. I've got pictures of them the year before I got involved with Penny and pictures of them now. And you can see the difference. Marsha looks really happy. And there's a genuine Petie smile that I have not seen since he was two. It really tells a tale.

I don't long for Sherry anymore, but there are things that Marsha does that remind me of her. Facial looks and mannerisms, how she wears her hair, how she loops it over her ear, little phrases . . . Even the way that Sherry tore toilet paper off a roll—very strange. I'm not a connoisseur of how people tear toilet paper off a roll, but Marsha does it exactly the same. And she had not been potty-trained by the time her mother died; she didn't learn it from her. I think there's more genetically built-in than we are aware of. And when I see these things, I think, Oh God, Sherry, I'd like you to see this.

And then I think, oh, I'm sure you do.

After Sherry died, you see, we had six or seven vivid contacts. I have to preface this by saying I never drank, or did drugs. I was never "sensitive" or had premonitions of any kind. Never read Kübler-Ross, still haven't. Don't know anything, straight arrow. And yet this happened to me.

The first night, when I lay down to sleep, I felt a heaviness over my body, like someone was lying on top of me and kind of melting in. And then there came this image, a very vivid image of Sherry in a flowing white gown with a radiant face. I opened my eyes and the image stayed. It was there. And it kind of transformed me.

We had a very neat conversation—not a verbal conversation—about all kinds of different things, every night as I'd go to sleep. These were actual visitations, as actual as you're going to get. And they were so complete that there was nothing to think about them. There was nothing to question, nothing to do. I felt so at peace with them that I didn't even tell anybody, I didn't feel the need to share it.

You want to know what she said? I asked her what Heaven was like. She said, nothing keeps us apart here. We are totally free to come into each other, to know the goodness that we each hold, and the reason that we are here. She used the word *comingling*, being able to enter into each other, comingling ourselves, our goodness, each other.

A year or two later, I shared this with a friend, another widowed person, and the information she got from her husband after he died was the same. And her husband was Mormon, not Catholic. This widowhood is a great leveler of beliefs. This experience of contacting Sherry after her death transcends my faith. My faith is based on my experience more than any teachings now.

I used to go to the grave at night, and at times, things have happened out there. Like one time I was on the way out and the fog was so thick you literally couldn't see five feet in front of the car. I could hardly find the gravestone. I'm having to actually feel for the stone, I'm thinkin' this is real eerie. But then the fog cleared. And I mean it *cleared*. There were no clouds anywhere, none. A full moon. Wonderful thoughts going back and forth. It lasted five minutes, and then it was completely fogged in again. Fogged in all the way home, thirty miles. No explanation. None needed.

Of course it has occurred to me that I might be widowed again, but I'm not afraid of it. I have a hard time worrying about tomorrow, about what might happen. I appreciate the depth of the day, the experience of today. I know I could be widowed again and survive. I know I could be handicapped or paralyzed or sick. I think I could handle depression. Somehow or other, I'd be okay.

When the surgeon told me Sherry was dying, I felt he had given *me* a death sentence. It wasn't Sherry dying, but *me*. My identity had become so entwined with hers that I didn't experience any separation from her. I cried for three days before I recognized it was *she* who was dying, not me. I met my own death for three days there, cried and grieved over my own death. It was real, I spouted it out loud before I caught myself. So I have the feeling I've met my own death and there isn't anything left to fear.

And I feel I have people on the other side who are waiting for me. I've got friends here, I've got friends there. I've got both sides covered. I've accepted my death as part of my life. And I've lived enough of life to know that all the sorrows that have come, have come with boundless joy and growth. And I wouldn't trade what I've got today for the way things used to be.

When Men Are Left Alone

W
HEN we started this book, we set out with the intention of gaining something more than simply a greater under-standing of widowerhood from it. We were also looking for what we might be able to learn about men in general by looking at how they handle this crisis.

Peter, more than anyone else, illuminates that connection. Not only does his story recapitulate the entire process of grief in very personal terms—including all the problems of a suddenly single father—it also details a process of growth which American men, as a group, are going through in a much more deliberate way.

When Peter talks about going down to the bottom of his loneliness and finding a new kind of strength there, he echoes the way men have often talked about the experience of war, about finding out what you're made of under a crisis situation. But Peter's war was a personal war, fought on internal territory, and the fighting of it called for an alto-gether different kind of courage.

In the past, men have been content, for the most part, to let their women handle the emotional work in life, along with the housework, the social work, and the work of raising the children. Because of that, as we've seen in this book, when men are left alone, without women, they often not only have to learn how to cook and clean and take care of the children—as well as learning how to maintain a social network on their own—they also have to learn altogether new skills in handling their emotions.

Peter's discussion of the ways in which men are handicapped in grief illustrates the point exactly. The range of emotional expression that men have been allowed in this culture is dangerously narrow. On a day-to-day basis, that narrow range may or may not matter much, but when faced with the inevitable flood of feelings that widowhood brings on—or that any other such crisis brings on—many men are utterly at a loss as to how to deal with it. And as we have seen, that lack of expertise can represent a serious hazard to their health.

But because the world of emotions is traditionally a woman's turf, traditionally men have been disinclined to press beyond the limitations that society imposes—even when those limitations are causing them extreme distress—for fear that growing in that way would mean giving something up of themselves, something of their identity and their validity in others' eyes. This "internal territory" on which Peter fought his personal war remains a new frontier for most men. The forging of it requires, in a way, a new kind of machismo.

In its focus on self-sufficiency and on the strength to keep on going in the face of adversity, traditional machismo is largely a matter of taking pride in remaining unaffected by life, in being able to press through with your will in spite of everything. But the "new machismo," if you will, that being left alone requires is more a matter of having the courage to embrace all the ways that life does affect you, because that means you are alive, and taking pride in your need for others, because that is part of what makes you human.

It isn't entirely easy to do. We have generations and generations of precedents to unlearn and our own reluctance to overcome. But the social climate in this country has changed enough now that more and more men are learning those lessons of aloneness, even if it's only because they no longer have a choice: as women become more involved in the workplace, and as divorce becomes more common, men are being left alone more and more to take care of themselves and their children.

According to Peter's experience, the growth that comes from that does not mean giving something up so much as it means developing something more. And the interesting thing about Peter is that he added it on all at once. The crisis of being left alone set the process in motion, and because he went through the process in crisis, his growth was concentrated and forced like a hot-house plant. In Peter we can see, as if in time-lapse photography, the process of growth and change that men in general are going through in this country.

Peter has, to a large extent, overcome his handicaps. He has learned not only how to cook and clean and run a household, and how to take care of his children, he has also come to know himself on much more intimate terms—to recognize and understand his emotional responses much more profoundly than he did before, and to handle them with greater consciousness and autonomy.

Many men, many people, will recognize Peter's description of how he used to feel when faced with being alone—he always just had to keep busy. A lot of us feel this sense of discomfort when we are alone. It's sort of the way you feel about being alone in a house that you haven't explored—you don't know what might be *in* there with you. But because he has explored his responses and his capacities, Peter knows who's in there with him and he knows that they are friends (or at least he knows that if they're not friends, he can handle them.) Because he knows himself and knows that he can handle himself in that way, he is not as dependent on other people as he once was. He doesn't have to have someone else there. He's comfortable with himself.

Part of the reason for that comfort is the fact that he is able to honor contradictory feelings at the same time, a feat that many men, in the past, have not been able to handle at all. Men have been befuddled for centuries by the frustrating "lack of emotional consistency" in women. But Peter is no longer befuddled to recognize that he can love his children and dislike them at the same time, that he can love his family and resent some of the things they've done, and that he can continue loving Sherry and love Penny simultaneously. It brings to mind Walt Whitman:

> Do I contradict myself?
> Very well then I contradict myself,
> (I am large, I contain multitudes.)

The extent to which men are handicapped in grieving—and in life—is the extent to which we have not allowed ourselves to contain those multitudes. And one of the biggest problems we face when we are left alone is the sudden need to make room for them.

If you have recently lost your wife, all of this may be about the last thing you want to hear. As Lou pointed out, for a while at least, things are only going to get worse, and thinking about how you have to change is not going to make them better. In the long run, widowhood is another stage of development, another phase in the life cycle like puberty and the mid-life crisis. Like any other developmental stage in the life cycle, it presents a new set of tasks to master. To the extent that you recognize that, and don't resist the growth that will be required to master those tasks, your experience with widowhood will be easier.

Of course, the fact that Peter was only 30 when he was widowed meant he had lots of time and room to grow, and if you are many years older than that, you may feel the chance has passed you by. But there is always room and time. Roger was 55 when he was widowed, and he grew. Lou was 62. He grew. Murray was 68, and he is still growing to beat the band. And Jim, at 94, is now throwing dinner parties on his own. It doesn't matter how old you are. It only matters that you are alive.

You are, in fact, alive, whether you feel like it or not. That is not as self-evident as it may at first seem.

Our dependencies on other people can cause us a lot of confusion. As very young children, we don't understand that there is a separation between ourselves and other people. And in fact as very young children, we haven't been separate very long, having lived so recently in the womb. But later on, when we begin to understand about separation, we learn that something can happen to someone else without its necessarily happening to us. Part of coming into this world, and becoming accustomed to this world, and growing in this world, is the growing awareness and acceptance and operating with the knowledge that we are separate entities.

But part of living in this world is also a matter of searching after and finding ways of being connected. It is a search we conduct all our lives, with varying degrees of success, and it is in marriage that many of us find our greatest success with that search. Marriage, even a bad one, can give you the feeling that you're not, in fact, separate, that somehow two have merged into one, that you have become one organism, two halves of one whole. Many men talk about this feeling, a feeling of having "been one" with their wives. And to the extent that you experienced that sense of "oneness" with your wife, you may well feel in some way that her death was in fact your death. George talked about that feeling when he described that sense of personal annihilation that came on him occasionally. And Peter talked about it in terms of feeling he'd met his own death.

So it is not as foolish as it may seem to emphasize that you are alive.

Because even though you may say, of course I'm alive, you may say it in the same way that Bill said, of course my wife is dead, and then was led to an understanding of that in altogether new terms. There is the matter of knowing something. And then the matter of *knowing* something.

Once you fully grasp the fact that you are separate from your wife— and that, in fact, you *are* still alive—you may be faced with feeling entirely ambivalent about it. Or feeling guilty about it. Or, God forbid, feeling *glad*. Or all of the above, and more.

No one said this was going to be easy.

But if we look at widowhood as a phase of the life cycle, it helps to make things a little bit easier. Life is a helix, you keep coming round to the same points over and over again at different depths of understanding, or different extensions of understanding. You may have experienced a profound understanding of separation before, but here it is again, demanding all over again to be learned.

And until you really come to grips with the fact that you're separate from your wife, you won't be free to go on living. In order to go on living, you have to reach a point where you can let go of your wife with confidence in the fact that you will remain intact. And you have to reach a point where you understand that in doing that you are not in any way loving her less. It doesn't happen overnight.

To a large extent, relearning this sense of yourself as a separate entity is a matter of renegotiating your relationship with your wife. That relationship, after all, is not ending, it is only changing. And you must come to a new understanding of who you are in relation to her. Are you still her husband? What does that exactly mean? How do you think it will change over time? How do you want it to change?

Relearning a sense of yourself as separate also involves renegotiating your relationship to yourself, another task that this stage of development presents you with. You have, as you have in all stages of life, a certain set of needs now. Some are the same as they've always been, and some are altogether new. But many of the needs you now have cannot be filled as they once were, because so many of those needs were fulfilled by your wife. And many of the needs that she didn't fulfill were fulfilled by your role as a husband. Your need to be a provider, perhaps. Your need to be seen as linked.

The business of renegotiating your relationship to yourself is the business of recognizing those needs and finding new ways to fulfill them.

Roger found altogether new ways of being a provider. Lou found new ways of being linked. It is the business of recognizing the new needs you may have and finding ways of fulfilling them. Mark found the need for solitude and bought himself a house in the country. Peter discovered the need to begin a whole new career.

Renegotiating your relationship to yourself is also a matter of being able to see yourself as another. To the extent that you recognize yourself as separate from other people, you can also recognize yourself as one of those other people. That's what Jan was talking about when he talked about his wife's murderer as one of "those strange people" that were known to lurk in the woods. He then went on to acknowledge that he was also one of "those strange people" that lurked about in the woods. That's stepping aside from yourself and looking at yourself as another person.

One way of doing that, as we have said, is by keeping a journal. You set yourself down on paper one moment, then come back at another moment and look at yourself as another, as if somebody else had written that, and you interact with yourself. That's a way to renegotiate your relationship with yourself—to come to a different understanding of who you are and what you need, by seeing yourself as somehow separate from who you are and what you need.

But as important as it is to renegotiate your relationship to yourself as another, you are only *one* other. You need others and others and others, too, to have yourself a life. And in the process of changing your relationship to your wife and yourself, you will probably find that that is changing the way you relate to the rest of the world. As Murray discovered, he rather liked relating to piano bars. And you may find you want to develop as many kinds of relationships with as many kinds of people as you can. As Lou discovered, by diversifying his dependencies, he was actually able to meet more of his needs than were met before.

You may also find, if you are a father, that you will have to renegotiate your relationships with your children, and that is no less true if your children are grown than it is if they're toddlers. In some ways, in fact, it may be more difficult if your children are grown because the balance of power is different, and grown-up children who have gone through the struggle to put their childhood behind them can find it extremely distressing to find that history being rewritten.

As adults, your children have managed to find a certain place for you in their understanding of the world, and that place is part of the foundation on which they've built their lives. If you now get up and start moving around—changing your style and your attitudes, changing your activities—those changes can shake them at their roots, and you may encounter a lot of resistance in them to any change in you. Because of that, they may in fact inhibit your attempts to accommodate your new circumstances. In fact, you may find yourself having to declare your independence from them just as they declared their independence from you in their adolescence. We all have claims on each other and sometimes those claims have to be renounced, or at least renegotiated.

If your children are still young, you face the further difficulty of helping them learn how to grieve. Peter's way of doing that was to allow himself to get on much more intimate terms with his children. Throughout the vigil, the wake, and the funeral, and the subsequent years of bereavement, he allowed his children's grief to be an integral part of his own. Not all fathers are willing to allow their children to see them grieve, but the fact that Peter allowed it not only helped all three of them through their grief, it also made their relationships much more rich than they might otherwise have been.

As Peter's experience illustrates, though, not everyone supports that approach. Some people believe that children should be kept apart from death because they can't cope with the concept of it, and that "until they are old enough" they should not go to funerals and wakes. But Peter's story suggests that no matter how old your children are, they can cope with death if they are prepared for it, and that they can handle wakes and funerals if the adults around them are supportive and understanding, and if the children aren't expected to exhibit their grief in a grown-up way.

Some people try to impose on their children some form of somber adult behavior at funerals and wakes. But Petie's running around at the wake not only allowed him to act as he felt, it also gave the gathering a sense of life in the face of death. In fact, the entire wake—with the baby book and the scrapbook and the stories—harkens back to George's Quaker-like memorial meeting for Carol and shows how much a wake can be about life as it is about death. If you think of wakes and funerals as ceremonies about life, the question of whether to let the children attend seems suddenly pointless.

Peter understood that he protected his children best by helping them to be part of Sherry's death, and not to be afraid of it. In doing that, he treated them with a great deal of respect. If he had pretended to them that things were somehow other than they were, he would have been suggesting to them that they were somehow deficient, unable to deal with reality, and, perhaps worse, that he was not a reliable source of information. And in the absence of real information, it's true, as Peter feared, that children can sometimes dream up something far worse. If they are sheltered from the truth, and not allowed to participate, they may become much more confused about death, and, more important, more afraid of it.

Peter talks of arriving, around the fourth year, at a point where he was comfortable as a single father, realizing he could manage his life alone and even be comfortable doing it alone. At this point, we could say that Peter had arrived at a "good outcome," that he had successfully renegotiated his relationships to Sherry and Petie and Marsha, and to himself, and to the world around him, and that his grieving was "over." Not that it was literally over—because it's never over—but when you start to feel satisfied with the present and to talk about the future with anticipation, you could say you've completed the transition.

As a stage of adult development, widowhood is, in fact, a transition. It is a process one moves through. With widows, we talk of that transition in terms of making a transformation from wife to widow to woman. It isn't quite so poetic to talk of a widower making a transformation from husband to widower to man, but that is what Peter has done at this point. His blooming as a single father marked the end of that transition. He'd arrived at a new sense of who he was, and he had a new way of doing things which was a reflection of that. At that point, he was "whole" again, and ready to consider remarriage.

Too often, we tend to look on remarriage itself as the "good outcome." But getting married again isn't really the end of the grieving transition. It is the start of a new transition. The "good outcome" of widowhood more likely comes before, and then you move on to another marriage as the start of a new phase. Peter is very fortunate he didn't move into that new phase within the first year or two. It would have been very easy, and it could have cheated him out of a lot of the growth he has achieved, growth that is now providing him with much of his happiness.

But as much as that growth can make you happy, it is very difficult to arrive at a point where one can say, I wouldn't be happy with her now if she came back as she was; I have grown and changed too much. It may be fear of arriving at that point that keeps some men from growing. "Outgrowing" their wives like that would make them feel guilty or disloyal.

For Peter, the freedom to grow may have come a bit easier than it does for some others because he had those several visitations from Sherry after she died. In those visitations, he was able to see that Sherry, in her "new life," was growing and changing as well. And because of that, he was able to see his own growth and change as something other than leaving her behind. He saw her death more precisely as a forking of their ways and came to believe that they were growing now in different ways.

You may not share Peter's understanding of the afterlife. And you may not believe that his visitations were anything more than hallucinations manufactured from his own need. But whether they really happened or not, their effect make his transformation complete. Peter's understanding of life, the afterlife, and the cosmos is now a product of his own experience. It is his understanding, his own, rather than a xerox copy of official dogma. When Peter was left alone, it even transformed him spiritually.

Peter did not arrive at this state of transformation easily. It took a lot of conscious work. One of the things that helped him most with that work was coming in contact with others who had been through what he was going through, because they could give him accurate feedback about the experience. Until then, while he was getting advice from other, well-meaning people, his grief work was much more difficult.

His experience with the anniversary of Sherry's death, for instance, is an example of how bad information can complicate the grieving process. If you are led to believe that things should be getting better after a year, and in fact you find they are getting worse, you end up not only feeling bad, but feeling bad about feeling bad—thinking there's something wrong with you. Peter's description of the cycles he went through in the subsequent year—some days good, some days bad—is much more accurate information about what to expect.

But people are quick to give bad advice. They want to help, and advice is one of the few ways they know how. It isn't their fault that they haven't been through it and don't know what they're talking about. And wrong information abounds, everywhere. It's interesting that the student who came to talk to Peter's widowers' group was being given wrong information even by her college professor: the professor assumed that women who exhibit masculine coping skills will do better in grief. As Peter pointed out, the opposite is more like the truth.

It is up to the man who is receiving advice to learn to filter it and pick out those parts that work for him. You needn't follow all of it, but you needn't reject it all, either. In fact, it may be a good idea to get as much advice as you can, then pick and choose, like a smorgasbord.

This book, in a way, has been a collection of indirect advice. Hearing others' experiences, though, is only part of the process. You need to take those experiences in and mix them up with your own until you can come to some informed understanding of what you want to do next. We hope that reading this book has helped you begin to reach such an understanding. But in the end, no book can take the place of face-to-face interaction. Because it is in the give-and-take of talking with another person that experiences really get thoroughly mixed.

Now that you've read all these stories, maybe it's time to tell your own—not just for the sake of telling it, but as a way of adding your experience to the pool of knowledge and getting something back from it. There are plenty of men who've been through this before you, and plenty going through it now, all of whom would be eager to hear what your experience with it is.

If, through talking with them, you eventually find yourself drawn into the position of talking to other men who are newer to this than you are, maybe that is a chance for you to take what has been a nightmare for you and turn it into a positive force, to make some contribution to somebody else's survival and well-being.

If you'd like to set that process in motion, there are a number of resources, listed at the end of this book, that can be of help in getting you started. Before we turn to them, a few last words about widowhood.

If you are recently widowed, no one needs to tell you that you are currently going through one of the hardest experiences that life has to offer. But you couldn't be experiencing the sense of loss that you feel now if you hadn't gained great riches before—if you hadn't learned to love and be loved, to give and forgive, to care. Having learned how to do those things, you still know how to do them, even though the person who taught you much of it is gone.

That knowledge, the knowledge of love, is the greatest power you hold right now. Having used that knowledge and power in the past to gather the warmth around you, there is no reason to think you won't be able to do it again, in new ways. There is pleasure to be taken in that, and solace and honor and comfort and hope. And there is no reason in the world you shouldn't take them all. Because even in this desperate time, life is still a good and great gift and carries with it the responsibility to use it well.

So go now and grieve, well and thoroughly. Love again, in every way that you can. Strive to be happy, in due time.

And in the meantime, be well.

Self-Help Organizations
and Readings

If you'd like to talk to another man who has been through what you're going through, call your local chapter of the **American Association of Retired Persons (AARP)** and ask if they have a Widowed Persons Service through which you could talk with a volunteer aide. Their services are available to people of any age, whether you are retired or not. If you find no local listing for them, get in touch with the Widowed Persons Service at the national headquarters, which will refer you to someone nearby. The address is 1909 K Street, NW, Washington, D.C. 20049, (212) 872-4700.

If you are interested in a group, the AARP also sponsors discussion groups and social activities. Ask around at local churches, funeral homes, hospitals, and hospice organizations, or have someone else ask around for you. Or try the **National Hospice Organization**, 1901 North Fort Myer Drive, Suite 307, Arlington, VA 22209, (703) 243-5900, for a referral to a group in your area.

If there are no active groups around and you want to set one up yourself, the **National Self-Help Clearing House** in New York can give you guidance. The address is 33 West 42nd Street, Room 1227, New York NY 10036, (212) 840-1259. The **New Jersey Self-Help Clearing House** can also be of help, even if you don't live in New Jersey. The address is St. Clare's Riverside Medical Center, Pocono Road, Denville, NJ 07834, (201) 625-9565.

You might also want to get copies of Dr. Silverman's books on the subject: *Widow to Widow* (Springer Publishing Company, 536 Broadway, New York, NY 10012, 212-431-4370) and *Mutual Help Groups: Organization and Development* (Sage Publications, 275 South Beverly Drive, Beverly Hills, CA 90212, 213-274-8003) which includes a step-by-step guide for organizing a program.

If you'd like to try keeping a journal and find that it doesn't come naturally to you, you can find some practical help, including particular techniques, in *The New Diary*, by Tristine Rainer (J. P. Tarcher, Inc., 9110 Sunset Boulevard, Los Angeles, CA 90069, 213-273-3274). Another book you might want to work with, which is specifically geared to bereavement, is *Time Remembered: A Journal for Survivors*, by Earl A. Grollman (Beacon Press, 25 Beacon St., Boston, MA 02108, 617-742-2110).

There are also people to call to help with more specific problems. If you're a suddenly single father, you can find support and information from your local chapter of **Parents Without Partners**. Try their national office, at 8807 Colesville Road, Silver Spring, MD 20910, (800) 638-8078, for a referral in your area.

If you're dealing with suicide, you can find out about self-help groups in your region by getting in touch with the **American Association of Suicidology**, 2459 South Ash, Denver, CO 80222, (303) 692-0985; or the **Suicide Prevention Center**, 184 Salem Street, Dayton, OH 45406, (513) 223-9096.